CANON LAW,
CONSULTATION AND CONSOLATION
Monsignor W. Onclin Chair 2003

KATHOLIEKE UNIVERSITEIT LEUVEN
Faculteit Kerkelijk Recht
Faculty of Canon Law

CANON LAW, CONSULTATION AND CONSOLATION

Monsignor W. Onclin Chair 2003

UITGEVERIJ PEETERS
LEUVEN
2003

ISBN 90-429-1294-4
D.2003/0602/52

© 2003, Uitgeverij Peeters, Bondgenotenlaan 153, B-3000 Leuven (Belgium)

INHOUDSTAFEL / TABLE OF CONTENTS

DE OPLEIDING KERKELIJK RECHT NA DE ROMEINSE HERVORMING. *PER ASPERA AD ASTRA?*

RIK TORFS

INLEIDING

Einde november 2002 werd een decreet van de *Congregatie voor de katholieke opvoeding* openbaar gemaakt. Het document, dat als datum 2 september 2002 draagt, en werd ondertekend door prefect Zenon Grocholewski en secretaris Giuseppe Pittau, beoogt de studies in het kerkelijk recht te reorganiseren[1].

De auteurs stellen een toename van het aantal studenten in het kerkelijk recht vast, maar tegelijk ook een kwaliteitsverlies op het vlak van de inhoud der studies. De kennis van het Latijn, die in 1931, ten tijde van de apostolische constitutie *Deus scientiarum Dominus* van Pius XI[2] nog volkomen adequaat was, gaat er stevig op achteruit. Bovendien concentreren hedendaagse seminaristen zich steeds indringender op theologische en pastorale disciplines, ten koste van het kerkelijk recht. Kortom, aankomende priesters zijn minder dan voorheen gewapend om studies in het kerkelijk recht aan te vatten.

Met de leken is het (uiteraard) nog treuriger gesteld. Zij melden zich vaak aan zonder enig theologische kennis.

Actie was dus noodzakelijk. De Congregatie voor de katholieke opvoeding deed een bevraging. Daarna organiseerde de Congregatie *plures consultationes,* om het te zeggen in een taal die voortaan aanzienlijk aan belang zal inwinnen. Ook de Congregatie zelf hield over het onderwerp plenaire vergaderingen in 1998 en 2002[3]. Uit al deze stappen vloeit het

---

[1] Decretum Congregationis de Institutione Catholica quo ordo studiorum in Facultatibus Iuris Canonici innovatur, 2 september 2002. Het decreet werd publiek gemaakt door de persdienst van de H. Stoel op 14 november 2002. Het werd inmiddels gepubliceerd in de verschillende edities van de *Osservatore Romano,* maar nog niet in de *Acta.*

[2] PIUS PP. XI, Constitutio apostolica *Deus scientiarum Dominus* de universitatibus et facultatibus studiorum ecclesiasticorum, 24 mei 1931, *AAS* 1931, 241-262.

[3] Zie hiervoor de verwijzing in de preambule van het decreet van 2 september 2002. Zie ook B. ESPOSITO, "Verso una riforma delle Facoltà di Diritto canonico ecclesiastiche? Pro e contra in vista di una prossima decisione", *Angelicum* 2002, 208.

decreet van 2 september 2002 voort. Het leidt tot een wijziging van artikel 76 van de apostolische constitutie *Sapientia Christiana* en van de artikelen 56 en 57 van zijn normen[4].

Hoe ziet de oogst van de vernieuwing er nu precies uit?

Het onderwijs in het kerkelijk recht wordt in drie cycli georganiseerd.

De *eerste cyclus*, die twee jaar of vier semesters beloopt, is verplichtend voor studenten die geen voorafgaandelijke opleiding in de filosofie of de theologie hebben gehad. Dat is automatisch het geval voor mensen die een graad in het burgerlijk recht hebben behaald. In detail wordt aangehaald op welke terreinen deze personen moeten worden bijgespijkerd. Het gaat om Latijn, fundamentele structuren van het kerkelijk recht, drie filosofische disciplines, en een negental theologische vakken. Essentieel voor de toekomstige kerkjurist zijn onder meer triniteitsleer, christologie en genadeleer. Theologen, maar ook alumni van de priesterseminaries, mogen onmiddellijk naar de tweede cyclus.

De *tweede cyclus*, met een duurtijd van drie jaar of zes semesters, behandelt het gehele kerkelijk wetboek alsook andere kerkelijke wetten, een introductie in de Oosterse Codex (CCEO), Latijn, optievakken, en tenslotte een reeks zogenaamde *disciplinae conexae*: theologie van het kerkelijk recht, rechtsfilosofie, fundamentele concepten van Romeins recht, elementen van burgerlijk recht, geschiedenis van de fundamentele canonieke structuren, geschiedenis van de bronnen van het kerkelijk recht, de relatie tussen de kerk en de profane samenleving, canonieke administratieve en gerechtelijke praktijk.

De *derde cyclus*, het doctoraat, duurt minimum één jaar of twee semesters. Daarbij dienen lessen te worden gevolgd in canoniek Latijn, en is er ruimte voor keuzevakken.

De nieuwe regeling betekent dus dat theologen voortaan *drie jaar* over kerkelijk recht moeten doen. Juristen, die er in België reeds vijf jaar studie hebben opzitten, moeten daar nog eens *vijf jaar* effectief aan toevoegen. Ten vroegste tien jaar na aanvang van hun universitaire opleiding worden zij licentiaat in het kerkelijk recht. Daarbij verovert ons vak een plaats aan de absolute top. Langer studeren is nauwelijks mogelijk.

---

[4] IOANNES PAULUS PP. II, Constitutio apostolica *Sapientia Christiana* de studiorum Universitatibus et Facultatibus Ecclesiasticis, 15 april 1979, *AAS* 1979, 469-499; SACRA CONGREGATIO PRO INSTITUTIONE CATHOLICA, Ordinationes ad Constitutionem Apostolicam «Sapientia Christiana» de studiorum Universitatibus et Facultatibus ecclesiasticis rite exsequendam, *AAS* 1979, 500-521.

Troost kan dan weer worden gevonden in de snelheid (één jaar) waarmee een doctoraatsdiploma kan worden behaald.

In wat nu volgt, wil ik op drie aspecten van de hervorming nader ingaan. Ik vang aan met een analyse van het licentiaatprogramma: twee of drie jaar. Wat zijn of, beter gezegd, *waren* de pro's en contra's. *Waren*, want *alea iacta est*. Toch veroorloof ik mij even een terugblik.

Vervolgens sta ik stil bij wat in het decreet van 2 september 2002 niet geschreven staat. Welke opties neemt de Congregatie zonder dat ze expliciet worden geformuleerd?

Tenslotte poog ik na te gaan hoe wij, binnen het bestaande kader van *Roma locuta, causa finita* toch aan een canoniek programma met allure kunnen werken. Of anders gezegd: hoe kunnen de drie verplichte licentiejaren zinvol worden opgevuld, waarbij enerzijds de Romeinse eisen worden ingewilligd, en anderzijds een toekomstgerichte visie op ons vak tot ontwikkeling kan worden gebracht?

Kortom, drie thema's komen aan bod: (I) de in het decreet gemaakte keuzes; (II) impliciete opties en onverwachte nevenwerkingen; (III) toekomstige ontwikkelingen met het nieuwe decreet als noodzakelijk kader. Hoeft het gezegd, de nu volgende beschouwingen zijn een louter persoonlijk, en geen facultair standpunt.

I. LICENTIEPROGRAMMA KERKELIJK RECHT: TWEE JAAR OF DRIE JAAR

Het decreet van 2 september 2002 verdient alle lof waar het opkomt voor een kwalitatief hoogstaand studieprogramma in het kerkelijk recht. Het heeft geen zin diploma's toe te kennen zonder dat daar bij de begunstigden een adequate kennis tegenoverstaat. Dé grote vraag is evenwel of die kennis het best wordt verworven door een verlenging van de studieduur. Er zijn immers valabele argumenten die voor het behoud van een tweejarig licentieprogramma pleiten. Tijdens een vergadering in Leuven op 31 augustus 2001 werkten decanen of andere verantwoordelijken van zeven canonieke opleidingen een argumentatie uit waarin voor het continueren van een tweejarig licentiaatsdiploma werd gepleit. De zeven betrokken instellingen waren de *Pontificia Università della Santa Croce* (Rome), de *Catholic University of America* (Washington), de *Katholieke Universiteit Leuven*, de *Pontificia Universidad Católica S. Maria* van Buenos Aires, het Institut de Droit Canonique van de *Université Marc*

Bloch in Strasbourg, de *Universidad de Navarra* (Pamplona) en *Saint Paul University* (Ottawa).

Zelf stuurde ik, volgend op de bijeenkomst, en na uitvoerige besprekingen met collegae Roch Pagé (Saint Paul) en John Beal (Catholic University of America) in Albuquerque, New Mexico, begin oktober 2001, en na schriftelijk contact (met vaak gedetailleerde antwoorden) met de andere decanen, op 21 januari 2002 een brief aan kardinaal Zenon Grocholewski waarin zeven problemen in verband met een studieduurverlenging worden gesignaleerd. Een kopie van de brief werd eveneens verzonden aan de decanen van de faculteiten die op 31 augustus 2001 in Leuven niet aanwezig waren. Onder meer in het *Angelicum* in Rome is deze brief wel degelijk aangekomen. Bruno Esposito maakt er uitvoerig melding van in zijn artikel *Le facoltà di diritto canonico ecclesiastiche tra passato, presente e futuro*, gepubliceerd in het tijdschrift *Angelicum* op het einde van 2002[5]. Of ook kardinaal Grocholewski de brief heeft ontvangen, is niet helder. Van hem ontving ik tot op heden (21 januari 2003, dus precies een jaar na datum) geen enkele reactie, ook geen bericht van ontvangst. Het is derhalve niet uitgesloten, ja zelfs waarschijnlijk, dat de brief, gezien de gebrekkige werking der posterijen, nooit bij de bestemmeling is aangekomen.

De zeven aandachtspunten in de brief, waarvan Bruno Esposito er vijf in zijn artikel aanhaalt, vermeld ik hier nog eens in hun geheel, met daarbij telkens een korte toelichting.

1. Indien het voorgestelde driejarige programma voortvloeit uit bezorgdheid over de gebrekkige kennis van Latijn of theologie bij studenten die de zogenaamde tweede cyclus aanvatten, zou dit probleem kunnen worden opgelost door het opleggen van een ingangsexamen of door striktere eisen met betrekking tot het volgen van de eerste cyclus. Een meer algemene opleiding hoort immers niet tot het takenpakket van de faculteiten kerkelijk recht.

Dit argument wordt ook door Bruno Esposito gebruikt. Hij pleit voor *conoscenze previe* versus *conoscenze complementari*. De basiskennis

---

[5] B. ESPOSITO, "Verso una riforma delle Facoltà di Diritto canonico ecclesiastiche? Pro e contra in vista di una prossima decisione", *Angelicum* 2002, 177-224; B. ESPOSITO, "Le facoltà di diritto canonico ecclesiastiche tra passato, presente e futuro", *Angelicum* 2002, 909-968. De analyse van mijn brief staat in het tweede artikel, 956-958.

dient op een aanvaardbaar niveau te staan vooraleer de studies in het kerkelijk recht worden aangevat.

2. *Een verplichtend driejarig programma is erg duur, vooral voor opleidingen met een hoog inschrijvingsgeld.*

Voor Noord-Amerikaanse faculteiten ligt dit punt erg gevoelig. Soms zijn de kosten tweevoudig. De kerkelijke overheid draagt reeds zorg voor de organisatorische omkadering van de instelling, en moet daar bovenop nog het inschrijvingsgeld voor haar seminaristen of priesterstudenten neertellen.

3. *Ofschoon drie jaren studies voor een grotere cohesie binnen de opleiding kunnen zorgen, kan de lange duurtijd ook afschrikken. Bisschoppen zullen misschien aarzelen om uitstekende studenten te sturen. Dat geldt vooral wanneer de potentiële studenten geëngageerde priesters met enkel jaren pastorale ervaring zijn.*

Dit probleem heeft met de specificiteit van de studie in het kerkelijk recht te maken. Deze laatste sluit vaak niet naadloos aan op, bijvoorbeeld, de theologische vorming. Canoniek recht is veelal een studie voor gevorderden, mensen van rond de dertig voor wie de binnenkant van de pastorale praktijk geen vreemde materie is. Het is voor een bisschop altijd een grotere stap om iemand studieverlof te verlenen in wiens *vervanging* hij moet voorzien, dan om iemand *verder* te laten studeren. Laatstgenoemde wordt *nog niet ingeschakeld,* wat psychologisch gemakkelijker is dan *iemand die reeds is ingeschakeld te vervangen.*

4. *Drie verplichtende licentiejaren kunnen een weerslag hebben op het aantal doctoraten, vooral op plaatsen waar het schrijven van een doctoraat drie jaren of langer duurt. Zes of zeven jaar studie van het kerkelijk recht wordt wellicht als erg lang ervaren. In ieder geval: een gering aantal doctoraten dreigt de wetenschappelijke status van het kerkelijk recht op termijn aan te tasten.*

De Congregatie opteerde voor een doctoraat met een minimale duurtijd van één jaar. Wanneer de kerkrechtelijke opleiding deel uitmaakt van een universiteit met enig maatschappelijk prestige, is een dergelijk summier doctoraat uiteraard volledig onaanvaardbaar. Vier jaar is daar vaak een normale duurtijd voor een doctoraat. Dat betekent dus dat iemand met een civielrechtelijke vooropleiding die doctor in het kerkelijk recht wil worden, als hij niet te veel treuzelt, er $5 + 5 + 4 = 14$ jaar over doet. Die lange duurtijd is het gevolg van een combinatie van de *kerkelijke eisen* aangaande een licentiaatsopleiding en de *profane eisen* die aan een wetenschappelijk verantwoord doctoraat worden gesteld.

5. *Een driejarig programma zou parttime programma's, gebaseerd op zomercursussen, tot een weinig realistisch project maken.*

Een licentie voor theologen zou immers al snel zes jaar, en een licentie voor juristen tien jaar in beslag nemen. Een optie bestaat erin om parttime programma's inderdaad te elimineren. Het zijn evenwel precies deeltijdse programma's die een combinatie werk/studie moge-lijk maken. En het is nu net deze combinatie die zowel potentiële (pries-ter)studenten als hun bisschoppen gemakkelijker over de streep kan halen.

6. *Vele opleidingen kunnen met hun huidige bestaffing geen driejarig programma aan. Nieuwe professoren moeten dus worden aangewor-ven. Dat stelt financiële, maar ook praktische problemen: hoogge-kwalificeerde professoren zijn dun gezaaid.*

Het moge duidelijk zijn dat niet iedere *doctor iuris canonici* in aan-merking komt om aan een volwaardige universiteit te doceren. Dat is *a fortiori* het geval wanneer het bewuste doctoraat op één jaar tijd is geschreven en dus niet beantwoordt aan de wetenschappelijke criteria die in andere universitaire disciplines worden opgelegd. De povere wetenschappelijke kwaliteit van sommige professoren, die zowel blijkt uit hun gering aantal wetenschappelijke publicaties als uit de bedenke-lijke kwaliteit van publicaties die er toch komen, dient openlijk ter discussie te worden gesteld. Het kwaliteitsprobleem dat kardinaal Grocholewski bij de studenten aantreft, is ook onder professoren op pijn-lijke wijze aanwezig. Canonieke wellevendheid verhindert vaak een adequate reactie.

7. *Elke wijziging van programma's dient te gebeuren in nauwe samen-hang met de bestaande profane wetgeving, die van land tot land ver-schillend is. Niet overal worden canonieke diploma's door de staat erkend, maar waar zulks wèl het geval is, moet alles in het werk wor-den gesteld om deze erkenning te behouden.*

De Romeinse démarches houden geen rekening met de evoluties die in het universitaire landschap plaatsvinden. De invoering van de nieuwe *bachelor-master*structuur in de landen van de Europese Unie, is voor de Congregatie een *non issue*. De vaak moeizaam verworven dubbele (profane en canonieke) erkenning van diploma's wordt lichtzinnig op het spel gezet. Alles wijst erop dat de kerk maatschappelijke erkenning met betrekking tot het niveau van haar opleiding niet langer belangrijk acht. Op het vlak van onderwijs en wetenschap lijkt de *revival* van de *societas perfecta*-gedachte werkelijkheid te worden. Kerkelijke opleidingen verwijderen zich langzaam van de universitaire *mainstream*.

Kortom, de omschakeling naar een driejarig licentieprogramma heeft nogal wat consequenties. Misschien was het, *after all*, toch niet zo'n goed idee. Jammer ook dat over deze problematiek nooit een grondig *publiek debat* werd gevoerd. Het zou de binnenkerkelijke debatcultuur hebben gesierd indien zoiets wel had gekund. Maar laten we vooral geen naïviteit veinzen. Gedane zaken nemen geen keer. De drie jaren zijn een feit. *Life goes on*. In een volgend hoofdstuk poog ik even tussen de lijnen te lezen. De *expliciete* opties die door het decreet van 2 september 2002 werden genomen, passeerden in de inleiding de revue. Maar welke zijn de *impliciete* opties? Of, iets beminnelijker uitgedrukt, welke zijn de nevenwerkingen van het medicament dat kardinaal Grocholewski aan de opleidingen in het kerkelijk recht heeft voorgeschreven?

II. IMPLICIETE OPTIES. OF: DE NEVENWERKINGEN VAN HET MEDICAMENT

Wie het decreet van de Congregatie voor de katholieke opvoeding vluchtig leest, komt mogelijk onder de indruk van het streven naar kwaliteit dat erin doorschemert. De liefhebber van grondigheid treft nogal wat aardigheidjes aan. Een langere opleiding. Meer theologie. Meer Latijn. Meer aandacht voor de in bepaalde kringen zo geliefde CCEO. Kortom, de canonisten van de toekomst zullen erudiete lieden op leeftijd zijn, mensen die respect afdwingen.

En toch heeft het decreet ook 'onzichtbare' consequenties. Die kunnen op twee vlakken worden gesitueerd. Vooreerst is de plaats van *kerkelijk recht in kerk en wereld* aan de orde. Vervolgens gaat het om de positionering van de *kerk in de wereld*.

1. De plaats van kerkelijk recht in kerk en wereld

De canonist van de toekomst is op de eerste plaats een theoloog. Profane juristen zullen zich, zeker als hen overal, bijvoorbeeld ook aan de Lateraanse universiteit, *effectief* een opleiding van vijf jaar te wachten staat om het licentiaat te verwerven, in de toekomst gedeisd houden. De invloed van het profane recht op het canonieke, en de wisselwerking tussen beide disciplines zal wellicht afnemen. De aandacht die in de tweede cyclus aan het hedendaagse profane recht wordt geschonken, is trouwens marginaal. Er is een vak met als titel *elementa iuris civilis*. Daarnaast is er nog een vak over de betrekkingen tussen de kerk en de civiele samenleving, een vak dat – voortbordurend op zijn benaming zelf – niet juridisch van aard dient te zijn, het kan ook gaan om filosofische bespiegelingen. Kortom, *Elementa iuris civilis* is een *disciplina conexa*, en beslaat blijkbaar één vak, zoals bijvoorbeeld het verplichte vak triniteitsleer in de eerste cyclus.

Betekent de verdere theologisering van het kerkelijk recht dan ook dat de binnenkerkelijke invloeden van het profane recht geringer zullen worden? Ik vrees het tegendeel. De toekomstige canonist, die vrijwel zonder uitzondering theoloog zal zijn, wordt wellicht minder ingezet in materies met een belangrijke profaanjuridische component. Aansprakelijkheid bij seksueel misbruik van clerici, arbeidsverhoudingen, de toetsing van kerkelijke procedures door de profane rechter, het beroepsgeheim van de clericus: al deze materies zullen in de toekomst wellicht exclusief door *profane juristen* worden behandeld. Ze zijn immers te *technisch*, en indien ze verkeerd worden aangepakt, tegelijk ook te *duur* om ze aan een juridisch gebrekkig geschoold canonist toe te vertrouwen. Op dit ogenblik kan iemand die tegelijk profaan jurist en canonist is nog met zulke zaken worden belast. Dat houdt aanzienlijke voordelen in. Het gaat immers om materies die zowat *à cheval* zitten tussen het profane en het canonieke recht. Wanneer brugfiguren die beide disciplines beheersen ten gevolge van het decreet geleidelijk verdwijnen, zal – ongeacht binnenkerkelijke ideologische voorkeuren die naar de andere richting neigen – door de gewijde herders ongetwijfeld voor de profane jurist en niet voor de theoloog-canonist worden gekozen.

Op die manier wordt een trend bevestigd die nu al zichtbaar is. Canonisten in bijvoorbeeld Nederland en de Verenigde Staten constateren vaak dat, wanneer het echt belangrijk wordt, de bisschop zijn goedkope kerkjuristen overslaat en kiest voor de competentie van een dure profane advocaat. De dossiers in verband met seksueel misbruik van clerici hebben op dit terrein een grote symboolwaarde.

De slotsom is duidelijk: het terugbrengen van profaanjuridische invloeden *ad intra* voert *ad extra* tot een functieverlies van het canonieke recht ten voordele van het profane.

Maar er is meer. De toenemende theologisering van het canonieke recht roept zelfs *ad intra* een verrassend mechanisme in het leven. Het kerkelijk recht wordt er ideëler en irenischer op, en poogt het conflictuele veld zo weinig mogelijk te betreden. Canonisten hebben, gezien de theologische context waarin ze arbeiden, wellicht steeds meer de neiging om conflicten op een theoretisch niveau weg te redeneren. Eerder dan in een chaotische sfeer naar billijke juridische oplossingen te zoeken, proberen zij een theoretisch kader uit te werken waarin voor chaos geen plaats wordt geclaimd. Tegenover *les mains sales*[6] van het conflictuele recht, staan *les mains propres* van de theoretische concepten met hun theologische glans. Het fraaie, hoogtheologische canonieke recht steekt schril af bij het kerkelijk recht uit de gore buitenwijken, het *suburban canon law* waaraan ik vele jaren geleden tijdens een conferentie aan de toen nog bestaande Katholieke Theologische Universiteit van Amsterdam mijn liefde heb verklaard[7].

Een exclusief theologische aanpak neigt naar een op deductieve leest geschoeide overaccentuering van het mooie. Anders uitgedrukt, de nieuwe canonist zal weinig moeilijkheden hebben met normen die de Romeinse curie *organiseren*, met de profielomschrijving van de bisschop, met de theologisch-juridische omkadering van boetesacrament, vormsel, eucharistie of ziekenzalving. Maar hoe gaat de theologisch gevormde canonist om met het *conflict* dat *niet* via de weg van verzoening of herderlijke aandacht tot een oplossing kan worden gebracht? Met andere woorden, er bestaat een risico dat het theologische monopolie binnen de canonistiek tot een grotere aandacht voor de *organisatorische* dimensie van het canoniek recht zal leiden, ten koste van zijn *conflictuele* aspecten. Het conflict is de pathologie van de organisatie. Maar *mag* het conflict wel uitbreken binnen een organisatie die, steunend op zorgvuldig uitgekiende theologische concepten, theoretische onberispelijk in elkaar zit? Accepteert een zuiver theologisch geïnspireerd

---

[6] J.-P. SARTRE, *Les mains sales*, Paris, Gallimard, 1948, 259 p. is verantwoordelijk voor deze uitdrukking.

[7] R. TORFS, "Het recht op vrije meningsuiting in de Kerk. Retoriek of reddingsboei?", in R. TORFS, R.G.W. HUYSMANS, R. BURGGRAEVE en W. KLIJN, *Het recht van spreken binnen de Kerk. Een benadering vanuit kerkelijk recht en de theologische ethiek*, Amsterdam, Katholieke Theologische Universiteit, 1991, 1-23.

canoniek recht ook in de toekomst het *paradigma van het conflict*? Het heeft immers alles om de klassieke theoloog niet te bevallen: disrupties, kromme lijnen, verstoorde logica, *ad-hoc*-oplossingen, onvriendelijke gelovigen, starre leiders. Nogmaals, durft een theologisch georiënteerd canoniek recht te leven met de chaos van het *conflictuele*? Heeft ze de moed om de irenische grandeur van de kerk als *organisatie*, van de 'andere Christus' te relativeren?

Inmiddels moge duidelijk zijn dat het decreet van 2 september 2002 voor het canonieke recht als vakgebied ernstige gevolgen dreigt te hebben. De toenemende theologisering van het vak leidt *ad extra* tot een terreinverlies van het canonieke recht tegenover het profane. *Ad intra* verschuift de klemtoon wellicht steeds meer naar de organisatorische dimensie van het canoniek recht, ten koste van haar conflictueel aspect.

2. De plaats van de kerk in de wereld

Bovenstaand titeltje klinkt gewichtig conciliair[8]. Staat er in het nieuwe *decretum* werkelijk zóveel op het spel? Overdrijven is nooit goed. Een wijziging in de opleiding kerkelijk recht stuwt de kerk als instituut niet meteen een andere richting in. Toch zijn een aantal punten in het nieuwe document symptomatisch voor trends die op dit ogenblik in de kerk de dienst uitmaken.

Vooreerst is er het (boven al gemelde) afscheid van de universitaire *mainstream*[9]. De kerk vaardigt nieuwe normen uit zonder ook maar een oogwenk in overweging te nemen wat de consequenties daarvan zijn voor de universitaire erkenning in de profane maatschappij. De logica van de *eigen beroepsopleiding* domineert het plaatje. Een bredere wetenschappelijke context is niet van belang. De groeiende afstand tussen universitaire opleidingen enerzijds en kerkelijke opleidingen anderzijds, is duidelijk zichtbaar in het programma. Negen theologische vakken staan tegenover slechts drie filosofische, namelijk metafysica, ethiek en filosofische antropologie. De kans is verre van denkbeeldig dat in dit laatste

---

[8] Zie hierover de pastorale constitutie *Gaudium et spes* over de Kerk in de wereld: Concilium Vaticanum II, Constitutio Pastoralis de Ecclesia in mundo huius temporis *Gaudium et spes*, 7 december 1965, *AAS* 1966, 1025-1120.

[9] Zie in dit verband J. Frank, "Wortkarge Abfuhr aus dem Vatikan. Warum Kirchenfürsten nicht wünschen, daß der Staat an der Universität Erfurt Theologie lehrt", *Kölner Stadt-Anzeiger*, 15 oktober 1998.

vak de zogenaamde *antropologia christiana*[10] zal worden aangeprezen, en sterk zal worden gewaarschuwd tegen de groeiende invloed van de humane wetenschappen. Deze laatste blijven trouwens, in hun geheel, opvallend afwezig. Psychologie, sociologie, economie of letterkunde behoren niet tot het studiepakket van de kerkjurist. Ook vergelijkende disciplines kennen geen succes. Zeker, wie de CIC bestudeert, moet ook iets over de CCEO hebben gehoord, en andersom. Maar van enige rechts-vergelijking met andere christelijke kerken of met wereldgodsdiensten is geen sprake. De opleiding is eerder *trechtervormig* dan *verbredend*.

Waarom *trechtervormig*? Reeds in de eerste cyclus wordt, met een strikt vitaal minimum aan filosofie, naar het funderende theologische denkkader toegewerkt. Daaruit wordt dan in de tweede cyclus het cano-nieke recht gededuceerd, met daarnaast enkele *diciplinae conexae* die op geen enkel ogenblik destabiliserend werken. Uitwaaierende (bijvoorbeeld rechtsvergelijkende) of ideologiekritische (bijvoorbeeld filosofische of psychoanalytische) vakken worden niet verplichtend opgelegd. Toegege-ven, ze zijn evenmin verboden, want er is in de derde cyclus ruimte voor *cursus speciales vel exercitationes ab unaquaque Facultate praescripta*.

Een mooie formulering, in een prachtige taal, het Latijn, en zo kom ik organisch uit bij een tweede optie die het decreet met betrekking tot de plaats van de kerk in de wereld neemt. Het Latijn wordt volledig in ere hersteld[11]. Canonisten gaan binnenkort weer vlot Latijn praten. In de eer-ste en tweede cyclus staat *lingua latina* op het programma, zonder dat daarbij van een exacte dosering sprake is. In de derde cyclus, het (moge-lijk) eenjarige doctoraat, moet een cursus in *latinitas canonica* worden verzorgd. Het Latijn is dus terug van weggeweest. Vroeger was de ken-nis van het Latijn bij elke West-Europese intellectueel, weliswaar tot op zekere hoogte, een evidentie. Nu niet meer. En of priesters uit Zimbabwe of China die in Rome komen studeren over een stevige basis in het Latijn beschikken, is niet honderd procent zeker. Deze lacune moet dus, in de logica van het nieuwe decreet, binnen de canonieke opleiding worden opgevuld.

De vraag is echter wat deze voorkeursoptie voor het Latijn precies bewerkt: gaat het om een heraanknopen met een bijna teloorgegane

---

[10] Zie hierover G. VERSALDI, "The Role of Experts in Marriage Procedures", *Forum* 1998/2, 83-98.

[11] IOANNES PP. XXIII, Constitutio Apostolica *Veterum sapientia* de Latinitatis studio provehendo, 22 februari 1962, *AAS* 1962, 129-135 waagde in die tijd, in een ander ver-band, reeds een poging om het Latijn te rehabiliteren.

traditie? Of schuilt onder de gemaakte optie een keuze voor een *ecclesiastical splendid isolation*?

De eerste hypothese, namelijk een wederaanknopen met de traditie, lijkt op het eerste gezicht de juiste. Het Latijn was altijd al de werktaal van de kerk. Verzwakkingen mogen dus niet worden geduld, zo zou de redenering kunnen luiden. Toch mag men niet vergeten dat Latijn nu, en Latijn in bijvoorbeeld de middeleeuwen, twee compleet verschillende zaken zijn. Latijn in de middeleeuwen was niet alleen de taal van de kerk, zij was tegelijk de *lingua franca*, de wereldtaal van de geciviliseerde en intellectuele wereld. Latijn was noodzakelijk om kerkvorst te zijn, maar ook een wereldlijk leider of een geleerde in gelijk welke discipline kon die taal best gebruiken. Het hoeft geen betoog dat het Latijn deze functie vandaag niet meer vervult. Engels is de *lingua franca* geworden. Frans, Duits of Spaans zijn ook nog belangrijk. Maar met de actieve kennis van het Latijn is het maar treurig gesteld. Zelfs voor wie dit verlies (terecht voor mijn part) beweent, is dit de harde werkelijkheid. Het gaat bovendien om een werkelijkheid die niet zonder consequenties blijft. Kort gezegd: wie in de middeleeuwen Latijn leerde, trad binnen in de intellectuele wereld; wie nu Latijn studeert, verschaft zich toegang tot de binnenkerkelijke subcultuur. Het actieve Latijn evolueerde van *wereldtaal* tot *binnenkerkelijke geheimtaal*.

Wat voorafgaat formuleer ik duidelijkheidshalve wat zwart-wit. Bovendien is, het weze herhaald, mijn persoonlijke sympathie voor het Latijn zeer groot. Wie Horatius nooit in de oorspronkelijke taal heeft gelezen, of Catullus, loopt onherroepelijk een flinke brok Westers cultureel erfgoed mis. Soms is Latijn zelfs een erg praktische taal. Zo herinner ik mij levendig hoe ik mijzelf in de zomer van 1998 in Shanghai, na vruchteloze gesprekspogingen in allerlei moderne talen, met een bejaarde prelaat ietwat gebroken Latijn hoorde spreken. Maar veel vaker dan een hulpmiddel, is Latijn vandaag een rem geworden. Kwatongen fluisteren dat sommige Rota-auditeurs hun benoeming vooral danken aan het feit dat ze het Latijn machtig waren. Enige canonieke kennis was mooi meegenomen.

Kan tijdens een (voor theologen) slechts driejarige opleiding Latijn grondig worden aangeleerd? Ik geloof het nooit.

Heeft het zin dat een kerkjurist, vooraleer hij eindelijk tot de studie van zijn vak komt, eerst een vrijwel volwaardig theoloog is geworden, alsmede een meester in de kerkelijke geheimtaal die het Latijn vandaag is? Ik durf het te betwijfelen.

Beide evoluties die ik boven schetste, namelijk het afscheid van de universitaire *mainstream* en de terugkeer van het Latijn, wijzen in dezelfde richting. De kerk gaat op intellectueel vlak haar eigen weg. Zij lijkt wel een *societas perfecta intellectualis*. Tegenover een *uitwaaierende* opleiding kiest zij voor een *trechtervormig programma* met veel theologie en weinig humane wetenschappen. Tegenover een resolute keuze voor de wereldtaal, het Engels, als voornaamste werktaal, poogt zij verbeten een heropflakkering van het Latijn in de hand te werken. De middeleeuwse *lingua franca* vervult voortaan de rol van binnenkerkelijke geheimtaal.

III. INNOVEREND DENKEN BINNEN HET NIEUWE KORSET

In een eerste hoofdstuk werd de nooit gevoerde discussie met kardinaal Grocholewski, aangaande het tweejarige of driejarige programma toch gevoerd. Daarna was het, in een tweede hoofdstuk, de beurt aan de impliciete keuzes en de nevenwerkingen van het nieuwe decreet. Die zijn niet onverdeeld positief. Maar inmiddels is de situatie duidelijk. *Roma locuta, causa finita.* Hoe kan, binnen het vrij rigide korset dat tengevolge van het decreet van 2 september 2002 wordt aangesnoerd, toch ruimte worden geschapen voor een aantal verfrissende en innovatieve ideeën?

Om het met een typisch evasief cliché te zeggen: *deze vraag vergt verdere, diepgaande studie.* Toch waag ik mij hier aan enkele summiere suggesties, en wel op drie terreinen. Vooreerst suggereer ik enkele mogelijke nieuwe *vakken*. Vervolgens ga ik kort in op *methodologische accenten*. Tenslotte komen *organisatorische strategieën* aan bod.

1. Nieuwe vakken

De ware vernieuwing van de opleiding in het kerkelijk recht moet wellicht niet zozeer op het terrein van het *secundum legem*, maar op het vlak van het *praeter legem* worden gezocht. Het nieuwe decreet legt weliswaar vast welke materies in ieder geval dienen te worden onderwezen, maar laat ook ruimte voor supplementaire accenten die de verschillende opleidingscentra zelf kunnen aanbrengen. Hoopgevend is het boven al geciteerde korte zinnetje dat als punt e) van de tweede cyclus staat vermeld: *disciplinae speciales et exercitationes atque seminaria ab unaquaque Facultate praescripta.*

Wie als faculteit gebruik maakt van deze mogelijkheid, verzwaart zijn programma nog. Maar voor wie een op zichzelf terugplooiend kerkelijk recht en een 'trechtervormige' opleiding wil vermijden, is er geen alternatief.

Welke vakken kunnen in het raam van de geboden ruimte worden aangeboden?

Vooreerst denk ik aan een *grondige* opleiding in de juridische verhoudingen tussen kerk en staat, in de normen van het profane recht met betrekking tot religie. Anders uitgedrukt: binnen de opleiding in *diritto canonico* moet ruimschoots aandacht worden besteed aan *diritto ecclesiastico*. De Siamese tweeling mag niet brutaal worden gescheiden. *Diritto ecclesiastico* is het kanaal dat het canonieke binnenmeer met de profaanrechtelijke zee verbindt. Het is de weg naar het ruime sop.

Vervolgens dient aandacht te worden geschonken aan *vergelijkend godsdienstig recht*[12]. Aandacht voor de van de CIC niet erg verschillende en op vele plaatsen maatschappelijk niet bijster relevante CCEO is onvoldoende. Verder reikende vragen mogen niet uit de weg worden gegaan. Vragen zoals: hoe kijken protestantse of orthodoxe kerken tegen het recht aan? Welke visie op recht komt uit de joodse en islamitische traditie te voorschijn? De echte *alteriteit* (om nog maar eens een theologisch modewoord te gebruiken) is eerder op dit terrein dan in de wenig opwindende CCEO te vinden. Wie het *specifieke* van het katholieke kerkelijk recht op het spoor wil komen, mag niet terugdeinzen voor een *verre* excursie.

Tenslotte ben ik een voorstander van vakken die de humane wetenschappen werkelijk *confronteren* met het canonieke recht. Ik pleit niet zozeer voor de invoering van een zeer algemeen vak sociologie, zelfs niet meteen voor een cursus godsdienstsociologie, maar voor een mogelijk erg confronterend vak *sociologie van het kerkelijk recht*, met vragen als: hoe werkt het systeem? Welke belangen beschermt het? Wie ontleent uit welke norm zijn macht en zijn status? Een kritische, soms ontmaskerende, sociologie van het kerkelijk recht vormt wellicht een gezond tegengewicht voor een al te *irenische* en al te *trechtervormige* theologische benadering die in het zog van het nieuwe *decretum* wellicht nóg meer dan vroeger *de bon ton* zal worden. Zulk een functie kan ook door andere, gelijksoortige, vakken worden vervuld zoals *criminologie van het kerkelijk recht*. Wat is het profiel van de kerkelijke crimineel, zoals de ketter of de deviërende theoloog? Herkent men de delinquent, in onvervalste *Lombroso*-stijl, aan de vorm van zijn schedel? Hoe kan

---

[12] Zie in dit verband onder meer de oprichting van het tijdschrift *Daimon. Annuario di diritto comparato delle religioni* in 2001 en het recente boek van S. FERRARI, *Lo spirito dei diritti religiosi*, Bologna, il Mulino, 2002, 304 p.

de kerkelijke misdadiger adequaat worden behandeld, zodat hij de kerk-gemeenschap niet langer bedreigt en tegelijk zelf weer beter wordt? Het lijkt mij normaal dat een rechtssysteem met een strafrecht dat laatste aan de hand van een criminologische benadering in sociaal-pastorale zin aanvult.

2. Methodologische ommezwaai

Tot ieders vreugde heeft Vaticanum II gezorgd voor betere dwarsverbindingen tussen theologie en canoniek recht. Op die manier werd korte metten gemaakt met mogelijke positivistische ontsporingen, die ten tijde van de technisch beresterke maar soms al té praktische CIC 1917 af en toe meer dan een louter denkbeeldig gevaar inhielden. Goed dus dat de theologie, zoals verder tijdens het tweede Vaticaans concilie ontwikkeld, aan het canoniek recht extra ondersteuning heeft weten te verlenen. Maar inmiddels blijft het canoniek recht zich wel nog altijd volledig onttrekken aan welke menswetenschappelijke invloed dan ook.

De toegenomen theologische omkadering droeg het hare bij tot een zeer theoretische en abstracte benadering. Weinig administratieve rechtspraak, veel *ius divinum*, afwezigheid van een echte scheiding van machten, zelfcensuur bij canonisten die hun vak niet wetenschappelijk-kritisch benaderen maar het zien als een handig opstapje voor een mooie binnenkerkelijke carrière: zie daar een aantal factoren die de 'braafheid' van het kerkelijk recht als vakgebied helpen verklaren, die er vaak voor zorgen dat de ultieme vragen *niet* worden gesteld. Die ultieme vragen slaan vaak op de context waarin het recht functioneert, zijn concrete toepassing, de resultaten die het bewerkt. De donkere zijde van het kerkelijk recht wordt verwaarloosd. Nochtans moet zij eerst verkend en vervolgens (in de mate van het mogelijke) overwonnen worden om van een volwaardige universitaire discipline te kunnen gewagen.

Het *decretum* van 2 september 2002 vermeldt de zogenaamde *praxis canonica administrativa et iudicialis* vreemd genoeg bij de *disciplinae conexae*. Dat betekent dat het recht en zijn toepassing als twee verschillende disciplines worden beschouwd. Door zijn toepassing verliest het recht de zuiverheid die het intrinsiek wèl heeft, zo lijkt de redenering te luiden. Welnu, deze stelling dient in een universitaire opleiding kerkelijk recht principieel te worden bestreden. Recht dat losstaat van zijn toepassing, is geen recht. Het is een wettekst, met de klemtoon op de laatste lettergreep. Het is dus vooral een tekst. Recht betekent: de studie van de norm en zijn werking.

3. Organisatorische strategie

Doorheen mijn analyse van het decreet van 2 september 2002 schemeren twee bekommernissen. Er moet meer aandacht gaan naar de *toepassing* van de normen. En de *kritisch-wetenschappelijke* analyse van het canoniek recht dient ongeremd en zonder al te veel *metus reverentialis* aan de oppervlakte te komen. De eerste optie bepleit meer aandacht voor de *praktijk*, de tweede streeft dan weer naar een diepgaander *theoretisch* kader. Het uitbouwen van een opleiding die aan de recente Romeinse normen gehoorzaamt, moet tegelijk nieuwe praktische en theoretische accenten leggen.

Op het *praktische vlak* dient ruimte ter beschikking te worden gesteld voor *stages* die van het opleidingsprogramma integraal deel uitmaken. Dat kunnen stages zijn bij kerkelijke rechtbanken of bij de diocesane administratie, maar eventueel ook elders: bij een kerkelijk of zelfs bij een gespecialiseerd profaan advocaat, bij katholieke instellingen of organisaties, eventueel in de media. Die praktische stage moet natuurlijk goed worden omkaderd en achteraf, bijvoorbeeld aan de hand van seminariesessies, grondig worden geanalyseerd. Indien mogelijk moet de stage een internationale dimensie vertonen. Een student uit de periferie kan in Rome iets leren. En, wat misschien verrast, ook het omgekeerde. *Urban* en *suburban canon law* kunnen elkaar bevruchten.

Op het *theoretische vlak* dient resoluut te worden geopteerd voor *elitevorming* binnen het bestaande opleidingsaanbod. Ook wanneer het nieuwe decreet strikt wordt toegepast, is een wetenschappelijk hoogstaand curriculum nog lang geen certitude. Zonder kritische reflectie is geen echte wetenschap mogelijk. Een al te trechtervormige programmering die voorbijgaat aan uitwaaierende componenten dreigt in een louter praktische opleiding te vervallen. Maar – en ik weet dat ik hier een gevaarlijk terrein betreed – niet alle professoren zijn intellectueel in staat om die kwaliteit te bieden. Ook niet alle professoren verbonden aan de sterkere universiteiten. De zoektocht naar canoniek talent verloopt overal moeizaam. Daarom pleit ik voor een derde jaar waarin, in het raam van een internationaal samenwerkingsverband, een beperkt aantal cursussen wordt gegeven door de beste professoren van de sterkste universiteiten. Dat vergt de creatie van een soort *premier league* van het kerkelijk recht, waarbij uiteraard geen kerkpolitieke, maar wetenschappelijke criteria centraal staan. Door de bestaande communicatietechnieken is het mogelijk een lezing te organiseren die interactief op diverse plaatsen ter wereld tegelijk kan worden gevolgd. Het uurverschil tussen Europa en Noord-Amerika is op dat terrein niet prohibitief. Onze universiteit beschikt over de technische en intellectuele vaardigheden om op dit terrein het voortouw te nemen.

Onnodig te melden dat een dergelijk hoog kwalitatief aanbod ook profaanrechtelijke erkenning dient na te streven. Voor doctoraatsstudenten moeten bovendien veel strengere eisen worden gesteld dan in het decreet wordt gevraagd. Men zou kunnen denken aan een minimale periode van drie jaar tussen het behalen van het licentiaatsdiploma en het verdedigen van het doctoraatsproefschrift. Doctoraten behaald na één jaar zijn immers niet verzoenbaar met het aanhouden van een aanvaardbaar wetenschappelijk peil.

BESLUIT

Het decreet van de *Congregatie voor de katholieke opvoeding* van 2 september 2002 poogt de kwaliteit van het onderwijs in het kerkelijk recht te verbeteren aan de hand van een (voor juristen zeer aanzienlijke) verlenging van de studieduur. Of dit een goed idee was, valt te betwijfelen, maar een dialoog hierover met de Congregatie was helaas onmogelijk. Laten we gewoon uitgaan van de realiteit: het decreet wordt opgelegd.

Dat het decreet een aantal onverwachte gevolgen dreigt te hebben, moge duidelijk zijn. De theologisering van het canonieke recht leidt, *ad extra*, zonder twijfel tot functieverlies ten voordele van het profane recht. *Ad intra* komt de klemtoon wellicht steeds meer op organisatorische, en steeds minder op conflictuele vragen te liggen.

Bovendien leiden de verwijdering van de universitaire *mainstream* en de vernieuwde sleutelrol van het Latijn in toenemende mate tot een kerk die zich als *societas perfecta intellectualis* profileert.

Toegegeven, dat klinkt allemaal niet zo fraai. En toch blijft innoverend denken binnen het rigide korset van het nieuwe decreet nog steeds mogelijk. Nieuwe vakken kunnen worden ingevoerd. Een methodologische ommezwaai wordt door het decreet niet verhinderd. Op het organisatorische vlak moeten nieuwe opties vooral op twee terreinen worden gezocht. Vooreerst dient meer aandacht te gaan naar de *toepassing* van kerkelijke normen, waarbij het opzetten van praktische stages een belangrijke factor kan zijn. Vervolgens moet op theoretisch vlak resoluut worden gestreefd naar *elitevorming* gebaseerd op louter wetenschappelijke criteria. Kortom, meer aandacht voor de praktijk en een hoger wetenschappelijk gehalte van het theoretische luik zijn de sleutelwoorden.

Heeft dit plan kans op slagen?

Wie de geruisloze *folklorisering* van het kerkelijk recht wil bestrijden, heeft de plicht om een laatste poging te wagen, waarna, bij mislukking, er zo nodig nog een volgt.

THE ROMAN REFORM OF THE CANON LAW
PROGRAMME. *PER ASPERA AD ASTRA?*

RIK TORFS

INTRODUCTION

In late November 2002 a decree from the *Congregation for Catholic Education* was published. This document, which is dated 2 September 2002 and was signed by Prefect Zenon Grocholewski and Secretary Giuseppe Pittau, aims to reorganise the study of canon law[1].

The authors note an increase in the number of students of canon law, but also a decline in the quality of programmes in terms of their content. Knowledge of Latin, which was still quite adequate in 1931, at the time of the Apostolic Constitution *Deus scientiarum Dominus* of Pius XI[2], is declining rapidly. Furthermore, today's seminarians are increasingly concentrating on theological and pastoral disciplines, at the expense of canon law. In short, priests who arrive at university are less well equipped than previously to begin a course of study in canon law.

The situation among lay people is still more lamentable (by far). In many cases they apply with no theological knowledge at all.

Action was therefore needed. The Congregation for Catholic Education organised a survey. The Congregation then organised *plures consultationes*, to put it in a language that will become significantly more important from now on. The Congregation itself held plenary meetings on this subject in 1998 and 2002[3]. The decree of 2 September 2002 is the result of all these steps. It gave rise to an amendment of Article 76 of the

---

[1] Decretum Congregationis de Institutione Catholica quo ordo studiorum in Facultatibus Iuris Canonici innovatur, 2 September 2002. The decree was made public by the press office of the Holy See on 14 November 2002. Since then it has been published in various editions of the *Osservatore Romano*, but not yet in the *Acta*.

[2] PIUS PP. XI, Constitutio apostolica *Deus scientiarum Dominus* de universitatibus et facultatibus studiorum ecclesiasticorum, 24 May 1931, *AAS* 1931, 241-262.

[3] See the reference in the preamble to the decree of 2 September 2002. See also B. ESPOSITO, "Verso una riforma delle Facoltà di Diritto canonico ecclesiastiche? Pro e contra in vista di una prossima decisione", *Angelicum* 2002, 208.

Apostolic Constitution *Sapientia Christiana* and articles 56 and 57 of its norms[4].

So how exactly do the fruits of the renewal look now?

Training in canon law is organised in three cycles.

The *first cycle*, which takes two years or four semesters, is compulsory for students who have had no prior training in philosophy or theology. This automatically applies to people who have a degree in civil law. There are detailed references to the areas in which these people need extra training. These include Latin, fundamental structures of canon law, three philosophical disciplines and nine theological subjects. The subjects which are essential for the future canon lawyer include trinitarian theology, Christology and divine grace. Theologians and seminary alumni are allowed to progress immediately to the second cycle.

The *second cycle*, which lasts for three years or six semesters, covers the entire code of canon law and other canon laws, an introduction to the Eastern Codex (CCEO), Latin, optional subjects and finally a series of so-called *disciplinae conexae*: theology of canon law, legal philosophy, fundamental concepts of Roman law, elements of civil law, history of the fundamental canonical structures, history of the sources of canon law, the relationship between the church and civil society, canonical administrative and judicial practice.

The *third cycle*, the doctorate, covers at least one year or two semesters. Classes in canonical Latin must be followed and there is scope for optional subjects.

The new regulations therefore mean that from now on theologians will have to spend *three years* on canon law. Lawyers who, in Belgium, have already completed five years of study, will have to add a further *five years* to their studies. They will receive their license in canon law no less than ten years after starting their university training. This gives our subject a place at the absolute top. It is barely possible to study for longer than that. Some comfort can be taken from the speed with which it is possible to obtain a doctorate (one year).

I would like to look in more detail below at three aspects of the reform. I will begin with an analysis of the licence programme: two or three

---

[4] IOANNES PAULUS PP. II, Constitutio apostolica *Sapientia Christiana* de studiorum Universitatibus et Facultatibus Ecclesiasticis, 15 April 1979, *AAS* 1979, 469-499; SACRA CONGREGATIO PRO INSTITUTIONE CATHOLICA, Ordinationes ad Constitutionem Apostolicam "Sapientia Christiana" de studiorum Universitatibus et Facultatibus ecclesiasticis rite exsequendam, *AAS* 1979, 500-521.

years. What are, or rather, *were* the pros and cons? *Were*, because *alea iacta est*. Nevertheless, I will allow myself a brief review.

I will then look at what is not written in the decree of 2 September 2002. What options has the Congregation taken without explicitly stating them?

Finally I will try to ascertain how we, within the existing framework of *Roma locuta, causa finita* can nevertheless work towards creating an attractive canonical programme. Or, to put it differently: how can we fill up a compulsory three-year licence programme in such a way that the Roman demands are met and a future-oriented vision of our discipline can also be developed?

In short, three themes will be addressed: (I) the choices made in the decree; (II) implicit options and unexpected side-effects; (III) future developments with the new decree as an essential framework. It must be said that the thoughts set out below are purely my own personal view, and not necessarily that of the Faculty.

I. PROGRAMME FOR THE LICENCE IN CANON LAW: TWO YEARS OR THREE

The decree of 2 September 2002 deserves every praise for standing up for a high-quality course of study in canon law. It makes no sense to award diplomas unless those receiving them have acquired an adequate knowledge. The great question, however, is whether that knowledge is best acquired through a longer course of study. There are, after all, valid arguments in favour of retaining the two-year license programme. At a meeting in Leuven on 31 August 2001 the Deans and other heads of seven canon law programmes set down an argument in which they called for the two-year license diploma to be retained. The seven institutions involved were the *Pontificia Università della Santa Croce* (Rome), the *Catholic University of America* (Washington), the *Katholieke Universiteit Leuven*, the *Pontificia Universidad Católica S. Maria* in Buenos Aires, the Institut de Droit Canonique of the *Université Marc Bloch* in Strasbourg, the *Universidad de Navarra* (Pamplona) and *Saint Paul University* (Ottawa).

I myself, after this meeting and after extensive discussions with my colleagues Roch Pagé (Saint Paul) and John Beal (Catholic University of America) in Albuquerque, New Mexico, in early October 2001, and after some contact in writing (often with detailed responses) with the

other deans, sent a letter on 21 January 2002 to Cardinal Zenon Grocholewski setting out seven problems in connection with lengthening the
study programme. A copy of the letter was also sent to the deans of the
faculties who were not present in Leuven on 31 August 2001. This letter certainly made its way to the *Angelicum* in Rome. Bruno Esposito
mentions it in detail in his article *Le facoltà di diritto canonico ecclesiastiche tra passato, presente e futuro*, published in the journal *Angelicum*
at the end of 2002[5]. It is not clear whether Cardinal Grocholewski also
received the letter. I have not received any response at all from him to
this day (21 January 2003, i.e. exactly one year after its date), nor even
an acknowledgment of receipt. It is therefore not impossible, and is even
probable that the letter, in view of our poor postal services, never reached
its addressee.

The seven points raised in the letter, five of which are mentioned by
Bruno Esposito in his article, are set out again here in full, with a brief
explanation of each one.

*1. If the proposed three year programme is inspired by the concern that
    students are now entering the second cycle of the licentiate programme
    lacking in knowledge of Latin or theology, this problem could be
    solved by imposing a preliminary examination or by more rigorous
    insistence on the completion of the first cycle. Providing a more gen-
    eral course is not part of the role of a faculty of canon law.*

This argument is also used by Bruno Esposito. He calls for *conoscenze
previe* versus *conoscenze complementari*. Their basic knowledge must
have reached an acceptable level before students begin studies in canon
law.

*2. A mandatory three year programme would be very expensive, espe-
    cially for students at schools with a high tuition fee.*

This is a very sensitive point for North American faculties. Sometimes
the costs are doubled. The ecclesiastical authorities already provide for

---

[5] B. Esposito, "Verso una riforma delle Facoltà di Diritto canonico ecclesiastiche?
Pro e contra in vista di una prossima decisione", *Angelicum* 2002, 177-224; B. Esposito,
"Le facoltà di diritto canonico ecclesiastiche tra passato, presente e futuro", *Angelicum*
2002, 909-968. The analysis of my letter is in the second article, 956-958.

the organisational framework of the institution, and the tuition fees must also be found for its seminarians or student priests.

3. *Although a three year programme can improve the consistency of canon law studies, the long duration may also be a deterrent. Bishops may hesitate to send excellent students. This is particularly true when potential students are committed priests with several years of pastoral experience.*

This problem is associated with the specific nature of the course in canon law. Often it does not fit in seamlessly with, for example, a theological education. Canon law is mostly a study for advanced students, people aged around thirty for whom the inside story of pastoral practice is not an alien subject. It is always a bigger step for a bishop to give study leave to someone whose *replacement* is his own responsibility, than to allow a person wishing to *continue* his studies. The latter person is *not yet engaged,* and this is psychologically easier than *replacing someone who is already engaged in his work.*

4. *A compulsory three-year license programme could endanger the number of doctorates, especially at centres where they take three years or more. Six or seven years of training in canon law will often be perceived as too long. In any case: a lack of doctorates could eventually harm the scientific status of canon law.*

The Congregation has opted for a doctorate with a minimum duration of one year. When the programme in canon law is given at a university with some social prestige, such a brief doctorate is certainly completely unacceptable. The normal period required for a doctorate in such places is four years. That means that a person with prior training in civil law who wants to become a doctor of canon law, if he is quick about it, will require $5 + 5 + 4 = 14$ years. The length of this period is a result of the combination of *ecclesiastical requirements* for a license programme and *civil requirements* imposed on an academically sound doctorate.

5. *A three-year programme would make part-time programmes based on summer courses a less than realistic project.*

A license for theologians would quickly run to six years, and a license for lawyers would take ten years. One option would be to eliminate part-time programmes. It is, however, precisely part-time programmes that make it possible to combine work and study. It is also precisely this combination that can make it easier for potential students (student priests) and their bishops to make the decision.

6. *Many faculties and schools cannot organise a three-year programme with their current teaching staffs. New professors would have to be hired. This entails both financial and practical problems: not many highly qualified candidates are available.*

It should be clear that not every *doctor iuris canonici* is eligible to teach at a respected university. That is true *a fortiori* when the doctorate in question has been written in one year and therefore does not meet the academic criteria that are imposed in other university disciplines. The poor academic quality of some professors, which is evident both from the small number of academic publications that they have written and the questionable quality of those publications, must be discussed openly. The quality problem that Cardinal Grocholewski finds among students is also painfully evident among professors. Canonical courtesy often prevents an appropriate response.

7. *Any reform of current programmes should take place in full harmony with the existing state legislation, which differs from country to country. State recognition of canonical degrees does not exist everywhere, but where it does, every effort must be made to maintain it.*

The Roman procedures do not take into account the changes that are taking place in the university landscape. The introduction of the new *bachelor-master* structure in European Union countries is a *non-issue.* for the Congregation. The double (state and canonical) recognition of diplomas is lightly set aside. There is every indication that the church no longer considers social recognition of the level of its training to be important. In the area of education and science, it seems that the *revival* of the *societas perfecta* idea has become a reality. Ecclesiastical programmes are gradually departing from the university *mainstream.*

In short, the transition to a three-year license programme will have considerable consequences. Perhaps it was not such a good idea *after all.* It is also a shame that there was never an in-depth *public debate* on this issue. It would have benefited the culture of debate within the church if such a thing had been possible. We must not, however, be naïve. What is done, is done. The three years are with us. *Life goes on.* In the next chapter I will try to read between the lines. The *explicit* options that were taken by the decree of 2 September 2002 were considered in the introduction. But what are the *implicit* options? Or, to put it rather more amiably, what are the side-effects of the medicine that Cardinal Grocholewski has prescribed for programmes in canon law?

II. IMPLICIT OPTIONS. OR: THE SIDE-EFFECTS OF THE MEDICINE

Anyone who reads the decree from the Congregation for Catholic Education fleetingly might be impressed by the striving for quality that shines through it. Lovers of thoroughness will find many things to their taste. A longer programme. More theology. More Latin. More attention to the CCEO, which is so well-loved in certain circles. In short, the canonists of the future will be erudite scholars of a certain age, people who command respect.

And yet the decree also has 'invisible' consequences. These can be identified in two areas. First of all comes the place of *canon law in the church and in the world*. Next it concerns the position of the *church in the world*.

1. The place of canon law in the church and the world.

The canon lawyer of the future is first of all a theologian. Civil lawyers will become rather shy of the course in future, certainly if even, *in practice* they face a five-year programme to acquire the license. The influence of civil law on canon law, and the interplay between the two disciplines, will probably decline. The attention devoted to contemporary civil law in the second cycle is quite marginal. There is one subject entitled *elementa iuris civilis*. There is also a subject that addresses relations between the church and civil society, a subject which – in accordance with its name – does not have to be juridical in its approach and may also consist of philosophical reflections. In short, *Elementa iuris civilis* is a *disciplina conexa* and clearly comprises one subject, like, for example, the compulsory subject of trinitarian theology in the first cycle.

Does the continuing theologisation of canon law therefore mean that the influence of civil law within the church will weaken? I fear the contrary. The future canon lawyer, who will, virtually without exception, be a theologian, will probably be less proficient in matters that have a significant component of civil law. Liability in sexual abuse by clergy, employment relationships, the testing of ecclesiastical proceedings by civil judges, professional secrecy of the clergy: all these issues will, in future, probably be dealt with exclusively by *civil lawyers*. That is because these subjects are too *technical*, and if addressed incorrectly, also too *expensive* to be entrusted to a canon lawyer with inadequate legal training. At the moment, someone who is a civil lawyer and a canon lawyer at the same time may be in a position to deal with these things. There are significant benefits associated with this. That is because the areas involved are rather *wedged* between civil and canon law. As bridging figures who master both disciplines gradually disappear as a result of the decree – despite ideological preferences in the other direction – ordained pastors will no doubt choose to use civil lawyers rather than theologian-canon lawyers.

Hence a trend which can already be seen, will be confirmed. Canon lawyers in the Netherlands and the United States, for example, often observe that when it really matters the bishop passes over his cheap canon lawyers and prefers to call upon the services of an expensive civil advocate. Cases in connection with sexual abuse by clergy, have great symbolic value in this domain.

The end-result is clear: a decline of the influence of civil lawyers *ad intra* leads *ad extra* to a loss of function of canon law in favour of civil law.

But there is more. The increasing theologisation of canon law gives rise to a surprising mechanism even *ad intra*. Canon law becomes more idealistic and irenic and seeks to avoid the field of conflict as far as possible. Canon lawyers, due to the theological context in which they work, perhaps always have more of a tendency to reason away conflicts at the theoretical level. Rather than looking for fair legal solutions in a chaotic environment, they try to work out a theoretical framework in which there is no room for chaos. In contrast with *les mains sales*[6] of the law in

---

[6] J.-P. SARTRE, *Les mains sales*, Paris, Gallimard, 1948, 259 p. is responsible for this expression.

conflict situations, we have *les mains propres* of theoretical concepts with their theological lustre. The delicate and highly theological canon law is in stark contrast to the canon law from the grimy suburbs, the *suburban canon law* for which I declared my love many years ago during a conference at the Catholic Theological University of Amsterdam, which still existed at that time[7].

An exclusively theological approach tends towards an over-emphasis of the beautiful, following a deductive pattern. In other words, the new canon lawyer will not have much difficulty with norms *organising* the Roman Curia, with the description of the profile of a bishop, with the theological and legal framework for the sacraments of penance, confirmation and Eucharist or the anointing of the sick. But how will the theologically trained canon lawyer deal with the *conflict* that *cannot* be resolved through reconciliation or pastoral care? In other words, there is a risk that the theological monopoly within canon law will lead to more attention being paid to the *organisational* dimension of canon law, at the expense of its *conflictual* aspects. Conflict is the pathology of the organisation. But is conflict *allowed* to break out within an organisation which, built on carefully refined theological concepts, has an impeccable theoretical structure? In future, will a purely theologically inspired canon law accept the *paradigm of conflict*? After all, it contains everything that the classical theologian does not like: disruptions, bent lines, disturbed logic, *ad-hoc* solutions, unfriendly believers, inflexible leaders. Once again, will a theologically-oriented canon law dare to live with the chaos of the *conflictual*? Does it have the courage to take a relative view of the irenic grandeur of the church as an *organisation*, of the 'other Christ'?

It should be clear by now that the decree of 2 September 2002 is at risk of having serious consequences for canon law as a subject. The increasing theologisation of the subject leads *ad extra* to a situation where canon law loses ground to civil law. *Ad intra* the emphasis may shift even more towards the organisational dimension of canon law, at the expense of the conflictual aspect.

---

[7] R. TORFS, "Het recht op vrije meningsuiting in de Kerk. Retoriek of reddingsboei?", in R. TORFS, R.G.W. HUYSMANS, R. BURGGRAEVE and W. KLIJN, *Het recht van spreken binnen de Kerk. Een benadering vanuit kerkelijk recht en de theologische ethiek*, Amsterdam, Katholieke Theologische Universiteit, 1991, 1-23.

2. The place of the church in the world.

This sounds like a weighty, Conciliar title[8]. Is there really so much at stake in the new *decretum*? It is never a good thing to exaggerate. A change in the canon law programme does not immediately push the church as an institution in a different direction. Nevertheless a number of points in the new document are symptomatic of trends which are currently dominant in the church.

First of all there is the departure (already mentioned above) from the university *mainstream*[9]. The church promulgates new norms without considering for a moment what their consequences will be for university recognition in the civil society. The logic of *its own professional training* dominates the picture. A wider academic context is not important. The growing distance between university courses on the one hand and church programmes on the other, can clearly be seen in the programme. In comparison with nine theological subjects there are only three philosophical ones, namely metaphysics, ethics and philosophical anthropology. It is far from imaginary to suppose that in the latter subject the so-called *antropologia christiana*[10] will be recommended, and there will be strong warnings against the growing influence of the humanities. The latter are, as a whole, conspicuously absent. Psychology, sociology, economics and literature are not part of the studies of a canon lawyer. Comparative disciplines are also not successful. Certainly anyone who studies the CIC must also have heard something about the CCEO, and vice versa. There is, however, no comparison with the law of other Christian churches or world religions. The programme is *funnel-shaped* rather than *broadening*.

Why *funnel-shaped*? Even in the first cycle, with a strict necessary minimum of philosophy, students work towards the foundational theological framework of thought. Canon law is then deduced from this during the second cycle, with a few *diciplinae conexae* which do not have a destabilising effect at any time. Subjects expanding from this (for example into comparative law) or critical of the ideology (for example philosophical or psychoanalytical subjects) are not imposed as compulsory.

---

[8] On this subject see the pastoral constitution *Gaudium et spes* on the Church in the world: CONCILIUM VATICANUM II, Constitutio Pastoralis de Ecclesia in mundo huius temporis *Gaudium et spes*, 7 December 1965, *AAS* 1966, 1025-1120.

[9] In this connection see J. FRANK, "Wortkarge Abfuhr aus dem Vatikan. Warum Kirchenfürsten nicht wünschen, daß der Staat an der Universität Erfurt Theologie lehrt", *Kölner Stadt-Anzeiger*, 15 October 1998.

[10] On this subject see G. VERSALDI, "The Role of Experts in Marriage Procedures", *Forum* 1998/2, 83-98.

It is true that they are not forbidden either, for in the third cycle there is space for *cursus speciales vel exercitationes ab unaquaque Facultate praescripta.*

This is a delightful formulation, in a wonderful language – Latin – which brings me neatly to a second option that the decree has taken with regard to the place of the church in the world. Latin has been completely restored to honour[11]. Canon lawyers will soon be speaking fluent Latin again. In the first and second cycle *lingua latina* is part of the programme, although the precise amount is not prescribed. In the third cycle, the (possible) one-year doctorate, a course in *latinitas canonica* must be provided. Latin has therefore been brought in from the cold. In the past, knowledge of Latin was taken for granted by every intellectual in Western Europe, at least up to a certain level. That is no longer the case. It is not a hundred percent certain that priests from Zimbabwe or China who come to study in Rome will have a strong foundation in Latin. According to the logic of the new decree, this gap must be filled within the canon law programme.

The question, however, is what precisely this preferential option for Latin will achieve: is it about re-establishing links with an almost defunct tradition? Or does this option hide another choice, in favour of *ecclesiastical splendid isolation*?

The first hypothesis, namely re-establishing links with tradition, seems at first sight to be correct. Latin has always been the working language of the church. So the reasoning may be that we must not allow our line to weaken. Nevertheless it should not be forgotten that Latin now, and Latin in, for example, the Middle Ages, are two completely different things. Latin in the Middle Ages was not only the language of the church, it was at the same time the *lingua franca*, the world language of the civilised and intellectual world. Latin was necessary in order to be a leader in the church, but secular leaders and learned people in all disciplines needed the language as well. It goes without saying that Latin no longer fulfils this function today. English has become the *lingua franca*. French, German and Spanish are also important. Active knowledge of Latin, however, is in a sorry state. Even for those who mourn this loss (quite rightly, in my opinion), that is the hard reality. What is more, it is

---

[11] IOANNES PP. XXIII, Constitutio Apostolica *Veterum sapientia* de Latinitatis studio provehendo, 22 February 1962, *AAS* 1962, 129-135, in a different time and a different context, made its own effort to rehabilitate Latin.

a reality that has certain consequences. In brief: anyone who learned Latin in the Middle Ages was entering the intellectual world; those who study Latin now, gain access to the subculture within the church. Active Latin has evolved from a *world language* into a *secret language within the church*.

For the sake of clarity, I have made the above statements in rather a black-and-white way. Nevertheless, I must repeat that I have a lot of personal sympathy for Latin. Anyone who has never read Horace in the original language, or Catullus, is inevitably missing an important part of our Western cultural heritage. Sometimes Latin is even a very practical language. I can remember very well how, in the summer of 1998 in Shanghai, after useless efforts at a conversation in various modern languages, I heard myself speaking in rather broken Latin with an elderly prelate. Latin today, however, has become a hindrance rather than an aid. There are vicious rumours that some Rotal auditors owe their appointment mainly to the fact that they had a knowledge of Latin. A little knowledge of canon law was a useful extra.

Is it possible to learn Latin thoroughly during what (for theologians) is only a three-year course? I do not believe it for a moment.

Does it make sense for a canon lawyer, before he finally comes to study his subject, first to have become virtually a fully-fledged theologian and also a master of the ecclesiastical secret language that Latin has now become? I dare to doubt it.

Both the evolutions that I have outlined above, namely the departure from the university *mainstream* and the return of Latin, point in the same direction. In the intellectual domain, the church is simply going its own way. It seems to be a *societas perfecta intellectualis*. In preference to an expansive programme it is choosing a *funnel-shaped programme* with a great deal of theology and not much in the way of humanities. Rather than making a firm choice in favour of the world language, English, as its main working language, it is stubbornly seeking to promote a revival of Latin. The Medieval *lingua franca* will from now on play the part of a secret language within the church.

III. INNOVATIVE THINKING WITHIN THE NEW CORSET

In a first chapter, the debate that never took place with Cardinal Grocholewski concerning the two-year or three-year programme was nevertheless conducted. Then, in the second chapter, we considered the implicit options and side-effects of the new decree. They are not exclusively positive. Now, however, the situation is clear. *Roma locuta, causa finita*. How, within the fairly rigid corset that has been tightened up following the decree of 2 September 2002, is it still possible to create room for a number of refreshing and innovative ideas?

To use a typically evasive cliché: *this question will require further in-depth study*. Nevertheless I will dare to make a few brief suggestions in three areas. First of all I will suggest a few possible new *subjects*. I will then look briefly at *methodological emphases*. Finally attention will be paid to *organisational strategies*.

1. New subjects

The real renewal of the programme in canon law should probably not be sought so much in the area of *secundum legem*, but in the area of *praeter legem*. It is true that the new decree lays down the subjects that must in any case be taught, but it also leaves room for additional emphases that the various educational centres may add themselves. One sign of hope is the brief phrase already quoted above, which is included as point e) in the second cycle: *disciplinae speciales et exercitationes atque seminaria ab unaquaque Facultate praescripta*.

Any faculty that makes use of this opportunity will increase the weight of its programme. For those who want to avoid a canon law that is turned in on itself and a 'funnel-shaped' programme, however, there is no alternative.

What subjects can be offered in the context of the scope that is available?

First of all I am thinking of a *thorough* training in the legal relationships between church and state, in the norms of secular law in relation to religion. In other words: within the training in *diritto canonico* plenty of attention should be paid to *diritto ecclesiastico*. These Siamese twins should not be brutally separated. *Diritto ecclesiastico* is the canal that links the lake of canon law to the sea of civil law. It is the route to the ocean waves.

Next attention should be paid to *comparative religious law*[12]. Devoting attention to the CCEO, which is not very different from the CIC and in

---

[12] In this connection see also the foundation of the journal *Daimon. Annuario di diritto comparato delle religioni* in 2001 and the recent book by S. FERRARI, *Lo spirito dei diritti religiosi*, Bologna, il Mulino, 2002, 304 p.

many places is not terribly socially relevant, is not enough. More far-reaching questions cannot be avoided. Questions like: how do Protestant or Orthodox churches view the law? What perspective on law appears from the Jewish and Islamic traditions? It is in this field that the real *alterity* (to use yet another fashionable theological word) is to be found rather than in the less than exciting CCEO. Those seeking the *specific* aspects of Catholic canon law should not shrink back from a *distant* excursion.

Finally I am in favour of subjects that really do bring the humanities into *confrontation* with canon law. I am not so much calling for the introduction of sociology as a very general subject, and not even immediately for a course in religious sociology, but for what is possibly a very confrontational subject *sociology and canon law*, with questions like: how does the system work? What interests does it protect? Who derives their power and status from which norms? A critical, and sometimes exposing sociology of canon law will probably provide a healthy counterbalance to an all to *irenic* and all too *funnel-shaped* theological approach which, in the wake of the new *decretum* will probably become *de bon ton* more than ever before. Such a function can also be supplemented by other, similar subjects such as *criminology of canon law*. What is the profile of the ecclesiastical criminal, such as the heretic or deviant theologian? Can the delinquent, in true *Lombroso* style, be recognised by the shape of his skull? How can the ecclesiastical offender be treated appropriately so that he no longer poses a threat to the church community and is, at the same time, improved himself? It seems normal to me that a legal system with criminal legislation should also supplement this with a criminological approach in a social-pastoral sense.

2. Methodological about turn

To everyone's joy Vatican II has ensured that better cross-connections exist between theology and canon law. In this way it dealt summarily with the perhaps positivistic excesses that were sometimes more than an imaginary threat in the time of CIC 1917, a document that was strong as an ox in technical terms but sometimes all too practical. It is therefore a good thing that theology, which was also developed further during the second Vatican council, has succeeded in offering extra support to canon law. Meanwhile, however, canon law is still withdrawing itself from any influence whatsoever from the humanities.

The increasingly theological framework has contributed towards a very theoretical and abstract approach. Not much administrative jurisprudence, a lot of *ius divinum*, the lack of any real separation of powers, self-censorship among canon lawyers who do not approach their subject in a critical academic way but as a handy step up to an attractive career within the church: these are a number of factors that help to account for the 'good boy' status of canon law as a subject and often result in the ultimate questions *not* being asked. Those ultimate questions often concern the context in which the law operates, how it is applied in practice and the results that it achieves. The dark side of canon law is neglected. Nevertheless it must first be explored and then (as far as possible) overcome in order to claim to be a fully-fledged university discipline.

The *decretum* of 2 September 2002, strangely enough, mentions the so-called *praxis canonica administrativa et iudicialis* among the *disciplinae conexae*. That means that the law and its application are seen as two different disciplines. The reasoning seems to be that through its application the law loses the purity which it truly has intrinsically. Well, this statement should be disputed in principle in a university canon law programme. Law that is separate from its application is no law. It is a legal text, with the emphasis on the second word. It is, above all, a text. Law means: the study of the norm and its operation.

3. Organisational strategy

Two concerns persistently appear through my analysis of the decree of 2 September 2002. More attention needs to be devoted to the *application* of the norms. What is more, the *critical and academic* analysis of canon law should be done without inhibitions and without too much *metus reverentialis*. The first option calls for more attention to be paid to *practical application*, and the second strives to create a deeper, *theoretical* framework. The development of a programme that is obedient to the new Roman norms must at the same time establish new practical and theoretical emphases.

In the *practical domain* space must be made available for *internships* which form an integral part of the training programme. These might be placements in ecclesiastical courts, with the diocesan administration, or perhaps elsewhere: with a canon lawyer or perhaps even a specialised secular lawyer, with Catholic institutions or organisations or possibly in the media. This practical placement must, of course, be well structured and subsequently analysed in depth, for example through the use of seminar sessions. If possible the internship should have an international dimension. There are things that a student from the periphery can learn in Rome. What is more, perhaps surprisingly, the converse is also true. *Urban* and *suburban canon law* can cross-fertilise one another.

In the *theoretical domain* a resolute choice must be made in favour of *forming an elite* within the existing range of programmes. Even if the new decree is applied strictly, a curriculum with a high academic standard is far from being a certainty. Without critical reflection, no real academic endeavour is possible. An excessively funnel-shaped curriculum that passes over more expansive components is at risk of deteriorating into purely practical training. However – and I know that I am treading on dangerous ground here – not all professors are intellectually capable of offering that quality. Not even all professors associated with the stronger universities. The search for canonical talent is everywhere a laborious one. I am therefore calling for a third year in which, in the context of an international co-operation framework, a limited number of courses are given by the best professors from the strongest universities. That would require the creation of a kind of canon law *premier league*, in which certainly not ecclesiastical-political, but academic criteria take central place. Through existing communication techniques it is possible to organise a lecture which can be followed interactively and simultaneously at different locations throughout the world. The time difference between Europe and North America is not prohibitive in this respect. Our university has the technical and intellectual skills to take the lead in this domain.

It goes without saying that such a high-quality offering must also seek to acquire recognition in the world of secular law. What is more, far more stringent demands must be placed on doctorate students than those required by the decree. One might imagine a minimum period of three years between obtaining the license diploma and defending a doctoral dissertation. That is because doctorates gained after one year are not reconcilable with maintaining an acceptable academic level.

CONCLUSION

The decree from the *Congregation for Catholic Education* dated 2 September 2002 seeks to improve the quality of education in canon law through an extension (very significant for lawyers) of the period of study. It is doubtful whether this was a good idea, but a dialogue with the Congregation on the subject was, unfortunately, impossible. So let us start with the reality: the decree is being imposed upon us.

It should be clear that the decree may have a number of unexpected consequences. The theologisation of canon law will no doubt lead, *ad extra*, to a loss of function in favour of secular law. *Ad intra* the emphasis will probably be increasingly on organisational and less and less on conflictual questions.

What is more, the departure from the university *mainstream* and the renewed key role of Latin will increasingly lead to a church that presents itself as *societas perfecta intellectualis* .

Granted, none of this sounds very nice. Nevertheless, innovative thinking is still possible within the rigid corset of the new decree. New subjects can be introduced. The decree does not prevent a methodological turnaround. In organisational terms, new options can, above all, be sought in two areas. Firstly more attention needs to be devoted to the *application* of ecclesiastical norms, where setting up internships can be an important factor. Secondly, in the theoretical domain, we must strive resolutely towards *the formation of an elite* on the basis of purely academic criteria. In short, more attention to practical application and more academic content in the theoretical section are the key words.

Does this plan have a chance of success?

Those who wish to combat the silent *folklorisation* of canon law, have a duty to make one last attempt, and if it fails, to make yet another.

THE LEGISLATIVE COMPETENCY OF THE EPISCOPAL CONFERENCE: PRESENT SITUATION AND FUTURE POSSIBILITIES

THOMAS J. GREEN

INTRODUCTION

In a relatively recent work on reforming the papacy[1] Archbishop John Quinn indicated that central to any realistic hope of Christian unity is a genuine and not simply symbolic exercise of collegiality within the Church. The way the pope exercises his primacy in relationship to his brother bishops within the Church indicates the way that he would do so in relationship to the Orthodox, Anglicans, and other Christians in the event of full communion with Rome. One significant dimension of the contemporary problematic of collegiality in the Church is the theological-canonical status of episcopal conferences (henceforth conferences), especially but not exclusively regarding their legislative competency and their teaching authority.

Numerous theological, canonical, and historical questions have been raised by the existence and functioning of conferences in the postconciliar Church. In 1985, the extraordinary synod of bishops called for a study of their theological status and doctrinal authority[2]. This prompted an international colloquium on episcopal conferences held in Salamanca in January 1988[3]. Meanwhile, the Vatican drafted a working paper on their theological and juridical status that was released by the Congregation for Bishops after the Salamanca meeting[4]. Some responses to this Vatican

---

[1] See John Quinn, *The Reform of the Papacy. The Costly Call to Christian Unity* (New York: Herder & Herder, 1999).

[2] Synod of Bishops, "Final Report," *Origins* 15 (December 19, 1985) 444-450, especially II, C, 8.

[3] For an English text of the papers resulting from this colloquium, see Hervé Legrand, Julio Manzanares, and Antonio García y García, eds., *The Nature and Future of Episcopal Conferences* (Washington, DC: Catholic University of America Press, 1988). Also *The Jurist* 48 (1988) 1-412. For a listing of some issues on conferences for scholarly inquiry articulated by the colloquium participants, see "Toward the Future: Perspectives and Proposals for Academic Research on Episcopal Conferences," ibid. 48 (1988) 397-401.

[4] "Draft Statement on Episcopal Conferences," *Origins* 17 (April 7, 1988) 731-737.

Instrumentum laboris from theologians, canonists, and conferences, including that of the National Conference of Catholic Bishops (USA) were quite critical[5]. After nearly a decade of further reflection and drafting by various Roman dicasteries, especially the Congregations for Bishops and for the Doctrine of the Faith, John Paul II issued the May 1998 motu proprio *Apostolos suos* clarifying the theological and juridical status of episcopal conferences as a guide to ongoing legal-pastoral practice[6]. Even given a

---

[5] For the text of the NCCB response see "Response to Vatican Working Paper on Bishops' Conferences," *Origins* 18 (December 1, 1988) 397, 399-402. For some initial critical American reflections on the draft, see the articles by Avery Dulles, James Provost, Ladislas Orsy, and Joseph Komonchak in *America* 158 (March 19, 1988) 293-304. Also Joseph Komonchak, "The Roman Working Paper on Episcopal Conferences," in *Episcopal Conferences: Historical, Canonical, and Theological Studies,* ed. Thomas Reese (*Episcopal Conferences*) (Washington: Georgetown University Press, 1989) 177-204. For a comprehensive examination of various issues on episcopal conferences in light of the *Instrumentum laboris,* see also *Die Bischofkonferenz Theologischer und juridischer Status,* ed. Hübert Müller and Hermann Pottmeyer (Dusseldorf: Verlag Patmos, 1989). Some articles are German versions of the Salamanca papers, whereas others are new works prompted by the *Instrumentum.* See also D. P. Lopez-Gallo, "Episcopal Conferences: a Reply and Comment on Instrumentum Laboris," *Monitor Ecclesiasticus* 114 (1989) 149-176; Julio Manzanares, "Reflexiones sobre el documento 'Estatuto teologico y iuridico de las conferencias episcopales," *Revista Española de Derecho Canonico* 46 (1989) 189-202; Herman Pottmeyer, "Was ist eine Bischofs-konferenz?" *Stimmen der Zeit* 206/7 (July 1988) 435-446; Heribert Schmitz, "Status theologicus et iuridicus conferentiarum episcopalium, Kanonistische Bemerkungen zu einem Arbeitspapier der Kurienkongregation für die Bischöfe," *Archiv für Katholisches Kirchenrecht* 156/2 (1989) 515-521; Felix Wilfred, "Episcopal Conferences-Their Theological Status," *Vidajyoti* 52/10 (October 1988) 470-494.

[6] See *Acta Apostolicae Sedis* 90 (1998) 641-658 (*AAS*).For an English text of the motu proprio see *Origins* 28/9 (July 30, 1998) 152-158. For some commentaries see Angel Anton, "La carta apostolica MP 'Apostolos suos' de Juan Pablo II," *Gregorianum* 80 (1999) 263-297; Ignacio Arrieta, "Le conferenze episcopali nel motu proprio *Apostolos suos,*" *Ius Ecclesiae* 11 (1999) 169-191; Winfried Aymans, "Geistlose Bischofskon-ferenz? Kritik an einen Beitrag von Ladislas Orsy über die Bischofskonferenzen und die Macht des Geistes," *Stimmen der Zeit* 218/6 (June 2000) 3-19; Alejandro Bunge, "Comen-tarios sobre el motu proprio *Apostolos suos* a la Luz del *Instrumentum laboris* del 1/7/87," *Annuario Argentino de Derecho Canonico* 6 (1999) 129-145; Peter Erdo, "Osservazioni giuridico-canoniche della lettera apostolica *Apostolos suos,*" *Periodica* 89 (2000) 248-266; Juan Fornés, "Autoridad y competencias de la conferencia episcopal. Un comentario al M. P. *Apostolos suos* de 21 de mayo de 1998," *Ius Canonicum* 39/78 (1999) 733-759; Gianfranco Ghirlanda, "Il M.P. Apostolos suos sulle conferenze dei vescovi," *Periodica* 88 (1999) 609-657; Ladislas Orsy, "Die Bischofkonferenzen und die Macht des Geistes," *Stimmen der Zeit* 218/1 (January 2000) 3-17; idem, "Episcopal Conferences and the Power of the Spirit," *Louvain Studies* 25 (2000) 363-375; Heribert Schmitz, "Neuen Normen für die Bischofskonferenzen. Kanonistische Anmerkungen zum Motu Proprio 'Apostolos suos' vom 21 Mai 1998 und zum Schreiben der Kongregation für die Bischöfe vom 13 Mai bzw. 21 Juni 1999," *Archiv für Katholisches Kirchenrecht* 169 (2000) 249-266; Francis Sullivan, "The Teaching Authority of Episcopal Conferences," *Theological Studies* 63/3 (2002) 472-493.

somewhat lengthy doctrinal part (pars. 1-13), the pope's legislative pre-occupations seem uppermost (pars. 14-24), especially a desire to remedy prior *lacunae iuris* regarding the exercise of conference teaching authority (c. 753). In a certain sense the motu proprio is somewhat like a delayed post-synodal exhortation following the 1985 synod; yet unlike those exhortations it is clearly legislative in character[7]. The motu proprio was followed a year later by a non-binding May 1999 circular letter of the Congregation for Bishops providing guidance to conferences in redrafting their statutes in light of the four complementary norms at the end of the motu proprio, especially regarding conference teaching authority[8].

The legislative[9] authority of episcopal conferences is an important canonical issue which has been treated in various sources[10]. Although the conference's ecclesial significance transcends its legislative prerogatives, for some observers the significance of these prerogatives symbolizes the

[7] For helpful descriptions of the process leading up to the issuance of *Apostolos suos*, see especially Anton, Ghirlanda, and Sullivan mentioned in the prior footnote.

[8] See "Congregation for Bishops Circular Letter: Doctrinal Declarations by Bishops' Conferences", *Origins* 29/7 (July 1, 1999) 113-114.

[9] In an earlier work the author spoke generically of the conference's "normative" function rather than more narrowly of its "legislative" function. This was because he judged that differentiating between conference 'laws' and 'general executory decrees' in the code was occasionally somewhat difficult. However, in retrospect this does not seem to have been necessary; hence the present article speaks simply of the conference's legislative or policy-making function. See Thomas J. Green, "The Normative Role of Episcopal Conferences in the 1983 Code," in *Episcopal Conferences*, 137-175 (Normative Role).

[10] See especially Winfried Aymans, "Wesensverständnis und Zuständigkeiten der Bischofskonferenz im Codex Iuris Canonici von 1983," *Archiv fur Katholisches Kirchenrecht* 152 (1983) 46-61; Juan Calvo, "Las competencias de las conferencias episcopales y del obispo diocesano en relación con el munus sanctificandi," *Ius Canonicum* 24/47 (1984) 645-673; Carmelo de Diego Lora, "Competencias normativas de las conferencias episcopales: primer decreto general en España," *Ius Canonicum* 24/47 (1984) 527-570; John Johnson, "Conferences of Bishops," in *New Commentary on the Code of Canon Law*, ed. John Beal, James Coriden, and Thomas Green (New York: Paulist, 2000) 359-363; 365-369; Bernard de Lanversin, "De la Loi générale à la Loi complémentaire dans l'Église Latine depuis le nouveau Code," in *Liberté et Loi dans l'Église Les Quatres Fleuves* 18 (Paris: Éditions Beauchesne, 1983) 121-134; Peter Leisching, "Die Grenzen der heiligen Gewalt. Erwägungen über die Bischofskonferenz als hierarchische Zwischenstruktur," *Oesterreichisches Archiv fur Kirchenrecht* 36/3 (1986) 203-222; G. Melguizo et al., "Las conferencias episcopales en el nuevo Código de Derecho Canónico," *Universitas Canonica* 3/7 (1983) 41-61; Francis Morrisey, "Decisions of the Episcopal Conferences in Implementing the New Law," *Studia Canonica* 20 (1986) 105-122; Donal Murray, "The Legislative Authority of the Episcopal Conference," *Studia Canonica* 20 (1986) 33-48; James Provost, "Conferences of Bishops," in *The Code of Canon Law: a Text and Commentary*, ed. James Coriden, Thomas Green, and Donald Heintschel (New York: Paulist, 1985) 368-373; F. Uccella, "Le conferenze episcopali nel nuovo codice di diritto canonico: prime riflessioni," *Il Diritto Ecclesiastico* (1986) I: 95-154.

strength or weakness, official acceptance or rejection of this relatively new institution in public ecclesial life. They are also important in enabling one to assess the health of Latin Church intermediary governance structures by comparison with their Eastern church counterparts as well as the extent to which the conciliar teaching on collegiality has reshaped the Church's institutional life[11].

The conference's legislative competence must be situated within the broader context of more notably decentralized governmental processes in the 1983 Code of Canon Law (hereafter Latin code)[12], which among other things enhances the legislative discretion of diocesan bishops in governing their particular churches[13]. Such expanded corporate episcopal legislative discretion is a good example of the code's implementation of the principle of subsidiarity[14].

An area of continuing tension during the 1917 code revision process was structuring the relationship between the Holy See, the episcopal conference, and the diocesan bishop regarding their possession of various governmental competencies: executive, judicial, and especially

---

[11] For a thoughtful discussion of the relevance of the postconciliar discussion of collegiality to episcopal conferences, see Patrick Granfield, "The Collegiality Debate," in *Church and Theology Essays in Memory of Carl J. Peter*, ed. Peter C. Phan (Washington: CUA Press, 1995) 100-108. For Granfield collegiality is a reality that is unique, complex, and in process. It is unique because it is a distinctly ecclesial reality not to be envisioned in purely secular political terms. It is complex since a proper understanding involves theological, historical, canonical, pastoral, and ecumenical dimensions. It is in process because numerous pertinent issues still have not been definitively resolved, e.g., universal Church-particular church relationship, promotion of collegiality, relationships between the Roman Curia and the particular churches, etc. Granfield also mentions the status of episcopal conferences as one of these issues. While *Apostolos suos* has clarified certain theological and juridical aspects of conferences, authors such as Anton, Bunge, Ghirlanda, and Sullivan note that there are still unresolved issues to be probed further. They base this in part on the official presentation of the document by Cardinal Ratzinger, which was reported in the July 24, 1998 edition of *L'Osservatore Romano*.

[12] Henceforth the 1983 Latin code will be cited as c. or cc. followed by the pertinent canon number(s). The 1990 Eastern code will be cited as CCEO followed by the pertinent canon number (s). The 1917 Latin code will be cited as 1917 code followed by c. or cc. and the canon number(s).

[13] See Myriam Wijlens,"'For You I am a Bishop, with You I am a Christian: The Bishop as Legislator," *The Jurist* 56 (1996) 68-91.

[14] See principle 5 for the revision of the 1917 code in *Communicationes* 1 (1969) 80-81. Also Thomas Green, "Subsidiarity during the Code Revision Process: Some Initial Reflections," *The Jurist* 48 (1988) 771-799. For an overview of various examples of particular law in the Latin code see F. Campo del Pozo, "El derecho particular de la Iglesia según el Código de 1983," *Estudio Augustiniano* (1985) 473-528. For some helpful reflections on this issue not long before the promulgation of the code see F. Morrisey, "The Significance of Particular Law in the Proposed New Code of Canon Law," *Proceedings of the Canon Law Society of America* (1981) 1-17 (hereafter cited *CLSA Proceedings*).

legislative. During that process, the conference's legislative competency was gradually reduced[15], partly because of code commission fears that such enhanced conference competency might jeopardize church unity by prompting an unhealthy nationalism and impairing the legitimate governmental autonomy of individual diocesan bishops[16]. Interestingly, the commission did not seem to express comparable fears of excessive centralization regarding the broad competencies of the Holy See dicasteries.

Although *Christus Dominus* 36 urged the revitalization of other intermediary level institutes such as particular councils (cc. 439-446), unfortunately this has not actually happened[17]. On the contrary, there has been a noteworthy, if not always steady, postconciliar enhancement of the legislative competence of conferences, the extent of which is still somewhat controverted. De facto, despite continuing questions about their theological and juridical status, the conferences increasingly seem to be the privileged vehicle of episcopal consultation and collaboration at the supradiocesan but infra-universal level[18]. Whatever be the pre-Latin code

---

[15] The conference's gradually diminished legislative competency during the revision process is a complex issue requiring more detailed study. For example, see Thomas Green, "The Church's Teaching Mission: Some Aspects of the Normative Role of Episcopal Conferences," *Studia Canonica* 27 (1993) 23-57 (Green, Teaching-Conferences); idem, "The Church's Sanctifying Mission: Some Aspects of the Role of Episcopal Conferences," in *Ius Sequitur Vitam Law Follows Life*, ed. James Provost and Knut Walf (Leuven: Leuven University Press, 1998) 57-88 (Green, Sanctifying-Conferences). See also Frederick McManus, "Local, Regional, and Universal Church Law," in *The Papacy and the Church in the United States*, ed. Bernard Cooke (*Papacy and Church*) (NewYork/Mahwah: Paulist, 1989) 179-183.

[16] For concerns about the possible impairment of the exercise of the episcopal office especially through an expanding conference bureaucracy see Paul Gouyon, "Les relations entre le diocèse et la conférence épiscopale," *L'Année Canonique* 22 (1978) 1-23. For some other thoughtful reflections on conference-diocesan bishop relationships see Hubert Müller, "The Relationship between the Episcopal Conference and the Diocesan Bishop," *The Jurist* 48 (1988) 111-129.

[17] For a brief history of particular councils, their status in the 1983 code, and their relationship to conferences, see James Provost, "Particular Councils," in *The New Code of Canon Law/Le Nouveau Code de Droit Canonique* (Ottawa: St. Paul University, 1984) 537-562. See also Juan Fornés, "Naturaleza sinodal de los concilios particulares y de las conferencias episcopales," in *La Synodalité La participation au gouvernement dans l'Église Actes du VIIe Congrès International de Droit Canonique Paris, UNESCO 21-28 septembre* 1990. (Paris: Letouzey et Ané, 1991) 305-348; Gianfranco Ghirlanda, "'Munus regendi et munus docendi' dei concili particolari e delle conferenze dei vescovi," ibid., 349-388.

[18] For a thoughtful consideration of such enhanced conference competence in the early postconciliar period see Giorgio Feliciani, *Le conferenze episcopali* (Bologna: Società Editrice Il Mulino, 1974) 529-545. In light of this development, section IV, 1 of the theological part of the *instrumentum laboris* observed somewhat questionably that canon

history of episcopal conferences[19], this article focuses on their current
legal status, especially in the Latin code (cc. 447-459)[20] and *Apostolos
suos*, which clarify their basic nature, structure, and functioning.
And more specifically the author wishes to explore the scope of the

law made more attributions to particular councils than to conferences ("Draft Statement,"
734). While the meaning of such "attributions" is not entirely clear, there is simply no
comparison between the two institutes in terms of the attention the code devotes to them.
The councils are dealt with almost exclusively in canons 439-446, which describe their
main features. On the contrary, the code makes numerous references to conference functions although some canonists such as McManus (n. 15) sought even broader provisions,
especially in the legislative area. The *instrumentum* seemed unwilling to broaden the conference's legislative competency because doing so would presumably accord it the same
dignity and authoritative power as particular councils and Eastern synods. Yet the *instrumentum* did not explain why this was unacceptable in principle. *Apostolos suos* does not
address this issue at any great length, especially given its primarily conference teaching
authority focus, but it does not at all sharply differentiate between such conferences, councils, and synods. In fact note 1 of the motu proprio indicates explicitly that it does not deal
with such synods and notes that no analogy may be drawn between them and conferences
(*Origins* 28/9 [July 30, 1998] 157.) However, this article will devote significant attention
to the similarities and differences between conferences and such synods.

[19] For a couple of particularly useful canonical discussions of conferences at Vatican
II shortly after the council see Frederick McManus, "The Scope of Authority of Episcopal Conferences," in *The Once and Future Church*, ed. James Coriden (New York: Alba
House, 1971) 129-178 and Klaus Moersdorf, "Commentary on Christus Dominus, c. III:
concerning the Cooperation of Bishops for the Common Good of Many Churches,"
in *Commentary on the* Documents of Vatican II, ed. Herbert Vorgrimler, 5 vols.
(New York: Herder & Herder, 1968) 2: 280-300. For a detailed listing of conciliar references to episcopal conferences see William Leahy, "References to Episcopal Conferences
in Conciliar and Other Related Documents," in *Once and Future Church*, ed. James
Coriden, 277-299. For a detailed discussion of the conciliar treatment of the conferences
see Feliciani, *Le conferenze episcopali*, 353-443. For the most thorough analysis of the conciliar debates on episcopal conferences see Remigiusz Sobanski, "The Theology and
Juridic Status of Episcopal Conferences at the Second Vatican Council," *The Jurist* 48
(1988) 68-106. For some brief but useful remarks on the canonical history of conferences
through Vatican II see Bernard Franck, "La conférence épiscopale et les autres institutions
de collégialité intermédiaires," *L'Année Canonique* 27 (1983) 69-80.

[20] For commentaries on these canons see the following: Juan I. Arrieta, "De las con-
ferencias episcopales," in *Código de Derecho Canónico*, ed. Pedro Lombardia and Juan
I. Arrieta (Pamplona: Ediciones Universidad de Navarra, SA, 1983) 319-327; Giuseppe
Damizia, "Le conferenze dei vescovi," in *Commento al Codice di Diritto Canonico*, ed.
Pio Vito Pinto (Rome: Urbaniana University Press, 1985), 262-269; John Johnson,
"Conferences of Bishops," in *New Commentary on the Code of Canon Law*, ed. John Beal
et al. (New York: Paulist, 2000) 350-371; Josef Listl, "Die Bischofskonferenzen,"
in *Handbuch des Katholischen Kirchenrechts*, ed. Josef Listl, Hubert Müller, and Heribert
Schmitz (Regensburg: Verlag Friedrich Pustet, 1983) 308-320; Provost, "Conferences of
Bishops," 350-377; Gordon Read, "Bishops' Conferences," in *The Canon Law Letter and
Spirit*, ed. Gerard Sheehy et al. (Collegeville: Liturgical Press, 1995) 250-257;
Juan Sanchez y Sanchez, "De las conferencias episcopales," in *Código de Derecho
Canónico*, ed. Lamberto de Echeverría et al. (Madrid: Biblioteca de Autores Cristianos,
1983), 245-252.

conference's legislative or policy-setting role as one notable, but hardly the only, indicator of the impact of collegial governance patterns in the postconciliar Latin Church. By way of comparison he will also explore the exercise of legislative authority by patriarchal synods[21] (henceforth synods) in the Eastern churches. Subsequently he will examine a few selected canons on conference and synod legislative competency in exercising the Church's teaching, sanctifying, and pastoral governance missions. An examination of similarities and differences in conference-synod functioning may help one assess the adequacy of postconciliar Latin Church collegial governance patterns. The complexity of the issues raised and limitations of space permit only an initial tentative examination of such concerns.

This presentation is divided basically into two main parts, a relatively short set of theological-canonical reflections, and some conclusions. The first more generic part of the presentation in turn is subdivided into two sections. The first section examines the place of conferences in the Latin code: their essential nature, purpose, and varied functions, their legislative competency especially, and their varied relationship to diocesan bishops, other intermediary level entities such as particular councils, and the Holy See. The second section examines the place of patriarchal synods in the Eastern code and considers themes such as the principle of subsidiarity and the significance of particular law, synodal legislative competency, and the relationship of synods to the patriarch and to the Holy See. The second more specific part of the presentation briefly explores a few examples of noteworthy conference and synod legislative activity in exercising the Church's threefold *munera*. Despite some common elements in that exercise, we highlight the somewhat more notable Eastern synodal legislative competency. Subsequently the article concludes by raising some theological-canonical concerns about such a disparity in implementing collegiality in light of a thoughtful critique of *Apostolos suos* by Ladislas Orsy including some very brief ecumenical considerations. Ecumenical relationships with both Eastern and Western Christians not in full communion might well be enhanced by more thoroughly implementing the principle of collegiality throughout the Church, e.g., through expanded conference legislative competency.

---

[21] What is stated regarding patriarchs and patriarchal synods is also generally applicable to major archbishops and major archiepiscopal synods (*CCEO* 152). However, to simplify any pertinent comparative law observations the author simply refers to the patriarch and the patriarchal synod.

I. SOME GENERAL REFLECTIONS

A. Latin conferences

1. The place and purposes of conferences especially in the Latin code[22]

Vatican II affirmed that the Church is a communion of churches –
a reality partly expressed through the providentially emerging groupings
of such churches[23] generally within a nation, but not necessarily so
(*LG* 23). The council called for a revitalization of such groupings for
greater pastoral effectiveness and a more unified approach to the Church's
teaching, sanctifying, and pastoral governance missions (*CD* 36 and 40).
The council fathers formalized the preexisting practice of bishops gath-
ering in conferences to exchange ideas and pastoral experiences, discuss
common concerns, and provide mutual support[24].

The Latin code, reflecting such conciliar concerns, situates the primary
canons on episcopal conferences (cc. 447-459) in a title on groupings of
churches (cc. 431-459) within the broader context of the law on the
diocese, between the canons on bishops (cc. 368-430) and those on other
diocesan, parish, and inter-parochial institutes (cc. 460-572)[25]. In the 1917

---

[22] For some brief but helpful reflections in this area see Provost, "Conferences of
Bishops," 350-351; 363-364.

[23] We should probably speak more precisely of *groupings of bishops* in light of the
nearly exclusive emphasis in this part of the Latin code on conferences with their largely
episcopal membership and in the Eastern code on Eastern synods given their nearly exclusive episcopal character.

[24] Feliciani succinctly expresses the significance of Vatican II for episcopal conferences: "Christus Dominus transformed conferences from unofficial meetings into instances
framed by the Church's constitutional law, from voluntary assemblies into *coetus* which
were now obligatory in terms of both establishment and participation, from meetings which
were heterogeneous in form and composition into essentially homogeneous *conventus*,
from organisms of merely moral authority into institutions capable of juridically binding
deliberations, even if these were limited to specific matters and under rather rigorous conditions." Giorgio Feliciani, "Episcopal Conferences from Vatican II to the 1983 Code,"
The Jurist 48 (1988) 12.

[25] For some comments on the Latin code commission discussion of intermediary level
governance structures see Thomas Green, "Critical Reflections on the People of God
Schema," *Studia Canonica* 14 (1980) 294-303; idem, "Persons and Structures in the
Church: Reflections on Selected Issues in Book II," *The Jurist* 45 (1985) 78-83. For some
thoughtful observations on Latin and Eastern intermediate level governmental structures,
see Myriam Wijlens, "The Intermediate Level in the Roman Catholic Church: An Organizational or Ecclesiological Category," in *Of All Times and Places Protestants and
Catholics on the Church Local and Universal*, ed. Leo J. Koffeman and Henk Witte IIMO
Research Publication 56 (Zoetemeer: Meinema, 2001) 95-130 (hereafter cited Wijlens,
Intermediate). For a very thoughtful examination of various aspects of the problematic of
collegiality including the inadequacy of the Latin code's treatment of intermediary level

code, by contrast, conferences did not enjoy their own proper status but were treated briefly as pastoral consultative organs within the larger context of particular councils[26]. Such councils were viewed not as exercising distinctly episcopal authority but as sharing in supreme church authority, comparable to the college of cardinals (1917 code, cc. 230-241), the Roman curia (1917 code, cc. 242-264), and papal legates (1917 code, cc. 265-270). On the contrary, the 1983 code treats both particular councils (cc. 439-446) and episcopal conferences separately from the aforementioned universal Church institutes and views the former as exercising distinctly episcopal power, reflecting the pastoral solicitude of individual bishops for the good of all the churches. The basic canons on episcopal conferences (cc. 447-459) constitute a fundamental legal framework facilitating conference activity; however, they must be complemented by conference statutes, spelling out the implications of that framework for individual conferences given their distinct setting and functioning (c. 451). Finally *Apostolos suos* (especially pars. 14-24 and the complementary norms) complements the code by providing certain technical refinements and clarifications especially, but not exclusively, regarding the conference's teaching function.

Both the code and *Apostolos suos* tend to view conferences primarily from a somewhat pragmatic, functional viewpoint as instruments of pastoral communication and coordination among the bishops of a given geographic area. They enable bishops to exercise their diversified ministry as fruitfully as possible in view of fostering the common good of the various particular churches. This is especially true given the breadth of issues transcending diocesan boundaries (*Apostolos suos* 15) in a time of notable societal transformations, e.g., complex phenomenon of globalization. The conferences can thereby foster a better integration of the particular churches within the life and ministry of the larger Church[27].

---

structures, see Hervé Legrand, "Les évêques, les Églises locales et l'Église entière," in *Le ministère des évêques au Concile Vatican II et depuis* (Paris: Éditions du Cerf, 2001) 201-260. Finally on the importance of revitalizing intermediary level structures, see James Coriden, "Necessary Canonical Reform:Urgent Issues for Action," in *Canon Law between Interpretation and Imagination* (Leuven: Uitgeverij Peeters, 2001) 13-19 (regional diversity of discipline).

[26] See 1917 code, cc. 281-292 on plenary and provincial councils. Canon 292 required meetings of the provincial bishops every five years to see what was to be done in their dioceses, to promote the good of religion, and to prepare for future provincial councils, technically to be held every twenty years (1917 code, c. 283).

[27] Besides the commentaries on the canons on episcopal conferences mentioned in note 22, see Aldo Acerbi, "The Development of the Canons on Conferences and the Apostolic See," *The Jurist* 48 (1988) 146-152.

2. The Nature of Conferences

Any discussion of conferences inevitably raises profound theological-canonical questions, e.g., relationship between universal Church and particular churches, the meaning and possible diverse realizations of collegiality, the ultimate theological-canonical grounding of such conferences and analogous realities such as Latin particular councils and Eastern synods[28]. These complex issues can hardly be adequately addressed within the limited confines of this article given its distinctly legislative competency and comparative law focus. However, a few general observations seem warranted regarding the nature of the conference – at least as regards two possible ways of viewing it theologically[29].

One way of viewing the issue starts with the college of bishops to determine the nature, competence, and authority of conferences; this generally seems to be the approach of both the code and *Apostolos suos*. Another way of considering them, however, is to see them as an expression of the communion of churches, within which the bishops are situated in positions of pastoral leadership and service.

If one takes the college as one's point of departure, one denies that conferences exercise for their territory the same power that the college exercises for the whole Church. The conferences do not exercise collegiality in the strict sense but embody a certain *affectus collegialis* or collegial spirit in their operations. Such a viewpoint does not view collegiality as a complex reality admitting of various forms and possibly being partially implemented. Such an approach seems to see the principle of subsidiarity in terms of the higher instance's determining the competency of lower instances. For it emphasizes the conference's dependency on supreme church authority for its establishment, allocation of competencies, and review (*recognitio*) or possibly approval (*approbatio*) of conference decisions. The bishops are viewed primarily as members of the episcopal college rather than as heading particular churches. This approach does not seem to take as seriously as it should the historic experience of intermediary governmental institutions such as councils and synods, which emerged more often from episcopal initiatives from below rather than from establishment from on high.

---

[28] For an especially thoughtful exploration of the complex theological issues underlying episcopal conferences, see the Anton article mentioned in n. 6, especially the brief summary on 297.

[29] See Wijlens, Intermediate, 127-129.

The other perspective, however, considers conferences in terms of the vital reality of the communion of churches. Each local church possesses within itself all the elements of 'ecclesiality'; however, it is not properly autonomous but realizes its mission only by maintaining communion with other such churches. There is an intimate link between the diocesan bishop and his local church since he facilitates its union with other churches. Bishops fulfill their pastoral tasks largely within their own dioceses; but an essential part of their office is to collaborate among themselves and with the pope, the center of their episcopal communion (*LG* 23; *CD* 36). Such a viewpoint situates the conference within the horizon of ecclesial communion; and its activities serving the bishops that compose it partially exemplify the complex reality of collegiality. This approach seems to be somewhat more congruent than the other viewpoint with the historic conciliar and synodal experience of the churches and the functioning of intermediate level institutions. It seems to apply the principle of subsidiarity in such a way as to leave bishops relatively free to find different ways of jointly exercising their pastoral mission as adequately as possible.

With due regard for the aforementioned differences in perspective, certain points can be made regarding the current legal status of conferences. Unlike particular councils, primarily legislative entities (c. 445: "... potestate gaudet regiminis, praesertim legislativa..."), conferences are viewed primarily as instruments of pastoral communication and coordination among the bishops of a given area, usually a nation but possibly a more or less extensive area (c. 447)[30]. The conference is an obligatory institutionalization of collegial episcopal responsibility for the welfare of the Church and the larger society. The conference significantly

---

[30] Instead of a general reference to competency in matters of faith and discipline not already determined by universal law – the competence of particular councils (c. 445) – the conferences can make binding decisions only on issues explicitly enumerated in the code or in virtue of a special Holy See mandate granted on its own initiative or upon conference request (*CD* 38, 4; cc. 455, §1-2). Such restrictive provisions for conference competency contrast with the broad provisions for possible conference decisional activity mentioned in the 1963 conciliar schema on bishops and governance of dioceses. This schema envisioned the possibility of juridically binding conference decisions in the following situations: 1) matters entrusted to the conference for a binding decision by common law or a special Apostolic See mandate; 2) more important public statements in the name of the conference; 3) matters affecting the whole country and warranting discussion with civil authorities; and 4) serious matters warranting common conference action and a juridically binding decision in the judgment of two thirds of the bishops with a deliberative vote. In this connection see Sobanski, 84-85.

expresses that mystery of ecclesial unity in diversity mentioned in *Lumen gentium* 23.

Among the pastoral benefits of conferences are the sharing of information and the possibility for collaboration on issues transcending diocesan and even regional boundaries. Numerous pastoral issues (*Apostolos suos* 15) require serious and sustained corporate study, discussion, and action if they are to be addressed knowledgeably.

Secondarily, but still rather significantly, the episcopal conference may exercise governmental authority in various areas, especially by issuing general decrees. Such activity, however, must respect the inalienable pastoral governance prerogatives of the Roman Pontiff and the diocesan bishops. Such conference decisions have a corporate character, for the conference is an entity distinct from the individual bishops who compose it (cc. 448, §1 and 450). Its authority is more than the sum of their individual powers in their respective dioceses[31].

The episcopal conference is a collegial subject of ordinary proper power (c. 131), whose implications are explicitated throughout the code and in various post-code documents such as the August 15, 1990 apostolic constitution *Ex corde Ecclesiae*[32] empowering conferences to legislate in church authority-academic institution-individual theologian relationships (c. 812). The conference as a whole is to exercise such power (c. 453 on plenary assembly), not subordinate organs such as the permanent council (e.g., USCCB Administrative Committee) (c. 457) or any individual committees (e.g., USCCB Committee on Doctrine)[33].

The conference can exercise delegated power if the Holy See authorizes it to issue general decrees in areas not specified in universal law. Such a mandate might result either from a Holy See initiative or a conference request (c. 455, §1)[34].

While *Apostolos suos* seems to view conference power as ultimately derived from supreme church authority (as in the 1917 code), one may

---

[31] See Julio Manzanares, "Las conferencias episcopales a la luz del derecho canónico," in *Las conferencias episcopales hoy* (Salamanca: Universidad Pontificia, 1975) 49-53.

[32] See *AAS* 82 (1990) 1475-1509.

[33] See June 10, 1966 response of Central Commission for the Coordination of Postconciliar Work and the Interpretation of Conciliar Decrees in *Canon Law Digest,* ed. T. Lincoln Bouscaren (Chicago: Chicago Province S.J., 1975) 7: 131.

[34] For a useful example of such a delegated legislative competency in connection with the current tragic clerical sex abuse of minors crisis in the United States, see "U.S. Bishops' Meeting Charter for the Protection of Children and Young People Revised," *Origins* 32/5 (November 28, 2002) 409; 411-415; "U.S. Bishops' Meeting: Essential Norms for Diocesan/Eparchial Policies Dealing with Allegations of Sexual Abuse of Minors by Priests and Deacons, Revised," ibid., 415-418.

wonder whether this is one of the still not definitively resolved issues regarding conferences[35]. That the Holy See regulates conference functioning in various ways noted above does not seem to make it any less an exercise of distinctly episcopal power than that exercised by the diocesan bishop, whose pastoral governance authority the Holy See also regulates in view of the unity and advantage of the universal Church (*CD* 8a; c. 381, §1), e.g., various papal reservations[36].

3. The Functions of Conferences

The bishops in the conference jointly exercise certain pastoral functions (*munera quaedam pastoralia*) for the good of the Church and society at large (c. 447). The precise meaning of such functions, which are church mission-related, can be discerned only after thoroughly examining the code, *Apostolos suos*, and other church documents. We emphasize the code here given the comprehensiveness of its provisions. The conference's legislative activity, however significant a focus of this article, is only one aspect of a much broader range of conference functions mentioned in those documents[37].

It is sometimes difficult to differentiate precisely various conference functions, partly due to the code's lack of terminological consistency in specifying them. For example, the code has no standard vocabulary to indicate when the conference may legislate for its territory (general decree in c. 29) as distinct from its issuing a general executory decree (c. 31) when a code provision needs more precise implementation[38].

In a general overview Joseph Listl helpfully articulates both some general rubrics and some specific examples of conference functions in the

---

[35] This issue will be briefly considered later in this article.

[36] In this connection one might note the tensions involved in a 1986 papal visitation of the Archdiocese of Seattle, Washington, USA and the appointment of an auxiliary with special faculties (c. 403, §2) because of alleged inadequacies in the archbishop's exercise of his pastoral governance role. In connection with this exercise of papal primacy, see a Canon Law Society of America interdisciplinary study of the history and current legislation and practice regarding episcopal rights on the occasion of such a visitation. See *The Jurist* 49 (1989) 341-567.

[37] For example, see no. 7 of the June 1, 1988 directory of the Congregation for Divine Worship on Sunday celebrations in the absence of a priest. The conferences may regulate such celebrations in greater detail in view of responding more effectively to the pastoral needs of people in different cultures and social conditions. Such decisions in turn are to be reviewed by the Holy See. Congregation for Divine Worship, "Directory for Sunday Celebrations in the Absence of a Priest," in *Origins* 18 (October 20, 1988) 301, 303-307.

[38] See, for example, Johnson, "Conference of Bishops," 359-360; Provost, in "Conference of Bishops," 369-370.

code[39]. He differentiates conference functions in terms of five general rubrics: 1) general decrees (c. 29); 2) general executory decrees (c. 30); 3) administrative competency; 4) a right of collaboration or consultation regarding Holy See decision-making; and 5) certain communication and information rights and duties in varied conference-Holy See-diocesan bishop relationships[40]. Listl then specifies areas of conference concern following the order of the code: decisions on clerical formation, altar service and priestly life (six instances); rights relative to church associations (three instances); determinations regarding relationships, communications, and mutual information pertinent to conference-Holy See relationships (six instances); conference competency regarding the particular churches (seven instances); cooperation between conferences and religious communities (one instance); conference competencies regarding the Church's teaching mission (fifteen instances), the Church's sanctifying mission (twenty-five instances), temporalities (eight instances); and finally procedures (eight instances)[41].

Other authors approach the issue of conference functions somewhat differently. Both de Lanversin[42] and Morrisey[43] use an Italian episcopal

---

[39] See Listl, "Die Bischofskonferenzen," 313-320.

[40] For a comparable analytical approach see Aymans, "Wesensverständnis," 51-54. He differentiates between 1) conference general decrees (e.g., c. 230, §1 on criteria of eligibility for lay lectors and acolytes and c. 242 on the preparation of a *Ratio institutionis sacerdotalis*), 2) the conference administrative powers in certain instances (e.g., cc. 312 and 320 on establishing and suppressing a national association of the faithful), and 3) conference collaboration rights regarding the activity of other canonical entities (e.g., c. 372 on its being consulted by the Holy See before the establishment of a personal particular church and c. 467 on its receiving the declarations and decrees from diocesan synods). Subsequently, Aymans lists forty-eight examples of conference general decrees (pp. 54-58), twenty-nine examples of administrative competencies (pp. 58-60) and thirteen examples of collaboration rights (pp. 60-61). Provost, in "Conference of Bishops," 368-372, differentiates between general decrees (c. 29) and general executory decrees (c. 30) and then lists various areas of conference functioning based on a two-fold division, i.e., its competence to issue general decrees (twenty-nine instances) and other code references to conferences (fifty-three cases).

[41] For a comparable effort to clarify similar types of conference functions see Melguizo et al., "Las conferencias." His examination of episcopal conferences in the code contains a relatively brief section on its general status (cc. 447-459) and juridic authority (pp. 42-46) and a more detailed section on its functions throughout the code (pp. 46-58). Two concluding appendices indicate areas where the conference's legislative role is not envisioned (pp. 58-59) and where it is called for (pp. 59-60). See also Uccella, "Le conferenze episcopali," 137-140. For detailed reflections on diverse conference functions in the early postconciliar period that help to contextualize comparable functions in the current law see Feliciani, *Le conferenze episcopali*, 529-561.

[42] See de Lanversin, "De la Loi Générale," 129-133.

[43] See Morrisey, "Decisions of Episcopal Conferences," 108-120.

conference schema on conference activities although each articulates its implications somewhat differently. First, as de Lanversin notes, a series of so-called 'informative canons' derives from the conference's function of fostering collaboration, planning, and communion among the particular churches. Second, another set of canons calls for in-depth conference studies of certain problems affecting the mission of the particular churches and church-state relationships. A third set of canons provides for conference legislation under certain conditions. There are also other ways of understanding the conference's manifold functions[44].

Further reflection on the code, *Apostolos suos*, and other church documents will surely lead to more satisfactory classifications of such functions. However, with the aforementioned functions in mind, we can examine the conference's legislative role more thoroughly.

4. The Legislative Role of the Conference

A proper understanding of the conference's legislative role presupposes an examination of canon 455, which specifies the conditions for issuing general decrees[45]. This canon, which *Apostolos suos* 20 basically

---

[44] For example, see Uccella, "Le conferenze episcopali," 142-143: "Di vero, ci sono canoni, in cui si explicitano le prerogative esclusive, concorrenti o addirittura surrogatorie rispetto alla potestà dei singoli vescovi diocesani e loro equiparati; oppure ove la competenza e attribuita ex iure che le raffigura come fonti di diritto oggettivo, certamente da non sottovalutare; o nei quali si evidenzia la loro attività latamente amministrativa anche a natura consultiva o di carattere coordinatorio con le singole diocesi; o nei quali l'esercizio della potestà legislativa è facoltativo. Infine, dalle norme si ricava anche la possibilità, per esse, di svolgere una notevole mole di lavoro informativo per il Popolo di Dio (cann. 825, par. 1 e 2, 838, par. 3, 775, par. 2, 3), perche si assicurino l'unità della fede e la disciplina dei costumi (can. 823, par. 2), nonchè di coordinare ed attuare una determinata politica ecclesiale (cann. 459, 708, 961, par. 3, 1316)."

[45] Another pertinent text on the conference's legislative role is canon 451. It requires the conference to formulate its statutes on various key issues such as membership/voting rights, plenary sessions, permanent council, and the general secretariat. See also *Apostolos suos* 20; complementary norm IV. The conference is largely free to shape its structure in accord with its own legal-pastoral needs since the code says little about such statutes, though they must be reviewed by the Holy See. The importance of conference discretion in formulating its statutes is particularly highlighted by Müller, "The Relationship between the Episcopal Conference and the Diocesan Bishop," 124-129. For a very useful presentation and analysis of European conference statutes, see Romeo Astorri, *Gli statuti delle conferenze episcopali I Europa* (Padua: CEDAM, 1987). For a similar work on conferences in the Americas, see Ivan Iban, *Gli statuti delle conferenze episcopali II America* (Padua: CEDAM, 1989). Due to space limitations the author will not consider this canon or canon 456 requiring the conference to forward the acts and decrees of its plenary sessions to the Holy See, the former for information purposes and the latter for *recognitio* pur-

restates, raises various questions regarding the relationship between the conference, the Holy See, and the diocesan bishop which need to be considered in clarifying the conference's legal status[46]. The key source of canon 455 seems to be *Christus Dominus* 38, 4, whose formulation occasioned sharp conciliar debate over the binding force of conference decrees. Both the conciliar text and the canon reflect a compromise position that attempts to integrate various values and ensure proper respect for the universal oversight role of the Holy See and the decisional preeminence of the diocesan bishop in his particular church. The code modifies the conciliar text by applying the conditions for conference legislating to 'general decrees' (*decreta generalia*), a somewhat more narrow term than the conciliar term 'decisions' (*decisiones*).

Provost succinctly summarizes canon 455. General conference decrees issued in accord with the canon have the force of particular law for the territory subject to conference authority (c. 29). Conference legislative authority extends to those matters specified in universal law or for which the Apostolic See has given special authorization. Two-thirds of conference members with a deliberative vote (c. 454; *Apostolos suos* 17), whether present for the vote or not, must approve such a general decree[47], and their action must be reviewed by the Apostolic See before the decree can be promulgated and bind those subject to conference jurisdiction. The conferences seem to function here as properly intermediary governmental instances between the Holy See and the diocesan bishop. Such a somewhat circumscribed legislative competency, rooted ultimately in episcopal consecration and canonical mission, hardly jeopardizes either papal primacy or the diocesan bishop's preeminent pastoral governance role in the diocese. Furthermore, barring explicit higher level

poses. This latter text further explicitates the cryptic reference to Holy See *recognitio* of conference decrees in canon 455, §2.

[46] The author is particularly indebted to Provost for his analysis of canon 455, yet other relevant insights will be integrated into the following observations.

[47] This two thirds rule affecting conferences is a more exacting requirement than the normal provision for a simple majority of those present to approve a collegial act (c. 119, 2°). Interestingly enough, the simple majority provision seems pertinent to the exercise of legislative authority by particular councils (c. 445). One wonders why there is such a notable difference between the rules governing legislative activity by the two comparable institutes although such councils, unlike conferences, are said to possess legislative authority. While this is clearly the *ius vigens*, it seems questionable whether such a rule does justice to legitimate expectations for a broader conference legislative role. It does not seem to follow through adequately on the conciliar view of the two entities as analogous providential realizations of the episcopal obligation to foster the communion of churches (*LG* 23).

authorization, the conference can act in the name of all the bishops only if all its members agree[48].

Four important issues should be treated briefly here because they help to clarify the thrust and rationale of canon 455/*Apostolos suos* 20. First, we consider the 'decrees' being regulated along with the kind of authority the conference exercises. Second, we comment on the highly important conference relationship to diocesan bishops. Third, we examine the respective roles of conferences and particular councils, whose legislative competency is notably more important theoretically than that of conferences, however relatively inoperative such councils are in practice today[49]. Finally, we address the central relationship between the conference and the Holy See, particularly the required *recognitio* of conference decrees[50].

a. The Decrees Envisioned in Canon 455

The code mentions two types of general decrees: general decrees issued normally by a competent legislator (c. 29) but exceptionally by an administrator with special authorization (c. 30) and general executory decrees issued by an administrator (c. 31). While it is occasionally difficult to determine to which type of conference decree the code refers,

---

[48] Provost, "Conferences of Bishops," 368. Canon 455 reads as follows: "1. Episcoporum conferentia decreta generalia ferre tantummodo potest in causis, in quibus ius universale id praescripserit aut peculiare Apostolicae Sedis mandatum sive motu proprio sive ad petitionem ipsius conferentiae id statuerit. 2. Decreta de quibus in 1., ut valide ferantur in plenario conventu, per duas saltem ex tribus partibus suffragiorum Praesulum, qui voto deliberativo fruentes ad conferentiam pertinent, proferri debent, atque vim obligandi non obtinent, nisi ab Apostolica Sede recognita, legitime promulgata fuerint. 3. Modus promulgationis et tempus a quo decreta vim suam exserunt, ab ipsa Episcoporum conferentia determinantur. 4. In casibus in quibus nec ius universale nec peculiare Apostolicae Sedis mandatum potestatem, de qua in 1, Episcoporum conferentiae concessit, singuli Episcopi dioecesani competentia integra manet, nec conferentia eiusve praeses nomine omnium Episcoporum agere valet, nisi omnes et singuli Episcopi consensum dederint."

[49] Interestingly enough, the current clerical sex abuse crisis in the United States has prompted some calls for the holding of a plenary council to deal with that concern and other pastoral issues. The last such council took place in 1884. See "Eight Bishops Call for a U.S. Plenary Council," *Origins* 32/12 (August 29, 2002) 201-206; "Church Magazine It is Time to Convene a Plenary Council," ibid., 206-207; Philip J. Murnion, "The Potential of a Plenary Council," *America* (October 28, 2002) 12-14.

[50] See the following commentaries on canons 455-456: Acerbi, "The Development of the Canons on Conferences," 148-151; Arrieta, "De las conferencias episcopales," 324-325; Damizia, "Le conferenze dei vescovi," 267-268; Sanchez, "De las conferencias episcopales," 250-251.

it normally envisions general decrees. General decrees are properly laws, and they either constitute new regulations in an area where there has been no preexisting norm or they modify existing norms. On the other hand, general executory decrees are subordinate to laws, whose correct observance they are to foster. At times the code requires a conference decree (e.g., c. 766 on lay preaching) while at other times such decrees are facultative or discretionary (e.g., c. 891 on an age for confirmation different from the age of discretion)[51]. Usually the conference is to legislate on its own (e.g., c. 1292, §1 on the minimum and maximum sums for the alienation of church goods). At other times, however, either the conference or the diocesan bishop may legislate (e.g., c. 844 on sacramental sharing).

The strict requirements of canon 455 including Holy See *recognitio* of conference decrees seemed at first to apply only to general decrees (c. 29) since these, unlike general executory decrees, are technically laws. Since canon 455 restricted the conference's legislative activity, a strict interpretation seemed warranted (c. 18). However, on May 14, 1985 the Commission for the Authentic Interpretation of the Code surprisingly ruled that canon 455 applied to all general decrees including general executory decrees. John Paul II confirmed this broad interpretation on July 5, 1985[52].

The conference exercises ordinary proper legislative power wherever the code or another universal law source so empowers it. In other words, it exercises that power as a collegial juridic person (cc. 115, 2; 116) in its own name in virtue of the law. The conference has indeed been established by supreme church authority as a hierarchic instance between the Holy See and the diocesan bishop with its own juridic personality (c. 449). Technically, however, the conference is neither delegated by the Holy See to issue such general decrees nor does it represent the Holy See in exercising the aforementioned legislative function. The fact that supreme church authority specifies certain conditions for the exercise of the conference's legislative function does not alter its proper character any more than the diocesan bishop's governmental discretion is necessarily impaired in principle by its subjection to certain universal law conditions.

---

[51] On November 8, 1983, just before the code took effect, the Secretariat of State forwarded to conference presidents a list of twenty-one instances in which conference decrees were required and twenty-two instances in which such decrees were optional. However, the secretariat did not differentiate between general decrees and general executory decrees. See *Communicationes* 15 (1983) 137-139.

[52] See *AAS* 77 (1985) 771.

Occasionally the conference exercises delegated legislative authority. Particular legal-pastoral situations in certain territories may warrant conference norms in areas not provided for in universal law. In this situation the Holy See may issue a particular mandate on its own initiative or at the conference's request, e.g., current clerical sex abuse crisis in USA.

b. The Conference-Diocesan Bishop Relationship

Limitations on the conference's legislative role reflect a code commission desire to respect the legitimate pastoral governance prerogatives of diocesan bishops and the Holy Father[53]. A brief consideration of those other authority figures may help us appreciate the rationale for these limitations.

An adequate understanding of the complex conference-diocesan bishop relationship requires a thorough analysis of the whole code and subsequent documents such as *Apostolos suos*. Yet a few general observations are pertinent here. First, canon 455 highlights the preeminence of the diocesan bishop's decisional role in his particular church. This exemplifies the conciliar rediscovery of the centrality of the particular church in the communion of churches and the bishop's divine-law based leadership role within it. For example, a two-thirds majority of all conference members with a deliberative vote must approve general decrees unlike the usual provision for a simple majority of those present in such situations (c. 119, §2), e.g., particular council decisions. Second, such general decrees can be approved only by the plenary meeting and not by a subordinate body such as the permanent council (e.g., USCCB Administrative Committee), which is to facilitate the activity of the whole conference but not replace it. Third, canon 455, §4, contained in neither

---

[53] See Acerbi, "The Development of Canons on Conferences," 148-151, especially 151: the right of an episcopal conference to legislate is regulated according to a principle which does not arise from its intrinsic nature, but from the need to avoid collision with other rights, namely those of the diocesan bishops such as are sanctioned in canon 381 and those of the pope which are recognized in canon 331. The code rejects the view of some authors that the episcopal conference should have all the power necessary to govern a determined portion of the church, between what is reserved to the pope and what is reserved to the diocesan bishop. While one may sympathize with the legitimate concerns underlying such a position, one may equally wonder whether the continuing challenges of inculturating the Church in various settings calls for more significant intermediate level policy-setting options. The special synods called by John Paul II at the end of the last millennium highlighted the extraordinarily diverse pastoral challenges facing the Church throughout the world. See, for example, Thomas Reese, "The Experience of Special Synods," *CLSA Proceedings* (1997) 26-46.

Christus Dominus 38 nor *Ecclesiae Sanctae* I, 41, states that if the strict
conditions for conference legislation in paragraphs one through three are
not verified, the conference or its president can act in its name only if all
the members approve. Finally, bishops, either individually or united in
conference, may not limit their own sacred authority in favor of enhanced
power for the conference or one of its constituent parts, e.g., permanent
council (c. 457) (*Apostolos suos* 20). Presumably only supreme church
authority can authorize such a limitation of a diocesan bishop's divine
law-based prerogatives by an ecclesiastical law-grounded reality such as
a conference. These provisions sharply restrict the options for juridically
binding conference decisions.

With due regard for the foregoing considerations, perhaps the juridically binding force of certain conference decrees should not be unduly
emphasized although such a competency is an especially important indicator of the conference's appropriate legal status. In fact the 1973 Directory on the Pastoral Ministry of Bishops[54] stressed the morally binding
force of conference pastoral orientations in areas other than such general
decrees. A spirit of fraternal charity and a concern for ecclesial communion might incline a bishop to follow such orientations in shaping diocesan policy even if he did not necessarily favor them or even opposed
them during a plenary meeting. While the Latin code carefully protects
the diocesan bishop's legitimate pastoral governance autonomy, this
hardly means that he can act totally in accord with his own discretion.
Quite the contrary, he governs within a network of ministerial relationships within the diocese and is expected to collaborate with his fellow
bishops in serving the *communio* of churches[55].

During the latter stages of the code revision process, questions were
raised about the conference's possibly impairing the integrity of the
episcopal office. Objections were posed against presumably excessive
provisions for conference competence in the original code commission
schemata. It is difficult to assess precisely the extent and significance of

---

[54] See Sacra Congregatio pro Episcopis, *Directorium de Pastorali Ministerio Episcoporum*, February 22, 1973 (Vatican City: Typis Polyglottis Vaticanis, 1973) 217, paragraph
212b. Congregation for Bishops, *Directory on the Pastoral Ministry of Bishops*. trans.
Benedictine Monks Seminary of Christ the King, Mission, B.C. (Ottawa: Canadian
Catholic Conference, 1974) 113.

[55] For some thoughtful reflections on the necessarily collegial exercise of the episcopal
office see Müller, "The Relationship between the Episcopal Conference and the Diocesan
Bishop," *passim*. However, one should avoid a view of collegiality that is insufficiently
sensitive to the importance of the individual bishop's exercising his own personal responsibility in the diocese. See de Lanversin, "De la Loi Générale," 127-128.

such concerns; however, they clearly moved the code commission toward adopting a gradually more restrictive posture vis-à-vis conference competency in the 1980 schema[56] and subsequent drafts[57]. The legitimacy of such a restrictive posture can be questioned in the light of the exigencies of a genuine collegiality to be operative at the intermediate level of church governance.

Yet, however questionable it may be, the current law seems to reflect Calvo's view that the legislative competency of the diocesan bishop is the rule and conference competency the exception. For him the conference fulfills an extraordinary and subsidiary function vis-à-vis the individual bishop in significant issues transcending diocesan boundaries. The principle of subsidiarity is said to be operative in conference-bishop relationships, perhaps even more so than in Holy See-conference relationships[58].

Nevertheless, far from impairing the diocesan bishop's irreplaceable autonomy, the conference may notably support diocesan bishops in their ministry[59]. In fact in the nineteenth century conferences arose spontaneously in Belgium and elsewhere from the initiatives of bishops

---

[56] See Pontificia Commissio Codici Iuris Canonici Recognoscendo, *Schema Codicis Iuris Canonici iuxta animadversiones S.R.E. Cardinalium, Episcoporum Conferentiarum, Dicasteriorum Curiae Romanae, Universitatum Facultatumque ecclesiasticarum necnon Superiorum Institutorum vitae consecratae recognitum* (Vatican City: Libreria Editrice Vaticana, 1980). In responding to criticisms of the 1980 schema, the code commission secretariat stated that limitations on the discretion of the diocesan bishop had been minimized in its reworking of the original schemata. Such limitations usually were related to the conference's legislative role. See Pontificia Commissio Codici Iuris Canonici Recognoscendo, *Relatio complectens synthesim animadversionum ab Em.mis atque Ex.mis. Patribus Commissionis ad novissimum Schema CIC exhibitarum, cum responsionibus a Secretaria et Consultoribus datis* (Vatican City: Typis Polyglottis Vaticanis, 1981) 13-14.

[57] For example, see Acerbi, "The Development of Canons on the Conference," 149-150; Provost, "Conference of Bishops," 364. Gouyon forcefully expressed concerns about the role of the conference, especially the risk of over-bureaucratization. See "Les rélations entre le diocèse et la conférence épiscopale," *L'Année Canonique* 22 (1978) 1-23. He noted that some bishops were somewhat reluctant to speak at plenary meetings, felt somewhat intimidated by the conference staff, and seemed to be prevented from taking proper pastoral initiatives in their own dioceses because they were waiting, perhaps unnecessarily, for conference action in a given area(s). How significantly such apprehensions influenced the structuring of the conference's role in the 1983 code is hard to assess, but they clearly influenced the present law. Furthermore, *Apostolos suos* 18 raises similar questions about possible conference bureaucratization that may hinder rather than help the pastoral ministry of diocesan bishops.

[58] See Calvo, "Las competencias," 663-667. His focus is the exercise of the *munus sanctificandi,* but his observations are probably applicable *mutatis mutandis* to the exercise of the other *munera.*

[59] See Angel Anton, "Le conferenze episcopali: un aiuto ai vescovi," *La Civiltà Cattolica* (1999) I: 332-344.

experiencing the need to pool their resources in confronting various common pastoral challenges. For example, various church-state problems were posed especially in a time of notable political transformations. Since numerous pastoral issues today transcend diocesan boundaries, common conference pastoral approaches and norms may likewise enhance an individual bishop's ability to deal responsibly with such issues. Notably different approaches to such pastoral problems may actually weaken episcopal authority in a given area[60]. In short, the challenge of respecting local diocesan autonomy and also assuring regular episcopal consultation and collaboration through the conferences is a continuing one which defies easy resolution. The present code and more recently *Apostolos suos* are two significant stages but hardly the last word in that ongoing process.

c. The Conference-Particular Council Relationship

Before discussing conference-Holy See relationships, we should consider the conference's relationship to another intermediate level entity, the particular council (cc. 439-446)[61]. Such councils, which preceded ecumenical councils historically and have occurred at irregular intervals throughout history, are classic examples of the fluctuating vitality of Latin church intermediary level structures. They reflect the not infrequent experience of bishops and other believers consulting, deliberating, and finally deciding on common courses of action in doctrinal and disciplinary matters affecting large groupings of the faithful. Such ecclesial gatherings in the Spirit preceded theological reflection on them or canonical provisions regulating their status and functioning.

While *Christus Dominus* 36 praised them and called for their revitalization, de facto in the postconciliar period episcopal conferences have assumed a privileged place in embodying the collegial episcopal spirit in service to the communion of churches. Despite the tendency of the *instrumentum laboris* (not repeated in *Apostolos suos*) to stress the significant role of such councils vis-à-vis the lesser status of conferences, de facto the latter institute has become the more significant intermediate level

---

[60] See Bruno Lettman, "Episcopal Conferences in the New Canon Law," *Studia Canonica* 14 (1980) 347-367. A concern for reasonably uniform episcopal policies in certain delicate pastoral issues underlies canon 1316, which calls for neighboring diocesan bishops to strive for uniform penal laws as much as possible. This is the only place where the Latin code expresses such a *caveat*.

[61] See Provost article in n. 17.

entity in practice, even if not in theory. It seems that the conferences have now assumed the historic leadership role of such councils – a reality certainly not appreciated by the *instrumentum* and perhaps not sufficiently so by *Apostolos suos*[62].

There are similarities between conferences and councils. For example, in both institutes bishops play a preeminent leadership role; both entities have a certain legislative competency; and both bodies require Holy See *recognitio* before their legislation takes effect. But perhaps the differences between them are more notable. Such councils are temporary realities; they have a more diversified ecclesial membership; and they have a broader legislative competency since they are viewed primarily as governmental entities. By contrast conferences are permanent realities with juridic personality; they have a primarily, if not nearly exclusively, episcopal membership; they are not primarily governmental entities but instruments of pastoral communication and collaboration; and their legislative competency is much more restricted[63].

Given the council's diversified ecclesial membership (clergy, religious, and laity) and the value of broad input into ecclesial decision-making, one might hope that the conciliar aspirations for its revitalization will be realized more seriously in practice. However, in light of the de facto viability and preeminence of conferences, it seems wise to consider upgrading their legal status, especially in the area of legislative governance, if they are to respond as effectively and as expeditiously as possible to contemporary pastoral concerns.

d. The Conference-Holy See Relationship

The values of affirming papal primacy (cc. 331; 333), fostering ecclesial and episcopal unity, and counteracting a possibly unhealthy legal diversity[64] underlie several canons stressing the significant role of the

---

[62] In this respect see the following studies which were part of the January 1988 Salamanca international symposium on episcopal conferences: Antonio Garcia y Garcia, "Episcopal Conferences in Light of Particular Councils during the Second Millennium," *The Jurist* 48 (1988) 57-67; Heinrich Sieben, "Episcopal Conferences in Light of Particular Councils in the First Millennium," *The Jurist* 48 (1988) 30-56.

[63] Perhaps one reason why the conference's legislative role is more limited vis-à-vis the council is because the conference meets regularly whereas such councils meet infrequently if at all. Hence the diocesan bishop's pastoral governance autonomy could possibly be jeopardized more significantly by an entity that meets more frequently.

[64] Holy See concerns about the possible formation of national churches may be operative in this general connection. Principle 5 for the revision of the Latin code mentioned such concerns in discussing the canonical relevance of the principle of

Holy See in the establishment and especially in the functioning of the conferences. For example, supreme church authority alone may establish, suppress, or change conferences (c. 449, §1), a particularly significant role if the conference does not encompass all the particular churches of a given territory as is customary (c. 448). Supreme church authority currently specifies the areas of legitimate conference legislative activity (c. 455, §1). Furthermore, Holy See *recognitio* is required before conference statutes (c. 451), general decrees, and general executory decrees may be promulgated (cc. 455, §2 and 456). However necessary such a *recognitio*[65] may be in implementing the Holy See's necessary ecclesial oversight function, it can generate significant tensions in Holy See-conference relationships. This is especially true when conference decrees are substantially changed during the *recognitio* process despite technically remaining conference documents.

For example, in November 1983 the National Conference of Catholic Bishops (USA) voted to permit individual bishops to specify the term of office for pastors (c. 522), yet during the *recognitio* process the Holy See insisted that the term be six years with a possible renewal at the bishop's discretion. Although one may welcome the enhanced protection of the right to stability of pastors, one may also question the Holy See failure to respect a conference decision in a significant pastoral matter[66].

subsidiarity, especially regarding particular law options. After noting the conciliar emphasis on leaving numerous decisions to particular legislators, the principle reads: "Yet it seems foreign to the mind and spirit of Vatican II – apart from the particular disciplines of the Oriental Churches – that there be in the Western Church special statutes which seem to be like the laws of national churches. But nevertheless this need not be taken to mean that greater broadness of power and autonomy is not desirable for particular legislation, especially when it concerns laws enacted by national and regional councils, so that the special characteristics of the individual churches should be clearly apparent." Interestingly no explicit mention is made of episcopal conferences in this particular law context although subsequently the revision principle speaks generically of 'regional authorities.' See "Principles Which Govern the Revision of the Code of Canon Law," in *Readings, Cases, Materials in Canon Law A Textbook for Ministerial Students*, ed. Jordan Hite and Daniel Ward (Collegeville, MN: Liturgical Press, 1990) 88-89.

[65] For a literate discussion of various issues pertinent to the history, rationale, and meaning of Holy See *recognitio* of lower level juridic acts, see Julio Manzanares, "Papal Reservation and *Recognitio*: Considerations and Proposals," *The Jurist* 52 (1992) 228-254.

[66] See Joseph Janicki, "Chapter VI: Parishes, Pastors, and Parochial Vicars," in *The Code of Canon Law: A Text and Commentary*, ed. Coriden et al., 422-423; John Renken, "Chapter VI: Parishes, Pastors, and Parochial Vicars," in *New Commentary on the Code of Canon Law*, ed. Beal et al., 693-694. Murray, "The Legislative Authority of the Episcopal Conference," 45 rightly questions whether in situations where the Holy See notably modifies conference decrees during the *recognitio* process the whole conference should be asked to discuss and vote on the amended decree.

What is the rationale for the *recognitio*, which is not a constitutive element of the legislative act, but an act of control, an extrinsic condition for an already constituted act? For some it protects the legitimate autonomy of diocesan bishops who will be bound by conference decrees although they may have opposed their approval. For others the *recognitio* involves a necessary review of lower level legislative acts to ensure that they respect the code's hierarchy of norms (c. 135, §2). For still others the *recognitio* reflects a concern for the harmonious activity of ecclesial communities throughout the world and a needed protection against conference initiatives possibly compromising the faith, church unity, or episcopal collegiality, although one wonders how realistic a concern that is today.

The *recognitio* of a conference decree does not change its nature as a distinctly conference document. The *recognitio* is required for legitimate conference functioning, yet in theory at least it seemingly implies a somewhat less noteworthy Roman intervention in lower level decision-making than Holy See *approbatio* of a program of seminary studies (*Ratio institutionis sacerdotalis*, c. 242) or a conference catechism (c. 775).

Legitimate questions are raised about the need for Holy See *recognitio* in so many areas, especially given the applicability of such a requirement to both general decrees (c. 29) and general executory decrees (c. 31). However valuable it may be at times[67], this requirement can pose serious problems for conferences, especially given the occasional lengthiness of the *recognitio* process. Difficulties also result from Holy See efforts to impose a uniform policy in countries as large and pastorally diverse as the United States, even when the code itself does not call for such uniformity. Greater flexibility seems warranted if the diverse legal-pastoral needs of the people of God living in various socio-cultural settings are to

---

[67] Numerous American canonists welcomed the need for Holy See *recognitio* of conference decrees in the case of the June 2002 USCCB document entitled *Essential Norms* addressing clerical sex abuse of minors. After the Holy See declined to grant the *recognitio*, a group of American bishops and representatives of various Roman dicasteries met in Rome in October 2002 to discuss various canonical concerns posed by the *Norms*, e,g, protection of rights of accused clergy, role of diocesan review boards in assessing allegations of wrongdoing, etc. This led to the crafting of a more satisfactory set of *Norms*, which were approved at the November 2002 USCCB meeting. Such revised *Norms* were granted Roman *recognitio* on December 8, 2002. Even given continuing questions about the adequacy of some norms, the *recognitio* process did in fact enhance the quality of the original text. However, when one reviews the 36 year history of NCCB/USCCB legislative activity, it seems eminently clear that this was a rather exceptional instance of American canonists' expressing serious concern about conference legislation.

be duly met. Hence a serious theoretical-practical examination of the continued applicability of this requirement in its present form is imperative[68]. This seems all the more true when we consider the somewhat less circumscribed legislative competency of Eastern patriarchal synods.

B. The Patriarchal Synod

We now briefly note some general points regarding the status and functioning of patriarchal synods (hereafter synods), particularly by way of contrast to Latin conferences. The issues to be explored are complex; however, limitations of space restrict us to broad reflections on the pertinent issues.

We will consider the following interrelated issues: (1) the synod as an ecclesial reality; (2) the synod and the conference as permanent institutions; (3) synod/conference membership and voting rights; (4) frequency of synod/conference meetings, quorum, agenda, majority for decision-making; (5) the juridical power of the patriarch and the conference president; (6) the legislative power of the synod in comparison with the conference (our key concern), and (7) the Eastern code revision process, the principle of subsidiarity, and the importance of particular law[69].

---

[68] See Morrisey, "Decisions of Episcopal Conferences," 112; Murray, "The Legislative Authority of the Episcopal Conference," 44-46.

[69] In structuring this section of the article the author basically follows the treatment of the respective issues by Paul Pallath in *The Synod of Bishops of Catholic Oriental Churches* (Rome: Mar Thoma Yogam The St.Thomas Christian Fellowship, 1994). He found rather helpful in varying degrees the following works: Winfried Aymans, "Synodale Strukturen im Codex Canonum Ecclesiarum Orientalium," *Archiv für katholisches Kirchenrecht* 160 (1991) 367-389; Kuriakose Bharanikulangara, "An Introduction to the Ecclesiology and Contents of the Oriental Code," in *The Code of Canons of the Eastern Churches: A Study and Interpretation* (Alwaye, India: St. Thomas Academy for Research, 1992) 11-38; Sabine Demel, "Die eigenberechtigte Kirche als Modelle für die Ökumene," in *Patriarchale und Synodale Strukturen in den katholischen Ostkirchen*, ed. Libero Gerosa et al. (*Patriarchale Strukturen*)(Münster-Hamburg-London: LIT Verlag, 2001) 243-270; John Faris, "Synod of Bishops of the Patriarchal Church," in idem, *Eastern Catholic Churches: Constitution and Governance* (New York: Saint Maron Publications,1992) 278-304; Kurt Koch, "Primat und Episkopat in der Sicht einer trinitätstheologischen Ekklesiologie," in *Patriarchale Strukturen*, 9-30; Ludger Müller, "Synodale Leitungsorgane im Ostkirchenrecht," in *Patriarchale Strukturen,* 141-168; Paul Pallath, *Local Episcopal Bodies in East and West* (Kerala, India: Oriental Institute of Religious Studies India,1997) 431-453; 485-498 (an exceptionally valuable source for this article); Dimitri Salachas, *Istituzioni di Diritto Canonico delle Chiese Cattoliche Orientali* (Rome: Edizioni Dehoniane, 1993) 171-184; Hugo Schwendenwein, "Das Patriarchat in der Katholischen Kirche," in *Patriarchale Strukturen*, 123-140; Cyril Vasil, "Le principe de la synodalité dans les Églises patriarchales selon la CCEO," *L'Année Canonique* 40 (1998) 87-117; Ivan Zuzek, "Particular Law in the Eastern Churches," in *The Code of Canons of the*

1. The synod as an ecclesial reality

Synodal structures historically have been an integral part of Eastern church governance; such primarily episcopal hierarchical organs have been a notable sign and instrument of ecclesial and episcopal unity. From the earliest days of Christianity church leaders in neighboring jurisdictions have gathered together in councils and synods, deliberated on doctrinal and disciplinary issues, tried to heal divisions within the churches, and promoted church reform under the guidance of the Spirit. A consciousness of communion/'collegiality' in the same Spirit prompted such initiatives. The Council of Jerusalem (Acts 15) was viewed as somewhat paradigmatic for such synodal undertakings. The patriarchates historically emerged out of these conciliar experiences since certain ecclesial settings were especially notable for their apostolic roots, their geographic preeminence, and the prestige of their episcopal leaders among other factors.

A fundamental unity of faith and church order has coexisted with diverse concrete local realizations of the synodal principle, grounded among other things in diverse historico-geographical factors[70]. The different Eastern rites (CCEO, c. 28) reflect different emphases and a varied liturgical, canonical, theological, and spiritual patrimony. Such synods have symbolized the Church as a horizontal-vertical communion comparable to the Trinity itself.

There is a fundamental constitutional difference between the three-tiered institutional structure underlying the Eastern code (eparchy-patriarchate-universal Church) and the basically two-tiered institutional structure underlying its Latin code counterpart (diocese and universal Church with due regard for certain intermediary level structures such as conferences). The former is a more nuanced way of highlighting the Church's catholicity. Eastern church synodal structures enable the various churches (especially represented by their bishops) to enrich the whole Catholic communion.

Vatican II called for the revitalization of a communion ecclesiology as well as older synodal patterns of governance; it recognized the importance

---

Eastern Churches, ed. Clarence Gallagher (Rome: Mar Thoma Yogam The Saint Thomas Christian Fellowship, 1991) 39-56.

[70] For a thoughtful examination of the similarities and differences between various canonical traditions, Latin and Eastern, in the first millennium, see Clarence Gallagher, *Church Law and Church Order in Rome and Byzantium* (Aldershot Hants, England: Ashgate, 2002).

of intermediary levels of governance as constitutionally relevant even while not discussing them at length; it also stressed the fundamental equality of the churches which enjoyed a basic right to develop in keeping with their distinctive traditions and patrimony (*OE* 4).

There is a need for a better balance in realizing the hierarchical and synodal principles in the Church as a whole. The Eastern code seems helpful here since, more so than the Latin code, it expresses a bit more adequately the vitality of canonical pluralism. The relative autonomy of the Eastern particular churches and their groupings and a more balanced primacy-synodality interaction in that code may help nuance the still noteworthy Latin code emphasis on the universal Church over the particular churches. This may help further to revitalize intermediary Latin instances such as conferences, particular councils, and provinces.

The Latin code does not really have a synodal structure comparable to the patriarchal synod, especially in its ongoing interaction with the patriarch. The conference is the highest infra-universal, supra-diocesan hierarchic instance in the Latin code and is somewhat analogous to that synod; however there are noteworthy differences between them. In the Latin code the pope's patriarchal office (mentioned in the *Annuario Pontificio*) somewhat blends into his primatial office for the whole Church. Accordingly it is hard to distinguish his properly patriarchal role for the Latin Church since it is not spelled out in as juridically clear a fashion as is true for the Eastern patriarch in his relationship to the synod[71].

2. *The synod and the conference as permanent institutions*

The conference is analogous to the patriarchal synod (*LG* 23) as an institution with a juridic personality distinct from its individual members which functions according to its statutes and the rules on juridic persons in the two codes (cc. 113-123; *CCEO*, cc. 920-930)

There is a new set of regulations on the synod in the Eastern code; it is treated in a separate chapter III on the patriarchal churches (*CCEO*, cc. 102-113: synod of bishops of patriarchal church). This highlights

---

[71] See 1983 code, c. 438 on the generally honorary status of Latin patriarchs. Although patriarchs are mentioned throughout the Eastern code, see especially *CCEO*, cc. 63-101 on the election of patriarchs and on their rights and obligations. For a thorough listing of Eastern code references to patriarchs, see Ivan Zuzek, *Index Analyticus Codicis Canonum Ecclesiarum Orientalium* (Rome: Pontificium Institutum Orientalium Studiorum, 1992) 245-249. For references to the patriarchal synod, see ibid., 329-331.

somewhat more sharply than was true in *Cleri sanctitati* (cc. 340-351: patriarchal synods) the fact that it is not a second level institution in service to the patriarch.

Among the common elements characterizing the synod and the conference are their episcopal character, their permanence, and a certain decisional capacity. Among the differences between them is the fact that the conference is a relatively new entity emerging in the mid-nineteenth century whereas the synod is ancient in character. The synod has been inspired by the ancient synods whereas the conference is somewhat influenced by more modern Latin church organizational patterns. The synod exercises a threefold governmental power, which is primarily legislative and judicial in focus. The conference, however, is primarily geared towards coordinating episcopal pastoral initiatives although it possesses some limited legislative and administrative governmental powers. The conference also is somewhat more elaborately structured than the synod in pursuing its varied purposes although obviously the complexity of conference organization varies depending on its size.

Such juridic persons must draw up statutes clarifying their purpose, constitution, government, and operating procedures (c. 94). However, the synod's relatively greater autonomy is clear from the fact that its statutes need not be forwarded to the Holy See for review (*CCEO*, c. 113) by contrast to its conference counterpart (c. 451).

3. Synod/conference membership and voting rights

The synod members with a deliberative vote are the ordained bishops representing the patriarchal Church as a whole as well as the episcopate; this is true whether or not they are constituted within the patriarchal territory. A significant criterion for membership is the exercise of the threefold pastoral functions (*munera*), which is grounded in their sacramental ordination. Particular law, however, may restrict the voting status of titular and retired bishops, less noteworthy leadership figures. Non-episcopal church leaders such as other hierarchs, clerics, and laity including religious superiors may be invited as experts to express their mind on synod issues. Such invitees are determined by particular law or by the patriarch with the consent of the permanent synod (*CCEO*, c. 102).

The key conference members with a deliberative vote are bishops, coadjutor bishops, and other leadership figures equivalent to diocesan bishops. Somewhat more so than in the Eastern code, the important criterion for membership is a significant diocesan pastoral leadership role and not simply episcopal ordination. Auxiliary bishops and titular bishops functioning in the conference at its request or at the request of the Holy See have a deliberative or consultative role according to the statutes but may not vote on their revision (cc. 450; 454). The statutes determine the role of non-episcopal persons invited as experts.

A continuing issue in both codes is assuring a more significant role for non-episcopal members of the people of God in synod/conference deliberations, analogous to the provisions for such diversified input in Latin particular councils (c. 443). If the conference de facto is to replace the particular council as an organ of governance, there needs to be appropriate decisional input from non-bishops in its deliberations even if only a consultative vote is envisioned at first. Only such a provision does justice to the corporate, broadly diversified nature of the people of God.

4. Frequency of synod/conference meetings, quorum, agenda, majority for decision-making.

The *frequency* of synod meetings is not left entirely to the patriarch's discretion. On the contrary, the synod must meet when an issue falls within its exclusive competence, the patriarch requires its consent to act validly[72], the patriarch convokes it with the consent of the permanent synod, or one third of the synod members request it. (*CCEO* 106, §1). Furthermore, particular law may require synod meetings at regular inter-vals, possibly even every year (*CCEO*, c. 106, §2). A much less detailed Latin canon 453 indicates that the conference is to meet at least every year and more often depending on circumstances according to the statutes.

The *quorum* for synod meetings is generally a majority of the bish-ops obliged to attend; however, two thirds of them are to be present for the election of a patriarch or bishop – obviously a major ecclesial mat-ter. Furthermore, particular law can specify a higher number for a quo-rum in other consequential matters – another interesting example of the importance of particular law in the Eastern code (*CCEO*, cc.107; 69; 149; 183, §1). The canons on conferences do not address this issue; however, canon 119, 2° on collegial acts requires an absolute majority of conference members to be present in principle for the body to act, yet

---

[72] For instances when the patriarch needs the synod's consent to act validly, see Pallath, *Synod of Bishops*, 189-194.

conference statutes or universal law (e.g., c. 455) may further qualify this rule.

The patriarch prepares the synod *agenda* after consulting its members, who, however, must approve it and may add additional items if at least one third of the membership consents; the Latin permanent council by contrast is to prepare the agenda for conference plenary meetings (c. 456); yet its statutes may make other provisions.

There is a notable difference in principle between the codes relative to the *majority* required for synod/conference decisions. Normally an absolute majority of those present is required for synod action, e.g., passing legislation (*CCEO*, c.924, §1). However, occasionally in major matters the Eastern code itself requires a higher majority, e.g., a two-thirds vote to elect a patriarch (*CCEO*, c. 72). Furthermore, the synod itself may establish its own provisions in this regard (*CCEO*, c. 107, §2). Interestingly enough, the conference, with due regard for its statutes, may also act at times by absolute majority of those present like particular councils (c.119, 2°). However, when the conference legislates, a two thirds vote not simply of those present, but rather of all with a deliberative vote is required for validity. The code makes no explicit provision for conference initiatives in drafting voting regulations.

5. *The juridical power of the patriarch and the conference president*

Unlike any comparable Latin code relationship, the patriarch and the synod are genuinely interdependent in exercising patriarchal church governance. There seems to be a certain constitutional irreversibility about patriarchal church structures even if they are not technically grounded in divine law as are the papacy and the episcopacy (*OE* 7).

The Eastern code commission did not express a preference for the patriarch or the synod as the key Eastern governance structure but simply allocated various competencies to each in an attempt to harmonize the synodal and patriarchal principles.

The patriarch is not a legislator except for his own eparchy, yet he promulgates synod laws in light of its determinations. The synod is superior in some respects in the patriarchate (i.e., legislative and judicial governance), while the patriarch is the preeminent administrative governance figure who presides over the synod (*CCEO*, c. 110). In exercising that administrative role he must occasionally consult or even obtain the consent of the whole synod or of the permanent synod (*CCEO*, cc. 110, §4; 115).

The Eastern code attempts to implement the conciliar call to restore the rights and privileges of patriarchs in light of genuine Eastern traditions while adapting them to contemporary circumstances (*OE* 9). The patriarch is viewed as father and head (*pater et caput-CCEO*, c. 55) of the patriarchal church, a *primus inter pares* vis-à-vis his brother bishops in synod. Besides his distinctly ecclesial role, at times he represents his church in difficult historical-social-political circumstances in the Christian East.

In a certain sense the conference president, like the patriarch, is also a *primus inter pares* in relationship to his brother bishops; yet the code says little about the president's role (c. 452), which must be clarified by examining conference statutes. It reflects a notably less monarchical vision of the president than the Eastern code has of the patriarch. The former's role is a relatively modest one by comparison with that of the patriarch[73]; and it is normally exercised only for a temporary period according to the statutes unlike the patriarch's lifetime status. Furthermore, the conference's governmental role, especially its legislative competence, is notably less comprehensive than that of the synod.

6. *The legislative power of the synod in comparison with the conference*

The relative autonomy of the patriarchal churches is particularly evident in the legislative autonomy of their synods – our key focus with due regard for their other competencies. There has clearly been a postconciliar effort to recapture some of their original autonomy that had been somewhat lost over the years. Contemporary canonical developments have recognized more adequately than before the need of more comprehensive governmental autonomy given the varied liturgical, historical, and canonical traditions and varied socio-cultural settings of the different *sui iuris* churches.

Only the synod, not its presiding patriarch, may enact particular laws for the patriarchal church, and not simply in areas in which the Eastern code specifically mentions the synod (*CCEO*, c. 110, §1). In complementing the common Eastern law, the synod must take into account the ecclesial hierarchy of norms, not legislating contrary to that common law, much less any legislation binding all the churches, Latin and Eastern, e.g., divine law.

---

[73] See, for example, 1983 code, c. 455, §4 on the conference president's inability to act in situations in which the conference is not empowered to legislate unless every bishop consents.

Such broad synod legislative self-determination is an especially notable difference from the comparable conference competency. As noted above, the conference can legislate only in areas explicitly authorized by the code, subsequent legislation, or a special Apostolic See mandate (c. 455, §1) Unlike the synod or even the Latin particular council, it is viewed primarily (and in the author's view somewhat questionably) not as an intermediary governmental structure but rather as an instrument of pastoral communication and coordination facilitating the sharing of episcopal experiences.

Furthermore, certain other differences between synodal and conference legislation are noteworthy. While both Eastern and Latin bishops surely seek moral unanimity in their decision-making, the law requires a two-thirds majority of all Latin bishops with a deliberative vote to pass legislation, be they present at the plenary meeting or not. By contrast an absolute majority of Eastern bishops present at the synod meeting suffices; and the synod itself has a certain decisional latitude regarding its voting regulations. While conference legislation may not be promulgated validly without Holy See *recognitio* (1983 code, cc. 455, §2; 456), comparable synod norms are simply forwarded to the pope for information, not review, confirmation, or approval purposes (*CCEO*, c. 111, §3) and perhaps to the other patriarchs to foster ecclesial communion. Like the conference (c. 455, §3), the synod determines the mode of promulgating its laws, but the patriarch actually expedites the promulgation (*CCEO*, cc. 111, §1; 112, §1). While the synod alone definitively interprets its laws, the patriarch may do so temporarily prior to the holding of the next synod (*CCEO*, c.112, §2). Finally, with due regard for the aforementioned synodal autonomy, the pope's inalienable prerogative to intervene in individual instances in virtue of his primacy remains intact (*OE* 9; *CCEO*, c. 45, §1).

One might note, however, a certain difference regarding the scope of synodal disciplinary and liturgical laws, for which there is no Latin parallel. Liturgical laws bind everywhere; however, disciplinary laws and other synod decisions bind only within the patriarchal territory unless the Holy see approves them or an extra-territorial eparch promulgates them in his territory (*CCEO*, c. 150, §§2-3).This is true even given the involvement of such extra-territorial eparchs in the legislative decisional process. This raises the complex and sharply controverted question of the patriarch's extra-territorial jurisdiction which we cannot address here[74].

---

[74] Authors such as Pallath propose that synod decisions should be operative wherever a given *sui iuris* church's hierarchy is established. This would better reflect the equality

In short, the synod and the conference differ more than they are similar – a position we will question later. Perhaps this is so because the pope exercises a genuinely patriarchal role in the churches of the West, however minimally the code explicitates such a competency; whereas he exercises a primatial, but not precisely patriarchal, role in the Eastern patriarchal churches.

7. *The Eastern code revision process*[75], *the principle of subsidiarity, and the importance of particular law.*

With due regard for ongoing controversies over the ecclesial applicability of the principle of subsidiarity[76], principle 7 for the revision of the Eastern code[77], without describing the principle, affirms that it has long been operative in the Eastern churches. This is true even if it has not been explicitly referred to. If the principle means in part a respect for the decisional competence of lower level governmental bodies, it is more noticeably operative in the Eastern code's structuring of inter-ecclesial relationships than in its Latin counterpart[78]. As we have seen, the synod may function fairly freely with relatively little Holy See involvement in its operations. This somewhat reflects the 1973 proposal of the Pontifical Oriental Institute faculty[79] that, within the parameters of the common law (*CCEO* 1493, §1), the Eastern churches have the faculty to create particular law (*CCEO* 1493, §2) that would serve the common good more effectively. However, the aforementioned principle

---

of all the churches and accord them appropriate self-governing recognition. Such territorial differentiations weaken ecclesial unity and impair the conciliar-inspired autonomy of the Eastern churches. The extra-territorial hierarchs, in his estimation, are too dependent on the pope for their appointment and functioning. See Pallath, *Local Episcopal Bodies*, 489-491.

[75] For a particularly helpful history of the Eastern code revision process, see Faris, *Eastern Catholic Churches*, 67-106.

[76] For a literate discussion of the extensive literature on various aspects of the principle of subsidiarity, see John Burkhard, "The Interpretation and Application of Subsidiarity in Ecclesiology: an Overview of the Canonical and Theological Literature," *The Jurist* 58 (1998) 279-342. Also Ad Leys, "Structuring Communion: the Importance of the Principle of Communion," *The Jurist* 58 (1998) 84-123.

[77] See *Nuntia* 3 (1976) 21-22. The principles are not numbered unlike their Latin code counterparts, but the five paragraph discussion of subsidiarity is the sixth point after the preamble.

[78] Principle 5 for the revision of the Latin code seems much more cautious regarding its applicability in that code than in Eastern code in part because of a fear of the possible emergence of national churches. See *Communicationes* 1 (1969) 80-81.

[79] See *Nuntia* 26 (1988) 107-108.

is also operative at the lower levels of such churches so that higher authorities such as synods or patriarchs should not undertake competencies proper to eparchs and those collaborating with them at the eparchial and parochial levels.

De facto the Eastern code leaves much room for legislative initiatives in the various patriarchal churches, prescinding from issues reserved to the Holy See. Its common provisions are said to be limited to what is absolutely necessary for the good of all the churches. The Eastern code is a useful example of canonical pluralism in the Church and reflects a healthier view of papal-episcopal relationships than a more centralized structure. If any papal interventions occur in eparchial life, however tension-producing, they are not to impair legitimate episcopal power but rather are to support it. Serious efforts to implement the values of collegiality, subsidiarity, and legitimate diversity are integral to sound ecclesial governance that is also ecumenically sensitive as well. This is especially important for Eastern law given its code commission's explicit ecumenical concerns[80]. However, such concerns are no less relevant to Latin law although unfortunately ecumenical priorities were not explicitly articulated in the Latin code revision principles.

While the Latin code reflects a more noticeably universal law focus, its Eastern counterpart more forcefully highlights the importance of particular law[81]. That code takes more seriously the principle of subsidiarity perhaps because of a healthier recognition of the heterogeneity of the twenty one *sui iuris* churches it governs. And yet the alleged homogeneity of the vastly larger Latin Church raises significant questions when one considers the notable diversity of pastoral situations revealed especially in the various special synods called by John Paul II in the late 90's to celebrate the new millennium. The 'relative brevity' of the Eastern code (1526 canons as opposed to the 1752 Latin canons) is due to the Eastern code commission's dropping many norms contained in the four motu proprios promulgated by Pius XII[82] in the late 40's and 50's and not restating numerous canons contained in the un-promulgated proposed

[80] See principle 4 on the desired ecumenical character of the Eastern code in *Nuntia* 3 (1976) 21.

[81] See Kuriakose Bharanikulangara, *Particular Law of the Eastern Catholic Churches* (New York: Saint Maron Publications, 1996).

[82] See Pius XII, motu proprio *Crebrae allatae*, February 22, 1949: *AAS* 41 (1949) 89-119; idem, motu proprio *Sollicitudinem nostram*, January 6, 1950: *AAS* 42 (1950) 5-120; idem, motu proprio *Postquam apostolicis*, February 9, 1952: *AAS* 44 (1952) 65-152; idem, motu proprio *Cleri sanctitati*, June 2, 1957: *AAS* 49 (1957) 433-603.

motu proprios of that period[83]. Apparently such canons were deemed simply unnecessary or at least not reflecting the disciplinary patrimony of all the Eastern churches.

II. SOME SPECIFIC REFLECTIONS ON CERTAIN ASPECTS OF LEGISLATIVE DECISION-MAKING BY CONFERENCES AND SYNODS

After offering some general reflections on conferences and synods, the author will highlight a few specific aspects of their respective legislative roles following the order of the Latin code, our key point of reference. We will indicate some areas where the value of collegiality might be better served were there a more noticeable parity between the codes in empowering conference and synod legislative initiatives[84]. This is to say nothing about the more basic issue of the appropriateness of the restrictions on conference legislative initiatives as differentiated both from kindred Latin institutes such as particular councils and Eastern institutes such as synods. This issue will be briefly addressed in the conclusions at the end of the article.

In the following areas one might question why conference legislative competency is not as broadly structured as its Eastern synodal counterpart[85]: 1) norms on priestly formation, 2) norms on ecumenical policy-making, 3) norms on catechetics, 4) norms on publishing and translating liturgical books[86], 5) norms on establishing marriage impediments,

---

[83] In this connection see Ivan Zuzek, "Les textes non-publiés du Code de Droit Canonique Oriental," *Nuntia* 1 (1975) 23-31. 1574 of the proposed 2666 canons were actually promulgated by Pius XII

[84] In an earlier work the author indicated various canons of the Latin code providing for the legislative competency of the conference and offered brief comments on whether such a competency was obligatory or discretionary, whether any other authorities such as diocesan bishops enjoyed a similar competency, and whether the potential scope of conference legislative competency was curtailed during the code revision process. See Green, "Normative Role," in *Episcopal Conferences*, 154-165; 168-175 (appendix listing said canons and earlier formulations during the code revision process). For a thoughtful exploration of the Latin code provisions for the legislative role of conferences and the specific ways in which different conferences have implemented them, see Jose T. Martin de Agar, *Legislazione delle Conferenze Episcopali Complementare al C.I.C.* (Milan: Giuffrè, 1990).

[85] Even to speak of the synod as the 'counterpart' to the conference may be to accord a greater canonical parity to the two institutes than is actually warranted.

[86] This is actually more of an administrative issue technically; but it raises comparable concerns about the legal status of the conference; and it has been a matter of particular controversy especially in the English speaking world.

6) norms on holy days and days of penance, and 7) norms on alienation of church goods, 8) norms on removing and transferring pastors.

1. Norms on priestly formation

a. Latin code[87]

Each nation is to have a conference-established program of *priestly* formation to be observed by all seminaries, diocesan and inter-diocesan, with due regard for supreme church authority norms (1983 code, c. 242)[88]. The legislator apparently views this as an especially serious issue since such a program requires not simply Holy See *recognitio* but rather its *approbatio*. This indicates a somewhat higher level of Roman involvement in the enterprise, which still technically remains conference legislation. Quite wisely the code calls for adapting the program to changing circumstances, and such adaptations also require Roman approval before being implemented. Such a program fundamentally is to define the main principles of seminary formation in view of the pastoral needs of various regions and provinces[89].

b. Eastern code

The patriarchal synod is empowered to issue a formation program for *clerics* implementing the common law more precisely for seminaries within the patriarchal territory (*CCEO*, c. 330). Eparchs outside the patriarchate are also required to develop further such a program for their own eparchies, with due regard for canon 150, §3 somewhat encouraging them to implement synod legislation. Any modifications of the aforementioned Eastern norms are within the competency of the respective synod/eparchs. Interestingly enough, no reference is made to Holy See involvement in developing pertinent norms on personal, spiritual, doctrinal, and pastoral formation. The Eastern code's consciousness of ecclesial diversity in a given area is evident in its authorizing common formation programs for a region, nation, or even diverse *sui iuris* churches with due respect for the uniqueness of the various rites.

---

[87] See Martin de Agar, 7.

[88] This likely refers both to the October 28, 1965 conciliar decree *Optatam totius* [*AAS* 58 (1966) 713-727] and the various postconciliar provisions on seminary formation issued by the Congregation for Catholic Education (*Pastor bonus* 112-113).

[89] Individual Latin bishops or groups of them are to approve a rule for their own seminaries, presumably further spelling out the implications of the conference program (c. 243).

2. Norms on ecumenical policy-making

a. Latin code[90]

Canon 755, §2 speaks first of diocesan bishops and subsequently of the conferences' possibly issuing practical ecumenical norms with due regard for the prescriptions of supreme church authority, the primary moderator of ecumenical activity[91]. The conference functions within this broader context, and, like the individual diocesan bishop, has an irreplaceable role in adapting such norms to national, regional, or local ecclesial situations according to the conditions specified in canon 455. More specifically canon 844, §5 indicates that both diocesan bishops or the conference may issue general norms on sacramental sharing with members of other Christian churches or ecclesial communities only after consulting their appropriate leadership figures. Canon 1126 calls for conference regulations regarding the declarations and promises required of the Catholic party in a mixed marriage, and canon 1127, §2 enables it to determine the formalities for granting dispensations from canonical form in such marriages.

Norm 5 of the original schema on the church's teaching office[92] referred only to the conference (and not to individual bishops) regarding norms both on the ecumenical movement and on common prayer for Christian unity. Norm 2 of the original sacramental law schema[93] spoke first of the conference's and then of individual bishops' discretion regarding norms on sacramental sharing. However, the 1983 code seems to focus more sharply on the individual bishop's ecumenical and interreligious responsibility and discretion (c. 383, §§3-4).

[90] See Green, Teaching-Conferences, 31-35; idem, Sanctifying-Conferences, 65-70; Martin de Agar, 19-20; 27.

[91] In this connection see especially the November 1964 conciliar decrees *Unitatis redintegratio* on ecumenism [*AAS* 57 (1965) 90-107] and *Orientalium Ecclesiarum* on the Eastern Catholic Churches [*AAS* 57 (1965) 76-85]. Two significant post-code ecumenical documents are the 1993 ecumenical directory [Pontifical Council for Promoting Christian Unity, *Directory for the Application of Principles and Norms on Ecumenism*, Vatican City, March 25, 1993] and the May 1995 encyclical of John Paul II, *Ut unum sint* [*Origins* 25/4 (June 28, 1995) 49; 51-72]

[92] See Pontificia Commissio Codici Iuris Canonici Recognoscendo, *Schema Canonum Libri III de Ecclesiae Munere Docendi* (Vatican City: Typis Polyglottis Vaticanis, 1977).

[93] See Pontificia Commissio Codici Iuris Canonici Recognoscendo, *Schema Documenti Pontificii quo Disciplina Canonica de Sacramentis Recognoscitur* (Vatican City: Typis Polyglottis Vaticanis, 1975).

b. Eastern code

Without explicitly referring to the synod, the Eastern canon 904, §1 calls for particular law to promote ecumenical initiatives in each *sui iuris* church, not surprisingly with due regard for the general ecumenical supervision function of the Roman Apostolic See. However, Rome need not grant *recognitio*, confirmation, or approval of such synodal norms although the Roman Pontiff, and perhaps other Eastern patriarchs, are to be informed of such synodal initiatives which may have broad ecclesial implications.

Unlike its Latin counterpart, the Eastern code provides for the setting up of a patriarchal commission of ecumenical experts at the level of the *sui iuris* church to facilitate the discharging of the aforementioned legislative task. Other hierarchs in the same area may be consulted for suggestions in this regard (*CCEO*, c. 904, §2).

The Eastern provisions for synod legislation authorizing sacramental sharing (*CCEO*, c. 671, §5) and implementing the *cautiones* in mixed marriages (*CCEO,* c. 615) are largely the same as their Latin counterparts except for the necessary Roman *recognitio* of conference norms. However, Eastern provisions for a dispensation from canonical form are much more restrictive than the Latin code. Particular law may not specify the conditions for granting such a dispensation, which is reserved to the Apostolic See (Congregation for the Eastern Churches) or to the patriarch, who in turn is not to grant such except for a most serious reason (*CCEO,* c. 835). Finally, not surprisingly, given the Eastern code commission's ecumenical aspirations[94], eparchial bishops are to be especially sensitive to ecumenical and interreligious concerns (*CCEO*, c. 192, §§3-4).

Finally, the 1993 ecumenical directory envisions an extensive range of legislative and administrative competencies for conferences and synods on the one hand[95] and for diocesan bishops on the other hand in fostering the varied aspects of the Church's ecumenical involvement. Interestingly enough, while understandably not mentioning the canonical differences as well as similarities between conferences and synods, the directory

---

[94] See note 81.

[95] A cursory review of the directory indicates approximately twenty six references to the legislative (primarily) but also administrative (secondarily) competency of conferences and synods in the following paragraphs: chapter 1 (search for Christian unity): 6, 21, 23, 28,36; chapter 2 (ecumenical organization): 39, 40, 46-47; chapter 3 (ecumenical formation): 55, 72, 81; chapter 4 (communion of life and spiritual activity): 94, 99e, 106 (implicit), 130, 142, 150,157; chapter 5 (ecumenical cooperation): 164, 168, 173, 175, 193, 194, 195, 212.

consistently speaks of them in the same context. This seems to be a per-
suasive argument for viewing such institutes increasingly in similar
canonical terms, thereby altering the current less satisfactory canonical
status of conferences as appropriate.

3. Norms on catechetics

a. Latin code[96]

During the code revision process, the conference's catechetical role
was notably curtailed, and the diocesan bishop's religious education
oversight prerogatives were highlighted commensurately. For example,
norm 26, 1 of the original schema on the Church's teaching office envisioned the conference's issuing catechetical norms for its jurisdiction,
seeing to the preparation and dissemination of a directory, catechisms, and
other catechetical materials and fostering and coordinating various catechetical undertakings.

However, canon 775, §1 of the Latin code envisions the diocesan
bishop as the proper legislator on catechetical matters with due regard
for Apostolic See prescripts (Congregation for the Clergy: *Pastor bonus*
94). Moreover, it does not restate norm 27, 1 of the original schema,
which called for diocesan bishops to exercise their role as catechetical
legislators within the larger context of conference catechetical norms.
Nor does canon 777 restate the original schema's reference to conference
norms guiding diocesan bishops in regulating sacramental preparation
and other forms of catechesis (norm 30). Unlike the original schema
(norm 26, 1), the Apostolic See must approve conference catechisms
(c. 775, §2), but not the catechetical initiatives of diocesan bishops
(c. 775, §1).

Nor must diocesan bishops consult the conference before publishing
their own catechisms, as had been proposed during the revision process
to reconcile conference-diocesan bishop catechetical prerogatives.
The code commission judged that the conference should not impose a
specific 'catechetical line' throughout its jurisdiction; rather it should
simply serve individual dioceses and bishops through a possible catechetical office (c. 775, §3), which, however, is not required as in the original schema (norm 26, 2).

---

[96] See Green, Teaching-Conferences, 39-43.

b. Eastern code

Canons 621 and 622 on the synod's catechetical role seem to embrace much of what the original Latin schema on the Church's teaching office envisioned. With due regard for supreme church authority provisions, the synod may issue catechetical norms suitably arranged in a directory (*CCEO*, c. 621, §1). This important document is to consider the special character of the Eastern churches[97], be biblical-liturgical in focus, and respect the varied patrological, hagiographical, and iconographical traditions of the various churches (*CCEO*, c. 621, §2). Without any reference to Holy See involvement, the canon also calls for synodal publication of catechisms adapted to the needs of various groups with appropriate catechetical aids and resources. The synod is also to promote and coordinate catechetical initiatives throughout the patriarchate (*CCEO*, c. 621, §3). To facilitate the achievement of the aforementioned objectives, the synod is to establish a catechetical commission, perhaps along with other *sui iuris* churches in the same territory or socio-cultural region. A catechetical center is also to be set up to serve both the commission members and especially the various churches in coordinating catechetical programs and providing catechist formation (*CCEO*, c. 622).

4. Norms on publishing and translating liturgical books[98]

a. Latin code[99]

A central text on liturgical authority is canon 838, which generically regulates the diverse competencies of the Apostolic See (Congregation for Divine Worship and the Discipline of the Sacraments: *Pastor bonus*

---

[97] This is a good example of a canon reflecting one of the key Eastern code revision principles, i.e., the need to highlight its properly Eastern character. See *Nuntia* 3 (1976) 19.

[98] The issue of approving liturgical texts and translations seems technically more a matter of administrative than of legislative governance, our primary focus. However, in this area one notes important Latin-Eastern law differences regarding the liturgical competencies of bishops. It seems interesting to review them briefly at a time characterized by various controversies over liturgical texts, especially between the Congregation for Divine Worship and the Discipline of the Sacraments and some English-speaking bishops and liturgists. This complex issue can hardly be explored here. However, see, for example, "Bishop Trautman/Pastoral Musicians Liturgical Renewal: Keeping the Virtue of Hope," *Origins* 32/15 (September 19, 2002) 256-260; "Bishop Taylor Statement Regarding International Commission on English in the Liturgy," *Origins* 32/13 (September 5, 2002) 217-218.

[99] See Green, Sanctifying-Conferences, 61-63.

62-66), the conference, and the diocesan bishop[100]. However, the broad implications of these provisions can be appreciated properly only by a serious study of Book IV and the various liturgical books. The canon seems to emphasize primarily the competency of the Apostolic See and the diocesan bishop with a somewhat lesser focus on the conference. The Apostolic See is competent to regulate the liturgy of the universal Church, publish the liturgical books, review their translations, and exercise a general liturgical oversight role (§2). The diocesan bishop may issue liturgical norms within the limits of his competence (e.g., c. 1002 on communal anointing norms), a fairly broad legislative reference reflecting his notable liturgical governance role within his own diocese (§4). The conference enjoys a certain legislative authority regarding the exercise of the *munus sanctificandi* e.g., canon 891 on the age of confirmation. However, canon 838, §3 affirms only its somewhat limited competency regarding the translation of liturgical texts. It is to prepare them and publish them after Holy See *recognitio*, while making appropriate adaptations envisioned in the liturgical books themselves

b. Eastern code

The competency of patriarchal church authorities regarding liturgical texts is more noteworthy than their conference counterparts. The approval of liturgical texts is understandably a major administrative issue; hence not surprisingly the patriarch alone is competent to do so; however, he must obtain the consent of the patriarchal synod, not simply the permanent synod. Furthermore, the *recognitio* of the Apostolic See (Congregation for the Eastern Churches: *Pastor bonus* 56; 58, §1) must precede such an act of patriarchal discretion (*CCEO,* c. 657, §1). The implementation of the principle of subsidiarity, however, seems more operative regarding liturgical translations. Here the patriarch with the consent of the synod approves the translation and notifies the Apostolic See of this fact; no Roman *recognitio*, confirmation, or approval of the translation is necessary.

---

[100] Interestingly canon 838, §1 reflecting *Sacrosanctum Concilium* 22, §1 speaks only of the Apostolic See and the diocesan bishop as liturgical authorities. It neglects the reference to the liturgical competency of territorial groupings of bishops such as conferences in *Sacrosanctum Concilium* 22, §2 and the varied references to conference authority in Book IV. See Green, "Normative Role," in *Episcopal Conferences*, 160-162; 171-174; Martin de Agar, 21-30.

5. Norms on establishing marriage impediments

a. Latin code

Unlike norm 262, 3 of the original schema on sacramental law which would have authorized the conference to establish marriage impediments, canon 1083, §2 permits it simply to establish a higher age for marriage than the code provides (c. 1083, 1), yet only for liceity; in short it cannot create a new impediment of age. Hence the Latin code once again reaffirms the exclusive competency of supreme church authority to establish such impediments for the baptized, which qualify the exercise of the basic human right to marry (cc. 1075, §2; 1058). The code also precludes possible conference expanding of the number of impediments to the reception or exercise of orders, which are comprehensively listed in canons 1040-1042 and 1044.

b. Eastern code

By contrast to the Latin code, the Eastern code authorizes the synod possibly to establish new marriage impediments. However, this is not to be done lightly presumably because of the qualification of the basic human right to marry (*CCEO*, c. 778). Rather such a notable legislative initiative requires a most grave cause, and the synod is to consult both interested eparchs of other *sui iuris* churches and the Apostolic See as well. Yet the approval of neither those eparchs nor the Apostolic See is required. Furthermore, no lower ecclesiastical authority such as an eparch may create such an impediment (*CCEO*, c. 792). Interestingly enough, however, like the Latin Church, the impediments to the reception or exercise of orders are comprehensively listed (*CCEO*, cc. 762-763); and particular law may not establish any new impediments.

6. Norms on feast days of obligation/days of penance

a. Latin code[101]

The conference's competency to regulate both feast days of obligation[102] and days of penance has been significantly circumscribed by

---

[101] See Green, Sanctifying-Conferences, 80-83; Martin de Agar, 28-30.

[102] The faithful's observance of their feast day/Sunday obligation means that they are to participate in the Mass and abstain from works and affairs precluding worship, the joy of the Lord's day, and appropriate relaxation (*CCEO*, c. 1247).

contrast to the original schema on sacred times and places/divine worship[103]. Canon 1246, §2 authorizes the conference with Holy See *approval* (not *recognitio*) to abolish or transfer to Sunday the observance of the ten feast days of obligation for the universal Latin Church besides Sundays (1983 code, c. 1246, §1). However, norm 45 of the original schema mandated only two such feast days of obligation, namely Christmas and a Marian feast to be determined by the conference. Other feast days were to be determined by the conference, which would have enjoyed significant latitude in this pastorally noteworthy area in light of local circumstances.

The Latin canons on days of penance begin by generically affirming the penitential obligations of the Christian faithful (c. 1249) and specifically highlighting Lent and Fridays throughout the year as distinctly penitential times (c. 1250). The conference may determine that some food other than meat may be the subject of the penitential abstinence obligation, which is also specified in canon 1251. After canon 1252 indicates who are bound to fast and abstain, canon 1253 allows the conference to determine more precisely the implications of that penitential obligation (cc. 1249-1252), even substituting other pious practices. However, the original schema would have accorded even greater legislative latitude to the conference in this regard (norm 48, 2).

b. Eastern code

The Eastern code differentiates between feast days of obligation[104] common to all the Eastern churches (*CCEO*, c. 880, §§1 and 3) and those proper to individual Eastern churches (*CCEO*, c. 880, §2). In principle only supreme church authority may establish, transfer, or suppress common feast days presumably because this issue transcends the competence of the individual *sui iuris* churches. Hence, not surprisingly in this area, the synods have the same basic competency as the conference regarding altering such feast days. They may likewise only suppress them or transfer them to Sunday with Apostolic See approval.

---

[103] In this connection see Pontificia Commissio Codici Iuris Canonici Recognoscendo, *Schema Canonum Libri IV de Ecclesiae Munere Sanctificandi Pars II De Locis et Temporibus Sacris deque Cultu Divino* (Vatican City: Typis Polyglottis Vaticanis, 1977).

[104] Interestingly here, unlike the Latin code, there is room for possible synodal discretion regarding the faithful's observance of the feast day/Sunday obligation. They are to participate in the Divine Liturgy (Mass) or in the celebration of the divine praises if legitimate church custom or particular law provides for such (*CCEO*, c. 881, §1).

Unlike the Latin provisions for conferences, however, the synod may alter the feast days proper to the individual Eastern churches. It may establish, transfer, or suppress such feast days. However, while no Holy See involvement is required in such a decision, the synod fathers are to take into account the various churches in their territory – another indication of the Eastern code's sensitivity to ecclesial diversity. Furthermore, in making such changes, the synod is to foster a faithful and accurate observance of the rite of the patriarchal church to ensure its organic liturgical development (*CCEO*, c. 40, §1).

Finally, a relatively brief Eastern code provision, somewhat comparable to the original Latin schema, determines that particular law (e.g., synod) is to specify the implications of the penitential obligations of the faithful (*CCEO*, c. 882). Presumably such a broad provision takes cognizance of the diverse penitential practices of the twenty one *sui iuris* Eastern churches.

7. Norms on alienation of church goods

a. Latin code[105]

Periodically the code envisions conference norms regarding temporal goods probably because such norms ensure better coordination of regulations in this complex area involving both civil law and financial variables (cc. 1254-1310)[106]. One notable example is the following legislative competency. The conference helps determine the authority competent to permit the alienation of church goods which constitute by legitimate designation the stable patrimony of a public juridic person (c. 116) and whose value exceeds the sum defined by law (c. 1291). The conference does so by defining the minimum and maximum values of goods whose alienation requires the permission of certain church authorities (c. 1292, §1). This may include the Holy See (Congregation for the Clergy: *Pastor bonus*: 98) if the value of the goods exceeds the maximum amount, if they are given to the Church by a vow, or if they are precious for

---

[105] See Martin de Agar, 33.

[106] See Pontificia Commissio Codici Iuris Canonici Recognoscendo, *Schema Canonum de Iure Patrimoniali Ecclesiae* (Vatican City: Typis Polyglottis Vaticanis, 1977). Principle 5 for the revision of the code referred to the law on temporal goods as an area of special applicability of the principle of subsidiarity or legislative decentralization: *Communicationes* 1 (1969) 81. Hence the commission's approach to the conference's normative role here is of particular interest. In this general context see Green, "Subsidiarity during the Code Revision Process," 785-789.

historical or artistic reasons. Such a conference definition requires the *recognitio* of the Holy See before being validly promulgated[107].

b. Eastern code

One notices somewhat more significant legislative and administrative alienation of goods competency for the patriarchal churches in the Eastern canon 1036. Legislatively speaking, the synod is to define the pertinent minimum and maximum values of goods whose alienation requires certain permissions. Interestingly enough, while the Latin code speaks only of minimum and maximum amounts with commensurately higher level authorities involved in granting such permissions, its Eastern counterpart speaks of minimum, maximum, and double the maximum amounts with equivalently more demanding requirements permission-wise. The canon also distinguishes between patriarchal churches (§§1-3)[108] and other Eastern churches (§4). In patriarchal churches the Holy See is not involved in specifying the minimum and maximum amounts by way of *recognitio*, confirmation, or approval although the pope is to be informed of synod action as soon as possible. Furthermore, administratively speaking, in patriarchal churches the Holy See is also not involved in granting any such permissions; rather it is the eparchial bishop (minimum) (§1), the patriarch with the consent of the permanent synod (maximum) (§2), or the patriarch with the consent of the patriarchal synod (double the maximum)(§3).

8. Norms on removing and transferring pastors

There seem to be relatively few areas in procedural law where conference and synod legislative discretion differ[109]. Although the Eastern

---

[107] During the revision process, fears were expressed that certain proposed conference legislative and administrative competencies unduly restricted local episcopal discretion. Hence the *coetus* on temporal goods decided that generally any norm that could be construed as implying such undue restrictions would be dropped, thereby enhancing the legal-pastoral prerogatives of the diocesan bishop in his particular church. For example, norm 37, 2 of the original schema would have provided a conference office to monitor the bishops' discretion in authorizing the alienation of church goods. This provision is dropped in the current law – a development illustrating the fear of unwarranted conference centralization. Furthermore, the practical ability of some conferences to discharge such a task efficiently was also questioned.

[108] This provision also applies to major archiepiscopal churches (*CCEO*, c. 152).

[109] For a brief overview of similarities and differences between Latin and Eastern procedural law, see Thomas Green, "Procedural Law: Some Comparative Reflections on the Latin and Eastern Codes," in *The Art of the Good and Equitable A Festschrift in Honor*

canons were presumably to reflect distinctly Eastern traditions, Eastern code revision principle nine also called for the structuring of a largely uniform procedural law for all Catholics, allegedly to ensure impartial justice but also to facilitate possible recourse to the pope, which is a basic Christian right in virtue of his primacy (*CCEO*, c. 1059; c. 1417)[110].

One notable difference between the codes concerns the removal and transfer of pastors (*CCEO*, cc. 1388-1400; cc. 1740-1752). In light of the above Eastern code commission preoccupations, the canons in the two codes rarely differ; however, the initial Eastern canon provides for the possibility of particular law such as synodal legislation modifying the code. However, interestingly enough such an initiative requires the *approval* of the Apostolic See – a rather unusual Eastern code provision and probably an indication of the seriousness with which the pastor's right to stability in office is taken.

III. REFLECTIONS OF LADISLAS ORSY ON APOSTOLOS SUOS

Earlier in the article the author referred to various commentaries on *Apostolos suos*[111] and mentioned some continuing theological-canonical issues regarding conferences that it does not seem to resolve definitively. Ladislas Orsy, of Georgetown University, Washington, D.C. provides some thoughtful reflections on some of those issues[112]. After some introductory observations his article is divided into two main parts followed by a conclusion. The first part discusses structural issues regarding conferences and doctrinal concerns in *Apostolos suos* (411-419). A key question is the following: do present conference structures and norms adequately reflect the power of the Spirit at work in the episcopate? The second part (a new vision of faith and new structures) explores various aspects of his continuing concern that ecclesial structures such as conferences be duly informed by and reflect our best theological insights (419-425). Two key questions here are the following: if the answer to the prior question is negative, what theological-canonical values can better

---

of Lawrence G. Wrenn, ed. Frederick C. Easton (Washington: Canon Law Society of America, 2002) 103-124.

[110] See *Nuntia* 3 (1976) 23-24.

[111] See n. 7.

[112] See Ladislas Orsy, "Episcopal Conferences and the Power of the Spirit," *The Jurist* 59 (1999) 409-431 (Orsy, Conferences-Spirit). This is a somewhat reworked version of the article in *Louvain Studies* referred to in note 6.

inform our structures and norms on conferences? And how can we fashion such structures and norms? He concludes by articulating some general principles underlying a more balanced approach to papal-episcopal
relationships while calling for a reshaping of the current canonical norms
on conferences (425-428). The complexity of his article and space limitations preclude a detailed examination of his observations. However, we
will highlight some of his key insights to reinforce our own judgment
that an enhanced conference status (similar to Eastern synods) will enable
the Church better to implement its conciliar insights on collegiality.
We will not deal with the important issue of the conference's teaching
authority but are concerned especially with its legislative status.

Initially Orsy affirms that at the heart of *Apostolos suos* is the teaching that conferences are permanent juridical entities ultimately created
by the Holy See, whose statutes it recognizes and whose operations it
controls. This significantly impacts the theory and practice of such conferences and the Holy See's relationship to them and to diocesan bishops.
The doctrine underlying this viewpoint is that conferences as such have
no corporate power in themselves based on the assistance of the Spirit
(Mt. 18:20).

The motu proprio differentiates between *effective* and *affective* collegiality. The former (proper episcopal power) is verified only in the episcopal college as a whole, e.g., when it gathers in an ecumenical council
(cc. 337, §1; 338-341) or when the pope declares or accepts as properly
collegial the joint action of the bishops dispersed throughout the world
(c. 337, §2). Such effective collegiality, however, is not verified in legitimate but partial episcopal gatherings such as conferences. Such groups
embody only an *affectus collegialis*, an internal disposition to deliberate
and act jointly, without, however, participating in the Spirit-inspired
power of the episcopate.

Orsy then raises a number of questions about the motu proprio.
Why does it deny the presence of the corporate power of the Spirit in conferences? It seems to admit only the power of the bishop acting in his own
diocese or that of the college as a whole, hence no gradations of collegiality seem legitimate[113]. Furthermore, the document does not admit a
close analogy between conferences (permanent entities) and particular

---

[113] This seems contrary to the insight of Jerome Hamer, O.P. during the council, who
described collegiality as admitting of 'modalities of infinite variety.' See idem, "Les con-
férences épiscopales, exercice de la collegialité," *Nouvelle Revue Théologique* 83 (1963)
966-969.

councils (temporary realities) despite the conciliar tendency to do so (*LG* 23) and a text such as canon 753 on episcopal teaching authority, which refers to both institutes as authentic, even if not infallible, teachers[114]. *Apostolos suos* does not treat Eastern synods *ex professo* probably due to its Latin church focus. However, in so doing it misses an ecumenically valuable opportunity to clarify the similarity between permanent entities such as conferences and synods as authentic expressions of the Christian tradition. While the motu proprio recognizes a certain corporate power in conferences, such power is not ontologically grounded in episcopal consecration but rather rooted in the Holy See's authorizing them to exist and function. Even given the radical need for bishops in the same socio-cultural region to deliberate and decide together for the sake of pastoral effectiveness, they can do so only as a Holy See-created institution. The mystery of unity in diversity is at the very heart of the reality of Catholicism (*LG* 13). The pope especially symbolizes the unity principle, and the bishops the diversity principle. However, unless the law leaves sufficient room for legitimate episcopal autonomy, the bishops will be unable to enrich the papacy with their original insights into revelation and their creative legal-pastoral initiatives in the various particular churches.

Orsy then proposes to draw from the richness of our theological-canonical tradition to structure more adequate papal-episcopal relationships for the good of the Church[115]. He notes the council's affirmation of the powerful presence of the Spirit in various gatherings of believers (*LG* 12). Such a presence is presumably operative in a special way in episcopal gatherings such as synods and councils in which they exercise their diversified pastoral mission. There seems to have been an instinctive sense from the beginning of the Church that such is the case even if not all the bishops were present as in an ecumenical council. In short it seems reasonable to affirm a limited participation of conferences in the power of the whole college.

There is a certain continuity in the Spirit's assistance to the episcopal college, ranging from the ecumenical council (most intense assistance) to partial assemblies such as conferences and particular councils (less intense

---

[114] See also c. 823, §2 also referring to the two institutes together as called to exercise doctrinal oversight regarding the integrity of faith and morals in the areas of publications and instruments of social communications.

[115] He takes pains to note that his critical assessment of the motu proprio relates not to matters of faith but rather to the area of disputed theological-canonical questions. See Orsy, Episcopal Conferences-Spirit, 421-422.

assistance). There seems to be no theological reason to deny such special assistance in principle to conferences and to acknowledge it for such councils even given certain current canonical differences between them. This also holds true for Eastern synods, which surely differ canonically from conferences, as we have noted above, and reflect sharply different historical experiences, especially during the second millennium. However, there is a profound theological likeness between them given their similar sacramental grounding, fundamentally episcopal nature, and varied but similar ecclesial purposes. Recognizing such a parity between conferences and such synods might well be ecumenically extremely important since the presence of more credible synodal governance patterns in the Latin Church seems indispensable for any genuine rapprochement with the Orthodox, to say nothing of Anglicans, and other Reformation Christians[116]. While the Holy See sets parameters for the legitimate functioning of conferences, it is not the fundamental source of their empowerment to act; rather that is the power of Spirit ultimately communicated to the bishops in episcopal consecration.

Finally Orsy articulates certain fundamental principles to be considered in structuring appropriate laws on conferences. Such laws presuppose the integration of a properly nuanced theological-canonical vision with the fruits of concrete legal-pastoral experience.

Any conference norms must serve the unity of the whole Church while facilitating the fullest possible functioning of the conferences and enabling

---

[116] See Walter Kasper, "Present Situation and Future of the Ecumenical Movement," in *The Catholic Church in Ecumenical Dialogue 2002* Articles by Members of the Staff of the Pontifical Council for Promoting Christian Unity (Washington: USCCB, 2002) 12-13: "…ministries in the Church…crucial point of the ecumenical dialogue. Particularly at stake is the episcopate in apostolic succession and – in answering the question and the request of Pope John Paul II in the encyclical *Ut unum sint* (no. 95) – the future exercise of the Petrine ministry within the new ecumenical situation. We should make it clear that both are a gift for the Church that we want to share for the good of all. But it is not only others who can learn from us – we, too, can learn from the Orthodox and Reformation traditions and consider further how best to integrate the episcopate and the Petrine ministry with synodical and collegial structures. Such an effort to strengthen and develop the synodical and collegial structures in our own church without giving up the essential nature of personal responsibility is the only way in which an ecumenical consensus could be reached about the Petrine and episcopal ministries." Also in *Origins* 32/5 (June 13, 2002) 79. For some thoughtful canonical reflections on the primacy-episcopacy problematic, especially in light of relationships with the Orthodox, Anglican, and Lutheran traditions, see John McAreavey, "The Primacy of the Bishop of Rome: a Canonical Reflection in Response to *Ut unum sint*," *Studia Canonica* 34 (2000) 119-154. The McAreavey article does not deal *ex professo* with conferences, but he mentions some of the issues that Cardinal Kasper raises. On the ecumenical implications of the exercise of authority in the Church, see also Cormac Murphy-O'Connor, "The Question of Authority," *Origins* 32/22 (November 7, 2002) 361-362.

the bishops of a given area to share their original insights and creative initiatives and those of their churches with the rest of the Church.

Universal law must acknowledge the fundamental consecration-based right of bishops to assemble for spiritual-pastoral purposes; such a right reflects the basic baptism-based Christian right to associate (c. 215).

Universal law should specify norms acknowledging conferences and situating them within the organic structure of the whole college. The Holy See should maintain an ultimate supervisory role over conferences, but as a last instance court of appeal in conflict situations rather than as an institution regularly involved in monitoring the ordinary day to day functioning of conferences.

In conclusion Orsy notes a certain imbalance in papal-episcopal relations with a strong emphasis on the primacy and a lesser emphasis on the episcopate. It is increasingly necessary that bishops in the same cultural area collaborate pastorally, and realistically only conferences afford them that option today. However, the Holy See still seems to play a too significant a role in their daily activities.

Orsy alludes to the particularly significant paragraph 96 of the 1995 encyclical *Ut unum sint*[117], in which John Paul II invites reflection on the petrine office and suggestions for possible reform with due regard for its substance. Orsy suggests that a particularly effective sign of a reformed primacy would be a renewed episcopate enjoying more noteworthy autonomy. Such a development would be welcome both within the Church and within ecumenical circles.

GENERAL CONCLUSIONS

1) From one viewpoint the conference's legislative role should not be unduly emphasized given its broad legal-pastoral competencies. In fact that role must be situated within the broader context of its fairly comprehensive place in the code. The author's primary focus has been the conference's enactment of general decrees or general executory decrees. However, it also enjoys certain administrative competencies; it has a right to collaborate with or be consulted by the Holy See in certain areas of Holy See decision making; finally, it has rights and duties regarding the sharing of information on issues affecting it, the Holy See, and diocesan bishops.

---

[117] See n. 92

2) However, from another standpoint the conference's legislative role is a significant indicator of its status in relationship to other hierarchical instances, especially at the intermediary level of church life, e.g., Latin particular councils and Eastern synods. In fact the conference's expanded legislative competency needs to be situated within the broader context of contemporary canonical efforts to encourage decentralized governance patterns, including an enhanced pastoral governance role for Latin diocesan bishops and particular councils as well as, Eastern patriarchs, other eparchs, and synods.

3) The conference still seems viewed primarily as an instrument of pastoral communications and coordination among the bishops of a given territory and secondarily as a distinctly governmental authority, e.g., issuing general decrees. In this latter situation the conference exercises episcopal authority comparable to other intermediary level Latin governmental institutes like particular councils although a more appropriate legal parity between the two institutes is desirable. Such legislative authority, be it preceptive (c. 1292, §1 on alienation) or discretionary (c. 844, §5 on sacramental sharing), is ordinary in the areas specified in universal law, be it the code or subsequent documents, and delegated in those exceptional instances involving a special Holy See mandate.

4) Canon 455 specifies the basic conditions for issuing conference general decrees (c. 29) and general executory decrees (c. 31). Such decrees in areas explicitly specified in law or pursuant to special Holy See delegation must be approved by two-thirds of conference members with a deliberative vote, present or not, at a plenary session. Moreover, such decrees must be reviewed by the Holy See (*recognitio*) before being juridically binding. Such conditions are more demanding than those for the decrees of particular councils, which, unlike the conference, are viewed as properly governmental and especially legislative entities. Such councils may legislate in any area of the code (c. 445); an absolute majority of its members present with a deliberative vote suffices to pass council decrees(c. 119, 2°); and such decrees also require Roman *recognitio* to be promulgated (c. 446).

5) The aforementioned limitations on the conference's legislative competency reflect the code commission's effort to protect both the diocesan bishop's decisional prerogatives and the necessary Holy See oversight role in fostering ecclesial and episcopal unity. Such limitations constitute the commission's response to episcopal concerns during the revision process, especially about the alleged risks of unwarranted conference centralization. However, one wonders how extensive such concerns actually

were during that process and how realistic they are today. Furthermore and more important, a proper understanding of the Spirit's presence in conference deliberations (expression of partial collegiality) and of the conference's fundamental similarity to particular councils argues for an enhanced legislative role. This is especially true given the de facto conference replacement of particular councils as significant Latin intermediary level instances[118].

6) The inadequacy of the conference's legislative competency in the current law becomes even more evident when one contrasts that competency with the relatively broad legislative options available to Eastern synods. The Eastern code has responded to a certain extent to conciliar and post-conciliar concerns about enhancing the relative autonomy of such hierarchic instances. This is because of the varied liturgical, historical, and canonical traditions and diverse socio-cultural settings of the different *sui iuris* churches.

In complementing the Eastern code such synods may enact particular law in any area with due regard for the ecclesial hierarchy of norms, i.e., not legislating contrary to that code or any legislation binding all the churches, e.g., papal primacy within broader context of supreme authority of college of bishops. Furthermore, while Eastern bishops like their Latin peers surely seek moral unanimity in their decision-making, an absolute majority of the synod fathers suffices to pass binding legislation; and the synod has a certain discretion regarding altering its voting regulations. A Roman *recognitio* of synod decrees is generally[119] not required before Eastern synod legislation takes effect; rather such decisions are

---

[118] The author has not had an opportunity to study in depth the discussions on the episcopate and more specifically on episcopal conferences at the recent Latin synod of bishops held in Rome from September 30, 2001 to October 27, 2001. However, synod proposal 28 forwarded to the pope seems pertinent in this connection: "Le conferenze episcopali come strumenti di collegialità: Numerosi Padri sinodali e numerosi circoli minori hanno affermato ripetutamente che oggi le Conferenze episcopali rappresentano uno strumento assolutamente necessario per esprimere e realizzare lo spirito collegiale dei Vescovi. Pertanto è indispensabile che vengano maggiormente accresciute le potenzialità di questo strumento di comunione e di collegialità (cfr. *Novo millennio ineunte* 44). Proponiamo che il dialogo tra il Sommo Pontefice e le Conferenze episcopali prosegua in modo tale che il Sommo Pontefice si degni di chiedere alle Conferenze episcopali suggerimenti che arricchiscano la trattazione di questa materia avviata nel 'Motu proprio' *Apostolos suos*." *Adista* (19 novembre 2001) 7. When the documentation on the synod and the expected post-synodal apostolic exhortation are finally available, a study of the treatment of episcopal conferences will be most valuable.

[119] In some exceptional situations Roman approval of synod enactments is required, e.g., suppressing or transferring to Sunday common Eastern feast days (*CCEO*, c. 880, §3) or enacting particular law in removal or transfer of pastor processes (*CCEO*, c. 1388).

simply to be forwarded to the pope (and possibly other patriarchs) for information purposes.

One unique Eastern legislative factor is the differentiation between synodal disciplinary and liturgical laws. While the latter bind everywhere, the former bind only in the patriarchal territory unless the Holy See approves them or an extra-territorial eparch approves them for his territory (*CCEO*, c. 150, §§2-3). As problematic as this differentiation is for some Eastern canonists, the broad legislative self-determination of the Eastern synod makes it notably different a canonical institute from the Latin conference. It is true that different Eastern and Latin historical experiences have shaped the two institutes and that there are notable differences in size between the Latin and the Eastern churches. However, one may still wonder why the status of the two entities cannot be more similar given fundamental likenesses in their sacramentally-grounded episcopal character and ecclesial purposes in realizing the threefold *munera* of Christ.

7) The preceding reflections have surveyed conference legislative competency in the Latin code and *Apostolos suos* and reviewed the comparable Eastern synod legislative competency in Eastern code. The author has highlighted the synod's more significant competency, especially by contrast to the conference but also vis-à-vis the Latin particular council. The Eastern code implements the principle of subsidiarity more thoroughly than its Latin counterpart. That principle is understood here as a more noteworthy respect for the legislative autonomy of intermediary level instances such as Eastern synods. Latin code commission fears of the possible emergence of national churches (Latin revision principle 5) that might jeopardize church unity do not seem to have influenced the Eastern code commission notably although its members undoubtedly would have been aware of that principle in formulating their own revision principles such as 7 on subsidiarity. It is interesting to note that the official Vatican study of the principle of subsidiarity envisioned by the 1985 synod has not materialized. However, be that as it may, one may ask why the Eastern commission respect for the relative autonomy and competency of intermediary level instances such as synods cannot be equally applicable to comparable Latin institutes such as conferences.

8) The article reviewed several comparative legislative competencies of conferences and synods in which the synod is currently a more significant intermediary legislative instance than the conference. Those competencies are the following: a) norms on priestly formation, b) norms on ecumenical policy-making, c) norms on catechetics, d) norms on publishing and

translating liturgical texts, e) norms on feast days of obligation and penitential days, f) norms on establishing new marriage impediments, g) norms on alienating church goods, and h) norms on removing and transferring pastors. These seem to be specific examples of areas in which a broader legislative implementation of the principle of collegiality in its varied expressions warrants greater parity between conferences and synods. However, a still more basic issue to be addressed is the disparity between the generalized particular law competency of such synods (and particular councils) and the more narrowly defined legislative competency of conferences.

9) The conference should at least enjoy the general legislative competency of a particular council without the current universal law constraints. This would put it on a surer footing as a hierarchic institution comparable to that council and the Eastern synod. In proposing this change the author is not moving beyond the parameters of existing legislation but simply trying to give more adequate expression to the fundamental theological similarity of three largely episcopal bodies even given existing canonical differences among them.

In doing so he is concerned, however, that certain issues be addressed. First, lest church decision-making be perceived as unduly episcopal rather than broadly ecclesial, there must be adequate provision in the conference legislative process for the diversified input of other clergy, religious and the laity as is currently provided for in particular councils (c. 443) and diocesan synods (c. 463). Second, allowance also needs to be made for an adequate hearing of possibly minority episcopal sentiment in such a process while not permitting such to undercut the legitimate voice of the majority. This seems indispensable to preclude the verification of possibly legitimate fears of an excessive conference bureaucracy overwhelming rather than serving the bishops. Finally, the author does not advocate multiplying conference laws or transforming conferences into parliaments or legislatures. Rather the *ius condendum* should recognize a legitimate and traditional level of subsidiary action in the Church and acknowledge the postconciliar ecclesial success of conferences empowered by the Spirit[120].

10) Integrating properly the values of unity and diversity in ecclesial life is a continuing challenge. Perhaps today, as Orsy suggests[121], an enhanced conference legislative role will enable us to focus a bit more clearly than

---

[120] In this connection see McManus, *Papacy and Church*, 182-183.
[121] Orsy, Conferences-Spirit, 428-430.

in recent years on fostering the value of institutional diversity. Such a thrust seems integral to the health of the communion of churches, ecumenically rather significant, and very pertinent to the ongoing inculturation of the gospel in various settings. Only then will the revitalization of intermediary level structures hoped for by *Christus Dominus* 36 become even more a genuine reality than is true at the moment.

...there cannot be successful evangelization without a respect for diversity. All human beings are God's creatures, all nations are waiting for the good news of redemption. But no matter how good the message may be, it will not touch the mind and heart of the people unless it blends with the culture in which it seeks incarnation. In this process the bishops of the region ought to be the principal agents in proclaiming the old truth in a new language and communicating the ancient tradition through fresh symbols. This divine task, however, they cannot do without due autonomy[122].

---

[122] Ibid., 429-430.

CONCORDATS IN THE EUROPEAN UNION:
A RELIC FROM THE PAST OR A VALID INSTRUMENT
FOR THE XXI CENTURY?

Iván C. Ibán

I. BY WAY OF INTRODUCTION: THE IMPRECISION OF PROGNOSIS IN THE SO-CALLED SOCIAL SCIENCES, SINCE THEY ARE NO MORE THAN HISTORICAL SCIENCES

Since the subject that I intend to develop has been proposed by me, I am thus the only party responsible, even though it has been approved by the corresponding authorities in the University of Leuven. However, the most significant consequence that arises from dealing with this subject is perhaps highlighting the attendant difficulties.

Without intending to go into detailed explanations that I would be unable to make, since gnoxology and the theory of knowledge are fields beyond my sphere of expertise, I feel that the difference between the so-called pure sciences and social sciences lies fundamentally in the inability of the latter to predict the future. A chemist may predict the existence of a new element without being able to identify it yet, an expert in astronomy may deduce that a celestial object exists in a certain place in the firmament that is still not possible to see; even in such an imprecise science as medicine, a doctor may guess that the application of a certain treatment to a disease will obtain positive results or the full recovery of a patient. But an economist is unable to forecast with any degree of accuracy whether any specific share will rise in the stock market, nor a political expert whether a certain political party will win the elections. For this reason, economists are not necessarily millionaires, nor political experts Prime Ministers.

Perhaps, together with historians, jurists are those who are least able to predict the future. An historian may explain in all sorts of detail the reasons why an independent Kingdom of Belgium was established, or why the Monarchy in Spain as a system of government was restored in the last quarter of the twentieth century, but he is unable to foresee with the slightest degree of certainty whether Belgium will split into two independent states, or whether a Basque Republic will be created in the north of Spain.

However, should these situations occur, he certainly will be able to explain why history has taken this course.

But if the ability of the historian to predict the future is minimal, things are even more complicated for the jurist. At least an historian can rely on certain unquestionable facts: we are all going to die, which, when translated to the field of historical studies has some significance. If you will allow me to use a Spanish example: Franco inevitably had to die at some time and that fact, would necessarily cause changes in the historical-legal panorama. Jurists are unable to rely on even that much.

Our raw materials are legal rules, regardless of their origin. Nobody ever knows how long a rule will continue to exist, or whether it will lose its enforceability. Let us look at another Spanish case: in our turbulent nineteenth century, which naturally finished well by starting the twentieth century, there are various constitutional documents that were written with a view to permanence and yet, lost all legal effects within a few years. Meanwhile, the former Civil Procedural Code (Ley de Enjuiciamiento Civil), which came into force on a provisional basis, yet remained law for more than a century.

The fact is that legal reality has very little ability to resist change. Of course, great political changes inspire a change in the legal reality, if one thinks about what still remains of the Law of the Soviet Union, or more markedly, of the German Democratic Republic. But a change in the point of view of the legislator is sometimes enough, but not always based on a social change, to produce the effect that millions of pages of legal treaties serve no greater purpose than to pack the shelves of the libraries in our universities. Just think of the best-known criminal lawyer of any country one century ago and place him in today's legal system in any European country faced with ecological or financial crimes, or sexual discrimination. Would you not agree that he would work with that material with less ease than a first-year law student of any current European law faculty?

*

*   *

What I believe is that in the field of social sciences, labels are applied to events that have already happened. One day, an economist decides to apply the name "inflation" to an unnamed phenomenon that has been taking place for centuries. Nobody decided when the Middle Ages had finished until a long time afterwards.

Millions of marriages, loan agreements, deeds of sale and even criminal or other civil processes had taken place before any of them ever received their official name. The jurist would just be a type of parish priest who baptised or gave this or that name, or a clerk in the Public Records Office who registered this or that name. But the child already existed beforehand. And this is a task that necessarily leads to failure, since society is always opposed to a jurist's classificatory or nomenclative vocation, proposing new characters all the time and, more recently, a legislator or a Parliament, with an unlimited law-bringing role. Social reality changes quickly, it causes accelerated changes in legal relations, and the legislator is always both following and altering the legal reality. The theorist of Law cannot keep up with the pace of change in the legal reality. Just think about tax legislation and the phenomenon of tax havens, or the new concepts created by large companies to reduce their tax costs, as stock options, leasing contracts, remuneration in kind, capital decreases for remunerative benefits for shareholders, and you will understand what I mean.

*

*   *

Moreover, I believe that when social scientists try to predict the future, they are fully aware of their own inability to do so. What they are attempting is to influence its form so that this resembles what they consider to be desirable. This specifically involves attempting an opinion close to what they personally consider to be best, while at the same time, trying to ensure that this opinion will become fact in the future. The political expert who sees a future in which the two main parties dominate Parliament is, in reality, proposing a change in the electoral rules whereby the minor parties disappear from political life. The economist who sees a world in which communications companies exist on a global scale is, in reality, proposing a system of deregulation in the communications market that achieves this purpose. The reverse is also true. Further examples exist in the legal world, but I do not feel it is necessary to cite them.

This task of deliberate forecasting can even be adapted to different audiences in order to be more effective[1]. The jurist who wishes for less

---

[1] In order to start dealing with the material that interests us, I will use an example of this type of behaviour. It is a case of an evaluation of the posture adopted by the Catholic hierarchy in relation to European integration: "Papes et évêques ont répété…[le] même

protective labour law legislation (or more protective, it does not matter) in respect of employees' rights will present this wish as an inevitable future certainty, but he will do this in a different way if he is presenting it to an association of businessmen than to a group of trade union representatives. Naturally, there is no actual guarantee that his proposals are going to become reality.

For all of the reasons above, I think that trying to predict the future in respect of the social sciences is a complete waste of time. In the first place, because there are decisive features of this future reality which due to the present state of scientific knowledge are quite simply impossible to know. And in the second place, because any attempt to predict the future is inevitably influenced by the personal opinion and preferences of the person formulating it.

*

*   *

Concordats and the European Union. Having said the above, you will be able to appreciate that to some extent I am trying to provide a far from categorical answer to the complex subject for whose two distinct expressions I have assumed the responsibility of uniting in this theoretical discourse. Considered individually, they are two changing realities. When considered together, they simply do not exist. We shall begin by analysing the second of the terms: the European Union.

No aseptic analyst could have possibly imagined when the European Coal and Steel Community or the EUROTOM were created, that, after a short period of time in historical terms, there would exist a single currency in circulation from Lisbon to Athens, or from Helsinki to Monte Carlo. It is probable that only those who wished to could imagine it, and those who did not wish it, did not imagine it. What will the European Union be like in several decades? Or, what is the European Union now? I still feel that we lack an exact term for naming purposes. It is now a state, but neither is it a free trade area or an international organisation such as we know it. The evolution of the European Union is so constant, that once a

discours en le modifiant selon les circonstances. Lorsqu'ils s'adressent aux catholiques, ils insistent sur la dimension propement religieuse de la culture et de l'histoire communes. Devant des auditoires non confessionnels, ils pointent dans le droit, la philosophie et la conception de l'homme les éléments sécularisés de la théologie chrétienne". VANDERMEERSCH, Edmond, WEYDERT, Jean, Le catholicisme, in BAUBÉROT, Jean (ed.), Religions et laïcité dans l'Europe des Douze, Syros, Paris, 1994, p. 145.

term is discovered to define it, that definition is already made obsolete by the reality.

Nor is it an easy task to define what a concordat is. It is an institution that has existed for centuries, but with a notable evolution in its functions and content. Whilst in the not so recent past they were defensive instruments, in the present, they are used in certain circumstances to improve the situation that the Church would have with general law[2], (since I do not believe that, unlike as was predicted by some authors[3], the doctrine advocated by the Second Vatican Council regarding Church-State affairs, has resulted in the non-existence of a special legal system for the Church). At least the post-Council concordats establish the possibility that some elements of Canon Law are recognised under the state legal system[4], albeit clearly separating the respective powers, or, if you will, trying to accurately distinguish religious ends and temporal ends[5], although on some occasions, the Church, through concordatory means, has assumed functions that some would not consider typically religious but rather

---

[2] "I nuovi concordati han cessato di essere dei mezzi soprattutto *difensivi* della *libertà della Chiesa*, per cominciare invece ad essere dei mezzi di *espansione* dell'area dei *diritti temporali* in godimento della Chiesa stessa". BELLINI, Piero, *Natura ed efficacia dei concordati ecclesiastici*, in BELLINI, Piero, *Saggi di diritto ecclesiastico italiano*, I, Rubbetino, Messina, 1996, p. 93.

[3] "Del antiguo complejo jurídico concordado, creador de un Derecho conjunto, integrado por normas generales y especiales, civiles y canónicas a un tiempo, por remisiones, referencias y reconocimientos de efectos, y construido a base de concesiones especiales mutuas de uno y otro ordenamiento, habrá que prescindir en el nuevo sistema. Y ello es de suponer que repercutirá también en la ciencia del llamado Derecho eclesiástico del Estado, que sólo se mantiene apoyado en la existencia, dentro del Derecho civil del respectivo país, de unas normas especiales, diferentes de su Derecho común, integradas en un régimen peculiar para las materias religiosas". MALDONADO Y FERNÁNDEZ DEL TORCO, José, *Reflexiones sobre la cuestión actual de los concordatos en su perspectiva histórica*, in AA.VV., *Lex Ecclesiae. Estudios en Honor del Dr. Marcelino Cabreros de Anta*, Universidad Pontificia, Salamanca, 1972, p. 600.

[4] "[I concordati attuali] hanno un denominatore comune, espresso, a seconda delle circostanze storiche e politiche date, in misura più o meno ampia: la trasposizione nell'ordinamento statuale o l'efficacia civile di alcuni istituti canonistici". COLAIANNI, Nicola, *Le valenze dello strumento concordatario*, in COPPOLA, R. (ed.), *Concordato e società italiana. Atti dell'incontro di studio promosso dall'Istituto di diritto pubblico della Facoltà di giurisprudenza dell'Universtità di Bari. Bari, 6 maggio 1981*, Cedam, Padova, 1984, pp. 35-36.

[5] "Il sistema di collaborazione fra Chiesa e Stato attuato coi moderni concordati si fonda su basi assai diverse da quelle su cui poggiavano i precedenti regìmi pattizi e tende ad attuare una delimitazione delle competenze fra le due potestà conforme alle caratteristiche dello Stato moderno, ispirato alla netta distinzione fra fini religiosi e fini suoi propi". CONDORELLI, MARIO, *Concordati e libertà della Chiesa*, "Il diritto ecclesiastico" ["DE"], LXXIX-I, 1968, p. 244.

temporal[6]. I am not one of those people who think that the doctrine of the last Council should necessarily imply the disappearance of concordats. From a certain point of view, it could even be thought that, having renounced, even if only for realistic reasons, the claim that state legislation should include the Catholic postulates, the concordats would acquire a more necessary role than before; since no expectation would thus exist that at some future point in time the states would yield to the postulates of the *Jus publicum eccelsiasticum*[7].

But the fact that I do not believe that the Council insists upon the necessary disappearance of the concordat as a relative instrument, does not mean that its functions should not be altered, or even its formal celebration. This is nothing new, during the course of history it has exercised the most varied of roles and has adopted many different external forms. Changes in both parties have occurred, there have been changes in both who the representatives have been and in the doctrines that they defended; and this will continue to happen. That is going to happen now. Changes in one of the parties may even happen, caused by the fact that the other party to which it is related has, in turn, changed. If one considers, for example, as has been mentioned[8], the citizen who is used to

---

[6] "I concordati cambiano: ma non nella direzione che si poteva immaginare negli anni settanta: e cioè nella direzione di divenire strumenti agili in difesa della libertà di tutti. Essi tendono ad evolversi semmai in una direzione opposta, che sottolinea questa funzione tutta squisitamente temporale dell'azione della Chiesa di «promozione del bene comune»". CAPUTO, Giuseppe, *La funzione del sistema pattizio nella storia*, "Anuario de Derecho Eclesiástico del Estado" ["ADEE"], IV, 1988, pp. 43-44. Although I am unable to comprehend what are the reasons that lead to the consideration of "freedom for all" as a typically ecclesiastical end, and not the "common good".

[7] "Le dichiarazioni conciliari in tema di relazioni tra Chiesa e Comunità politica si allontanano dai consueti schemi del *jus publicum ecclesiasticum*, alla stregua dei quali era possibile un giudizio negativo sui sistemi concordatari, considerati come meri espedienti cui la Chiesa si adattava per il mancato adeguarsi degli Stati moderni al regime che doveva essere peculiare di rapporti tra entità ineguali". CATALANO, Gaetano, *Attualità e anacronismo dei concordati*, in AA.VV., *Individuo, gruppi, confessioni religiose nello Stato democratico. Atti del Convegno nazionale di Diritto Ecclesiastico. Siena, 30 novembre-2 dicembre, 1972*, Giuffrè, Milan, 1973, p. 875.

[8] "Si potrebbe...prefigurare una collaborazione particolarmente felice tra Chiesa e Stato, se non fosse che al conflitto tra Stato e Chiesa si sono sostituite tensioni ed attriti tra le Chiese e i loro membrii. Il dibattito si svolge su due diversi terreni. In primo luogo vi è una tendenza generale verso una maggiore democrazia. Il progresso democratico che i cittadini esigono nello Stato, l'esigono anche nella Chiesa, in qualità di fedeli...Il credente non si allinea sempre con gli organi dirigenti della sua Chiesa, che non per questo desidera necessariamente abbandonare...Accanto a questa questione più genericamente politica, è indubbiamente in atto anche un dibattito a livello dei diritti fondamentali. Anche se la libertà religiosa è considerata generalmente come un diritto fondamentale, essa non è più valutata...come intangibile...Può accadere che non si possa rispettare la libertà

certain levels of democratic participation in State affairs, starts to claim also certain democratic participation in Church affairs. That is to say, the fact that a concordat applies to an individual who belongs to two societies, will inevitably result in one of them (the Church) modifying itself along the lines of the participating mechanisms adopted by the other (the State).

But state societies are not uniform and it is likely that what the members of one claim is not the same as what members of the other claim. Upon subscribing to a concordat, the Church, to a certain extent, appears as the representative of the corresponding local Church. This causes different degrees of approximation and may even result in the negotiating bodies of the Church being other than the traditional ones[9]. In this way, the participation of national bishops in the negotiation of a concordat, something that in the past was a purely theoretical issue[10], perhaps should start to be viewed as an essential requirement, should the intention be that the concordat has to provide the solutions to the problems that are found in a certain society.

On the other hand, it should not be forgotten that, unlike what happened in the past, the bilateral concordat is not the only instrument of written International Law that the Holy See resorts to; its ratification of multilateral treaties is ever more frequent[11].

---

religiosa fino alle estreme conseguenze, perché (ad esempio) si renderebbe impossibile la libertà di espressione". TORFS, Rik, *Stati e Chiese nella Comunità europea,* "Quaderni di diritto e politica ecclesiastica" ["QDPE"], 1993-1, pp.20-22.

[9] "In una prospettiva giuridica è indubitabile...che la S. Sede in tanto stipula accordi con uno Stato in quanto fondamentalmente intenda stabilire condizioni e garanzie certe a tutela della libertà religiosa...di quei soggetti appartenenti al suo ordinamento giuridico...che, per l'essere contemporaneamente sudditi di un ordinamento statale, a questo sono sottoposti: essa assume...quella che può in certo senso definirsi una rappresentanza di interessi immediatamente propi delle Chiese locali, necessariamente differenziati in relazione alle diverse circostanze di tempi e di luoghi. Quest'ultima considerazione...deve farci riflettere se oggi non sia più rispondente, anche sotto il profilo giuridico, alla attuale fase di «aggiornamento» che i nuovi accordi vengano stipulati dalle autorità ecclesiastiche locali come, ad esempio, le Conference episcopali con potere di intervento della S. Sede nel corso delle trattative, fatta sempre salva la necessità di una sua successiva ratifica". CASUSCELLI, Giuseppe, *Concordati, intese e pluralismo confessionale,* Giuffrè, Milan, 1974, pp. 54-55

[10] "[Il] potere dei Vescovi...di concludere o di ratificare un concordato, oggi è soltanto una questione teorica, che ancora è discussa presso i canonisti; in pratica si preferisce la risposta negativa, riservando il diritto di concludere i trattati solo alla S. Sede". CASORIA, Giuseppe, *Concordati e ordinamento giuridico internazionale*, Officium Libri Catholici, Rome, 1953, p. 99.

[11] "La S. Sede...superando alcune pregiudiziali remore, che la spingevano a prediligere accordi bilaterali di immediato interesse per la Chiesa (i concordati),...via via, sottoscrive

All that I have intended to say up to now, which is not a claim to provide a definition, is that the very recent reality that we call the European Union and the ancient institution known by the name of the concordat, are none other than names of something that have changed through the passing of time and which will undoubtedly alter even more significantly in the near future.

*
*   *

The problem of definition is exacerbated if we take into account that, as I mentioned before in passing, any attempt at definition is tainted by one's own personal opinions. Of course, the debate is not strictly technical, but rather, to a great extent, political. I would even dare state that the debate at European Union level is essentially political. But the intentions of those who are in favour of "more Europe" or those opposed to it are far from clear. I do not think that I need to turn to primary sources in order to explain this. It is enough to simply think about what is written in the newspapers at the time of general elections in any European country, a time at which pro-European fervour seems to wane; or in the political debate about the position towards the United States in relation to a military attack on Iraq, or any other political topic of note.

I think that the political debate about the European Union revolves around the relation between the institution itself and each Member State. But this cannot be seen in simplistic terms, by virtue of which some want a stronger Union with weaker States, that is, wanting the State to disappear, and placing those who want a stronger State and the disappearance of the European Union in the opposing camp. Things are much more complex than that. Without attempting to explain it, since I am not an expert in the field, I shall try to give a logical overview of the panorama.

In some cases I think that the intentions are to have a stronger Union, paradoxically so that the Member State itself becomes stronger. That would be the case of some of the smaller countries many of whom are candidates to join the European Union. States that have recently been formed and who have a very short history of independence in real terms

o aderisce e ratifica anche alcuni Trattati multilaterali, che introducono nella comunità internazionale un diritto scritto, diretto a regolare la cooperazione tra gli Stati in diversi settori operativi". Petroncelli HÜBLER, Flavia, *Chiesa cattolica e comunità internazionale. Riflessione sulle forme di presenza*, Jovene, Naples, 1989, p. 154.

could find their national identity and their own independence up before powerful neighbours precisely by becoming integrated in the Union. I do not think it is necessary to give examples, which, among other things, may wound national pride. But it is not only the case of the smaller countries that have recently made a first appearance on the international scene; it also happens with others of more influence and tradition. In an international reality in which there is clearly only one superpower that in terms of economics and armaments, etc. is way ahead of its immediate successors, probably the only way in which the rest of the states can subsist is by allying themselves. Here I have no qualms about giving examples, since it affects all of us. For Germany, France, Belgium or Spain to exist alongside the United States, it is necessary that they be allied. In short, there are those defenders of the European Union who, in reality, are defending the Member States.

But there also exist those defenders of the Union who are opposed to the State. Or, to be more exact, who are opposed to the actual States, but in reality, continue to be fervent defenders of the formula.

In my opinion all the great principles set in motion by the French Revolution of 1789 and established by Napoleon I have been put in doubt. The last of those being centralisation. Regionalism, in its various names and forms, is spreading through Europe in an increasing and unstoppable fashion. Legislative chambers in Scotland, individual treaties for Corsica, it makes no sense to quote more examples since I am here in Belgium. The vast majority if not all of the regionalist, independentist, secessionist movements, etc. want more Europe. A Europe of the regions. A Europe in which the place that is currently occupied by the states would change to be occupied by new entities, who would inevitably metamorphose into states. When a sector of Spanish-Basque society, or a minimal sector of French-Basque society, or at least their political representatives, ask for "more Europe", what they are looking for in reality is the disappearance of Spain or France.

But there are also those in favour of more Europe who do not wish to defend the actual states or the actual regions, cantons, länder, self-governing regions, etc., rather they want the suppression of everything that went before in order to create a new State that would substitute all of that. This State would be Europe.

Therefore, my perception of the current situation is that, since it could not be any other way, all political debate and also all doctrinal debate about the European Union is a debate about the future of an institution called the State, although probably, in the end this will end up by disappearing, at least in its present form. But everyone defends his or her own personal choice.

*

*   *

If the "more Europe" – "less Europe" debate is not uniform, neither do I think that we can consider the "concordat yes" – "concordat no" debate to be any clearer.

"La justification du concordat réside dans son utilité; c'est aussi dans la mesure où il conservera cette utilité qu'il gardera sa raison d'être dans l'avenir"[12]. It is not possible to disagree with this statement made by one of the most important scholars in the field in modern times. I do not believe it is a necessary institution due to the fact that the Church claims to be a legal entity at the level of International Law[13]. Its use, for some, could be found in the fact that it enables a peculiar reality to receive specific treatment, which means that an enlarged system of agreements with the religious denominations is defended[14]. Their response to the proposal that such specific treatment could end up in unilateral state legislation is that it is not possible due to the difficulties that the State encounters in gaining such characteristics[15]. Or if they accept that such unilateral

---

[12] WAGNON, Henri, *L'institution concordataire*, in AA.VV., *La Institución Concordataria en la Actualidad. Trabajos de la XIII Semana de Derecho Canónico*, Instituto San Raimundo de Peñafort. Consejo Superior de Investigaciones Científicas, Salamanca, 1971, p. 21.

[13] I believe that that is the intention of the following words: "A mi entender, la Iglesia católica no pide relaciones a nivel concordatario por una cuestión de garantías -en esto no tiene por qué recibir un tratamiento diferente de cualquier otra sociedad religiosa- sino por coherencia con su propia afirmación de su carácter internacional, derivado de la tesis de la sociedad jurídica perfecta en el ámbito del iuspublicismo eclasiástico, y de las tesis de los ordenamientos jurídicos primarios dentro del dogmatismo italiano". DE LA HERA, Alberto, *El futuro del sistema concordatario. Entrevista*, "Ius Canonicum", XI, 21, 1971, p. 15.

[14] "In un sistema pluralista basato sulla partecipazione, gli accordi esplicano la funzione di dare risposte specifiche alle esigenze delle singole confessioni. Questa specificità si rifletterà negli accordi e potrà caratterizzare la disciplina di ciascuna materia regolata, di modo che essa potrà risultare diversa rispetto alle regolamentazioni concordate tra Stato e altre confessioni nelle medesime materie; o ancora potrà risultare che diverse siano le materie di volta in volta regolate". VITALI, Enrico, *Accordi con le confessioni e principio di uguaglianza*, "ADEE", IV, 1978, p. 84.

[15] "In linea di massima... la soluzione preferenziale mi sembra militare in favore dell'istituto concordatario. Una normativa invero unilaterale statale regolatrice di tali rapporti sarebbe auspicabile e da preferire se lo Stato si trovasse in grado di disciplinare il fenomeno religioso nel novero indiscriminato e indistinto degli altri fenomeni sociali e se avesse la possibilità di sottoporre le instituzioni confessionali relative a un puro e semplice

legislation is possible, they would point out that a concordat offers a greater guarantee that such regulations are respected[16].

In all the positions that defend the concordat, there is, whether expressly or tacitly, an ultimate intention to recognise the privileged status of the Church, even though on some occasions it should be pointed out that the State also obtains certain advantages from the said agreement[17]. This reaches the extreme of sustaining that the absence of bilateral instruments between the State and the churches would result in a situation of social tension[18]. Perhaps in the present day the Church no longer holds an express position of superiority over the State, but this is present to some extent in much of the reasons that are favourable towards the concordatory thesis[19].

In other words, I believe that in general terms, the supporters of the concordat consider that it is a necessary (or at least convenient)

---

jus commune generale alla stregua di tutte le altre formazioni sociali intermedie esistenti e operanti nel suo ordinamento...una simile soluzione non è possibile o non è, quanto meno, consigliabile per un complesso di ragioni che all'atto pratico impongono a ogni Stato la necessità di disciplinare il fenomeno religioso e le instituzioni relative con un nucleo più o meno vasto e rilevante di *jus singulare* ecclesiastico distinto del diritto comune generale". D'AVACK, Pietro Agostino, *Trattato di diritto ecclesiastico italiano. Parte generale*[2], Giuffrè, Milan, 1978, p. 221.

[16] "La diversa funzione di un Concordato rispetto a una legge unilaterale avente lo stesso contenuto è insomma una funzione di garanzia, ma non per l'inmediato bensì per il futuro". ONIDA, Francesco, *Considerazioni sul sistema pattizio alla luce dell'esperienzia comparatistica*, "ADEE", IV, 1988, p. 48.

[17] "[Le concordat] comporte une consécration et parfois une protection par l'État des droits des citoyens en matière religieuse, souvent aussi l'attribution à l'Église de certains privilèges qui l'aident à atteindre plus facilement sa fin. Tous les avantages d'ailleurs ne sont pas pour l'Église. L'État en a sa part, ne serait-ce que le bénéfice de la paix religieuse que les concordats contribuent à créer ou à garantir". NAZ, R., voz *Concordat*, in NAZ, R. (ed.), *Dictionnaire de Droit Canonique*, III, Letouzey et Ané, París, 1942, c. 1355.

[18] "Per chi non creda connaturale ad un sistema democratico l'ottica della «strategia della tensione» permanente tra comunità religiose e società civile, occorre valutare serenamente l'ipotesi della soluzione dei conflitti di lealtà di cui è portatore il *civis-fidelis* attraverso strumenti «concordatari» o, più in generale, pattizi". CASUSCELLI, *Concordati...*, cit., p. 121.

[19] "Quante volte l'istituto [concordatario] venga riguardato alla luce della tradizionale concezione della superiorità della Chiesa sullo Stato quale subordinazione giuridica di questo a quella, esso non può trovare posto se non fra le anomalie e le eccezioni ad un ordinato sistema di relazioni fra le due potestà. Qualora invece la tesi della superiorità della Chiesa venga in qualche modo attenuata [sic] in favore di una più realistica considerazione dell'atteggiamento dello Stato moderno, allora il concordato può essere valutato alla stregua della realtà storica dell'epoca attuale, nella quale...la connessione della società civile con la ecclesiastica non si atteggia più ad unione interiore ed intrinseca, ma a collegamento esteriore e formale, nei modi consentiti dal concetto laico della sovranità dell'ordinamento statale". CONDORELLI, *Concordati...*, cit., p. 245.

instrument for obtaining that favourable treatment for the Church to which it is entitled. It is not a state concession, but rather the recognition of certain specific characteristics. It is an instrument in defence of the Church and since it is considered that it should receive specific treatment, then it is better guaranteed by means of an agreement than by means of unilateral legislation.

However, it would be wrong to identify between those who are not supporters of a concordatory system and those who are opposed to the privileges of the Church. In such classical proponents of the *Ius publicum* so clearly favourable towards the interests of the Church, such as CAPPELLO, we can find statements of the following tenor: "Concordatum certe non est necessarium *absolute*, ut Ecclesia finem suum consequatur"[20]. In other words, ecclesiastical ends can be achieved without the need of a concordat. For many, part of the proponents of the *Ius publicum* or, if you prefer, for the more traditional Catholic way of thinking, the State must adapt its legislation to ecclesiastical doctrine, and in this way, in that situation of total harmony derived from the State submission, the concordat would be an unnecessary instrument[21]. The concordat is only resorted to when it is understood that the *potestas indirecta in temporalibus* is indefensible in practice[22], (which would be, I repeat, the stance of a good part of the creators of the *Ius publicum*)[23]

---

[20] CAPPELLO, Felice M., *Summa Iuris Publici Ecclesiastici*[3], Universitatis Gregorianae, Romae, 1932, p. 402.

[21] "Es obvio decir que no se realizan concordatos cuando ambos poderes viven en estado de hostilidad, así como tampoco cuando ambos estén en armonía perfecta. Surgen los concordatos, la necesidad de llevarlos a cabo, cuando los Gobiernos se inmiscuyen, se entrometen en asuntos eclesiásticos, o también, cuando se desvían de la Iglesia". HERRANZ, Pedro, *La Teoría Concordataria*, in AA.VV., *El Concordato de 1953*, Facultad de Derecho de la Universidad de Madrid, Madrid, 1956, pp. 24-25.

[22] "La Santa Sede non ha atteso i deliberati del Vaticano II per accorgersi che la sua *potestas indirecta in temporalibus* sopravviveva soltanto nei manuali canonicisti e per valutare in conseguenza come talune esigenze ecclesiali non avrebbero potuto realizzarsi prescindendo dal conseguimento, per via pattizia o altrimenti, dall'assenso dello Stato". CATALANO, Gaetano, *Sulle vicende dell'istituto concordatario nell'età contemporanea*, "DE", CIII-I, 1992, p. 30.

[23] "[Per certi autori] soltanto il mancato adeguarsi degli Stati a questi princìpi [potestas indirecta] giustifica il ricorso ai concordati, i quali, costituendo un espediente pratico di cui la Chiesa si avvale per la tutela dei propri diritti violati, debbono quindi essere riguardati non già come «*iuridice necessaria, ut Ecclesia finem suum adipiscatur*», sebbene come il frutto di una scelta politica, dettata dalle circostanze dei tempi e diretta al fine di evitare mali maggiori con l'ottenimento della garanzia patticia di almeno alcuni fra i diritti spettanti alla Chiesa *iure proprio* (Note: Giudizi di questo tenore appaiono nella maggior parte delle trattazione di *ius publicum ecclesiasticum* tra fine Ottocento e primi del Novecento...)". CONDORELLI, *Concordati...*, cit., p. 234.

It is interesting that some people consider that the concordat should be an instrument to enable the ecclesiastical postulates to prevail in civil society[24], which would mean, in the case of fully achieving these objectives, the disappearance of the concordat.

Therefore, and as I have already mentioned, some may not be in favour of the concordat but in favor of the Church receiving specific treatment, and in the final extreme, that the State subordinates itself to the Church. They seem to be obsolete postures, but there is something about them that is underlying in certain current positions. And all that without forgetting that some people are not in favour of the concordat, but rather defend other channels of relations with no difference save the name itself[25].

A more modern approach is the one that holds that the concordat is unnecessary, not as a result of the State having maintained the postulates of the Church in its legislation, but because the state legal system has created certain areas of freedom in which the Church finds itself comfortable enough. This would signal the end of the concordats; at least for those democratic countries that have established a protective framework for fundamental rights[26], even the existence of a special unilateral Law

---

[24] "La soluzione concordataria potrà…risultare il mezzo efficace perché la Chiesa abbia a svolgere un'azione stimolatrice presso la società civile, facendo penetrare in essa i suoi principi ed i suoi istituti". SPINELLI, Lorenzo, *Sistema concordatario e costume democratico*, in AA.VV., *Individuo…*, cit., p. 1091.

[25] "Hoy día se puede hablar de una *superación de los concordatos como sistema de relaciones Iglesia-Estado y como régimen normativo en el sentido* de su transformación, por parte de los sujetos interrelacionados y de las materias convenidas, *y de su integración en la figura más amplia de régimen convencional eclesiástico-estatal como forma normativa de legislar en materia religiosa y eclesiástica"*. CORRAL SALVADOR, Carlos, *La regulación bilateral como sistema normativo de las cuestiones religiosas*, in AA.VV., *Constitución y relaciones Iglesia-Estado en la actualidad. Actas del Simposio hispano-alemán organizado por las Universidades Pontificias de Comillas y Salamanca (Madrid, 13-15 of March 1978)*, Universidad Pontificia, Salamanca, 1978, p. 216.

[26] "[En opinión de algunos] el Estado pluralista sólo es coherente consigo mismo cuando no realiza ni establece acuerdo alguno con la Iglesia católica o cualquier otra confesión. Obviamente, un pluralismo con tales exigencias no habría de liberar al Estado del deber de respeto y tutela de los derechos de las minorías…En esta hipótesis, si queda por completo en manos del Estado el dictar per se unas normas que sustituyan a las nacidas del legislador eclesiástico, quedando confiada la tutela de los derechos de las minorías a lo que he llamado permeabilidad del legislador estatal, la situación a la que llegamos es del todo nueva: es el fin del Derecho Público Eclesiástico externo y del Derecho Concordatario; los concordatos habrán dejado de ser necesarios, pero no por la vía prevista por Ottaviani de que el Estado se atenga por completo al Derecho divino, sino porque el Estado es un reflejo fiel y exacto de la sociedad cuya forma política representa, y así cada minoría encuentra en el Estado y en su legislación una representación también exacta y fiel". DE LA HERA, *El futuro del sistema…*, cit., p. 16.

for the subject would be unnecessary[27]. It is even worth imagining a hypothetical new role of the concordats whereby their purpose would not be to create privileges for the Church, nor to procure special treatment for Catholics, but rather to assert the claim for universal freedom[28]. It seems to me that the transformation of the attitude towards the concordat from an instrument of imposition of "Catholic unity" to that of the defender of the "rights of Catholics"[29] represents an historic change that does not alter the fundamental nature of the institution, but I would find it difficult to imagine a concordat that did not contain any special treatment of the Catholic Church or of its members, and that was limited to assert the claim for universal freedom. I see a political instrument for such a purpose emanating from the Church, but I cannot perceive a bilateral legal instrument of such a kind.

If one thinks carefully, it is possible to observe that the "technical" difference, if the expression is admissible, between those followers of the *Ius publicum* who maintain that the concordat was unnecessary since state legislation should be a true reflection of the *Ius divinum*, whereby *libertas ecclesiae* was guaranteed, and the current jurists who maintain that state legal systems offer sufficient framework to include the Church, is practically irrelevant. It is quite simply a case of substituting the *Ius divinum* for this new Law, superior to the Law itself, which is a set of fundamental rights. But this is not the moment to analyse the phenomenon, too little studied from my point of view, of the transposition of

[27] "Si las normas de…Derecho especial no hacen más que repetir lo que tiene establecido el Derecho civil común para todos los súbditos del Estado no hay razón que justifique esa repetición para un grupo determinado de éstos y si se introducen unas normas diferentes de ese Derecho común, de las cuales se beneficie sólo un tal grupo determinado, por razón de su pertenencia a la Iglesia católica, es decir, en cuanto grupo precisamente religioso, uno entre los varios que presenta el pluralismo de la sociedad de hoy, habrá de ser mirado como una legislación estatal particular, referida precisamente a la Iglesia o a sus miembros, y entonces se cae de lleno en la figura de una legislación civil privilegiada y discriminatoria, de las que la propia doctrina de la Iglesia quiere apartar a los ordenamientos jurídicos estatales". MALDONADO, *Reflexiones sobre la cuestión…*, cit., p. 597.
[28] "Fu in quegli anni [postconciliari] che vi parla…enunciò l'idea che se non era inevitabile l'eclìssi dello stesso sistema concordatario, era possibile e desiderabile la sua novazione, attraverso la delineazione di un nuovo tipo di concordato, il concordato di separazione, col quale la Chiesa si limitasse a rivendicare la libertà: e non solo la libertà per sè, ma la libertà per la coscienza religiosa *tout court*, per la coscienza religiosa di tutti". CAPUTO, *La funzione del sistema…*, cit., p. 43.
[29] "Lo scopo dei concordati non sarebbe più la tutela privilegiata della verità cattolica da parte dello Stato, ma quella della libertà e identità religiosa dei cattolici e della Chiesa". MARTIN DE AGAR, José T., *Passato e presente dei concordati*, "Ius Ecclesiae ["IE"]", 12, 2000, p. 629.

techniques, practically without modification, of Natural Law to the current theories about public liberties.

Naturally, apart from those who consider that that the concordat is unnecessary for one or other reason, but who are either not opposed to special treatment for the Church, or consider that this special treatment is not even necessary so that in a democratic State it can carry out its mission, there are others who are opposed to the concordat for other reasons. They are the ones who are opposed to the Church having a sphere of action. I do not feel that such attitudes are present in the cultural and political sphere in which we are moving and therefore, I consider it unnecessary to describe who they are.

*
* *

The intention of everything up to now is to reflect my idea that we are moving in an area in which the conceptual imprecision is enormous, the potential options are numerous and the strong influence of personal "political" ideas when trying to accurately define concepts or propose solutions is clear. For that reason, it seems to me a minimum requirement of faith to briefly and sweepingly summarize, what my personal position is. And that shall be done before continuing with my discourse, so that you can appreciate the level of subjectivity present.

As far as my position is concerned in relation to the path that the European Union should take, I will demonstrate this in a clear way. I am absolutely in favour of "more Europe", and as I am not capable of inventing new classifications, I shall have to employ those that currently exist, and the one that is appropriate to use is that of the State. I feel that that the best scenario would be that the process concluded with the appearance of a State comprised of the Member States. Whether the formula should be that of a federation, a confederation, or some other seems to be to be a minor issue. Naturally, this process would necessarily be slow and not revolutionary. This new State would acquire the powers of the present states[30], which does not mean that it would exercise them directly.

---

[30] Also their international agreements, and in the area that we are interested, I understand that the present concordats would not be considered to be extinguished as may be interpreted from the following statement: "Si…à la suite de modifications survenues dans un État concordataire…l'État vient à s'éteindre ou à perdre sa souveraineté dans les matières qui font l'objet du concordat, cet accord doit nécessairement disparaître. Il ne peut passer comme «héritage» à l'État succeseure". WAGNON, Henri, *Concordats et Droit*

I am talking about a merger of sovereignties, not the centralisation of powers.

The first reason that urges me to desire this model is strictly practical. I think that on a global scale, even the territorially largest of the present states is far too small, and in respect of the smaller states of the present Union and even more so those about to join, they quite simply lack the minimum dimensions necessary to attend to the functions required of a modern state.

There is a more ideological idea behind my personal choice. I firmly believe that the protection of fundamental rights that has been achieved in democratic countries is the result of a struggle of the individual against the State. But not a neutral and aseptic State, rather a heavily ideologised State. This hypothetical State that would replace all the former ones, should necessarily be less ideologised, since it could not be biased towards one or other option in those cases in which the present states hold different positions. I shall give an example connected with our subject in order to make my position clear. It seems obvious to me that in Italy, Spain and even France, the Catholic Church holds a more favourable position in the legal system than other churches. The Orthodox Church is more highly valued under Greek law than other denominations. I believe that this is not desirable. I feel that this is due, for historical, sociological or whatever other type of reason, to the fact that the corresponding State has an ideological base that is closer to Catholicism, Protestantism or to orthodoxy. A European state, for pure reasons of subsistence, would necessarily have at its core a larger number of ideological opinions, as it could not operate using the criterion of the social majority, since this would not exist, and hence would be less ideological. You may well say to me that a certain level of ideology would always survive. And I could not agree more; in the example given, this new State would have a Christian basis and, therefore, would favour the Christian churches. Although the situation would not be ideal, this would suppose a positive advance for at least two reasons. In the first place, because Christian denominations would all at least enjoy the same level of equality. And in the second place, because the rest of the religious movements

---

International. Fondement, élaboration, valeur et cessation du Droit concordataire, J. Duculut, Gembloux, 1935, pp. 351-352. In any case, see also ibidem, p. 355 onwards. I think that in the hypothesis that I am laying out as preferable, this new State would assume those concordatory agreements, although obviously it would be necessary to adapt them to these new circumstances, this being an intermediary phase which would be followed by its substitution for a global one or its disappearance.

would indirectly benefit, since a less ideologised State, as this would be, is beneficial to minorities that are not in tune with the dominant ideology. Perhaps this is one of the reasons why the present pontiff is a firm believer in the idea of nationhood[31], since he is aware that in a strong European Union, the Catholic Church may hold a less favourable position than it currently does in Spain, Italy, Poland, etc.

My position in relation to what the future of the concordats should be, is less adamant. I believe that it is a fundamentally technical concept, and when dealing with technical instruments, ideological choices lose their weight[32]. On the one hand, at least in the area of language, the intentions of the Catholic Church in its relations with the State have varied[33]. We can say that it does not currently see the existence of the concordat as something fundamental to establish its position at the core of the legal system. And, as I have already mentioned, in reality, in democratic states, little more is obtained via concordats than what is conferred upon the Church by unilateral legislation[34]. There are even those who have stated

---

[31] "Avec Jean Paul II, le concept de *nation* retrouve une centralité dans le discours européen de la papauté…[dans le] discours prononcé à l'UNESCO à Paris, Jean Paul II exaltera «cette souveraineté fondamentale que possède chaque nation en vertu de sa propre culture» (2 juin 1980)". CHENAUX, Philippe, *Le Saint-Siège et la Communauté Européenne (1965-1990)*, in BARBERINI, Giovanni (ed.), *La politica internazionale della Santa Sede. 1965-1990. Atti del Seminario di studio. Perugia, 8-9-10 novembre 1990*, Edizioni Scientifiche Italiane, Naples, 1992, p. 63.

[32] Naturally I am fully aware that historically the choice in favour of or against the concordat has been a political choice. The instrument of relations (the concordat) symbolically constituted something much deeper: supporting (or not) the Church. I believe that that is not now the case.

[33] "La nueva base de relación entre los Estados y la Iglesia ha ido trasladándose progresivamente desde la doctrina tradicional del Derecho público eclesiástico -que traduce a categorías jurídico-políticas el principio filosófico de la *societas perfecta*- hacia la cultura contemporánea de los derechos del hombre. Conforme a esta nueva fundamentación, la *libertas ecclesiae* no radicaría tanto en el reconocimiento de un privilegio, cuanto en la idea de que la autonomía de la Iglesia en el cumplimiento de sus funciones es una forma de expresión de los derechos de libertad religiosa". PALOMINO, Rafael, *El acuerdo básico entre la Santa Sede y la OLP en el contexto de la práctica concordatoria reciente*, "Revista Española de Derecho Canónico", LVIII, 2001, p. 279. Although we should ask ourselves whether the concept of autonomy as it is interpreted by some would not be the same as *societas perfecta*.

[34] "Osservate alla luce dell'esperienza di altri sistemi e di altri ordinamenti, le norme che troviamo negli ordinamenti a sistema pattizio in genere non differiscono gran che rispetto a quelle emanate unilateralmente dalla maggior parte degli Stati". ONIDA, *Considerazioni sul sistema…* cit., p. 58. Although the following sharp reflections that the author goes on to make should not be forgotten: "Ma i sistemi pattizi aggiungono la nota negativa delle assai maggiori difficoltà a modificare quelle norme per adeguarle nel tempo all'evoluzione della società: nota negativa che in realtà, in uno stato democratico, appare proprio lo scopo fondamentale perseguito dalla Chiesa attraverso la richiesta di addivenire a un Concordato". Ibidem.

that mediated law may be even more restrictive than general law[35], although I think that this hypothesis is more theoretical than real, since those individuals or institutions that enjoy a special legal framework can always opt for what is laid down in general law, should they so choose. In other words and to conclude, it seems that in the current democratic systems, the Church has sufficient sphere of activity without having to resort to a concordat.

On the other hand, I cannot perceive the reasons why, should this not be the case, that is to say, in the hypothesis that the framework granted by general law were not sufficient, that the Catholic Church should enjoy a privileged framework in comparison to other denominations worthy of the same respect.

Now, all the above are my political opinions, which could be summarised using two expressions: "more Europe" and "the concordat is not necessary". Notwithstanding this, I do not believe that the role of a legal theorist, and I do not claim to be otherwise, is that of expressing his opinions and desires. The function of a jurist is to try to describe the current rules and, perhaps, to try to predict the future. That is what I shall try to do presently, being fully aware that, in all probability, the future will not coincide with my wishes. But being also aware that any hypothesis of the future will be overridden by a reality that is unimaginable now.

II. THE FIRST CORNERSTONE OF THE RELATION:
    STATE (AND THE EUROPEAN UNION) AND RELIGION:
    FROM EXISTING ECCLESIASTICAL LAWS TO A
    NON-EXISTENT AND INEVITABLE ECCLESIASTICAL LAW

It is clear that the concordat is a legal instrument to relate the Catholic Church to the State. It is no less clear that the subject of relations between the State and the Church is nowadays situated within the ample scope of what the Italians call "diritto ecclesiatico" and in Germany is called "Staatskirchenrecht", and that in English has no precise name. Let us

---

[35] "Si intravede una svolta storico-normativa di grande significato nelle relazioni tra Stato e Chiese. Una svolta per la quale, mentre un tempo il *diritto comune* era considerato tradizionalmente *restrittivo* rispetto alle concessioni che le confessioni potevano ottenere in sede di contrattazione bilaterale, oggi esso sembra divenire -almeno per alcuni aspetti- più appetibile, cioè più favorevole e liberale, rispetto ai diversi testi o accordi pattizi". CARDIA, Carlo, *Concordati e diritto comune*, "QDPE", 1999-1, p. 151.

say, although it is not absolutely correct, that it is situated within the framework of the legal treatment of religion by the civil authorities[36], and that is conventionally called "Church and State", although perhaps it would be more appropriate to start to think of a more aseptic and descriptive name for a reality that has now changed[37]. Therefore, it seems to me a quintessential task to make a brief summary of what is the said legal treatment in the Member States of the European Union, as well as the way in which the European Union has approached the said phenomenon. Let us begin with the Member States.

The first temptation is that of trying to outline different classificatory tables, grouping countries together according to the similarities of their models. Even though I am aware of the futility of the attempt, I shall attempt to propose a classification.

The first classification will be strictly sociological, and it should be said that there exist Catholic countries and Protestant countries in Europe. In the former block we have Ireland, France, Portugal, Spain, etc. and in the latter Finland, the United Kingdom, Denmark, etc. In imprecise geographical terms, a Reformed north and a Catholic south. Such a classification is imprecise, incomplete and useless. This would leave out Germany and Greece. It does not take into account the growing numbers of citizens who do not belong to either of the said churches. But, above all, it is impossible to deduce any legal consequence of any weight from that. Do the Church and State systems in Ireland, France or Italy have anything in common? No, nothing. Is the Greek system not more similar to the Danish one than the latter to the British one?

A second proposal that appears to be more technical is that in which the separatist countries should be grouped together on the one hand and those countries that maintain a system of co-operation on the other. Apart from the difficulties that arise in establishing the boundaries of such a

---

[36] I feel that it is not exact since it represents making an assumption, which for the time being should not be made, about the place that concordatory law occupies in the order of things in the different legal systems. I am thinking about the following types of question: Concordatory Law as part of International Law, or not; Concordatory Law as an internal or external element of Canon Law and of national legal systems, etc.

[37] "Can the whole of ecclesiastical law in Europe in 1995 [I imagine the question remains in 2003] be better classified under the broader heading *State and religion* than under the classic title *Church and State*? According to us the former is to be preferred. The necessity of an equal treatment for all religions and religious groupings and the growing interest for non-Christian religions, symbol, rites and practices seem to demand it". DE FLEURQUIN, Luc, *Ecclesiastical law in the European Union in 1995: A cautious move from* Church and State *to* State and Religion, "European Journal for Church and State Research / Revue Européenne des Relations Églises-État" ["EJCSR"], 3, 1996, p. 140.

principle of co-operation[38], the classification itself is completely useless since you would have to place fourteen Community states in one group and France in the other, and even nowadays, it would be highly arguable as to whether the French Republic could be considered separatist.

It does not seem problematic to identify the components of the two groups that could be established should we resort to a classification of maximum objectivity: countries with a State or national Church and countries where this does not occur. It would be enough to turn to their respective constitutional documents and the classification is automatic. However, things are not quite so simple. Where would you place Finland, which has two officially recognised national churches? What would you do with Italy and Spain, which specifically mention the Catholic Church in their respective constitutions? Should we take into account, to these effects, the reference to the Holy Trinity in the Irish Republic's Constitution? But, above all, and once more, such a classification would lack any practical purpose: do not the reformed churches in Germany receive more state aid than the Church of England receives from the British State? Does the lack of reference to the Catholic Church in the Belgian Constitution yet its inclusion in the Spanish one mean that it receives better treatment in Spain than in Belgium? Quite simply, nowadays, such differences lack any real significance.

Finally, let us move on to the classification that ought to be the most useful for our purposes: concordatory countries and non-concordatory countries.

Once more, the classification is clear only in appearance. The fact that Denmark, Sweden and the United Kingdom do not have any concordatory agreement in force with the Holy See is not an issue. Nor is it an issue that Portugal, Spain, Italy and Austria have concordatory systems. Germany is undoubtedly a concordatory country, but I do not believe that its model for relations can in any way be considered identical to that of the other concordatory countries. In relation to France, as is well known, it would be considered a non-concordatory country in which a part of the territory is concordatory. Regarding Belgium, it is probably not concordatory, in the same way that Luxembourg probably is; but in both cases we can only speak about probabilities and not certainties. We are thus not talking about a precise classification.

---

[38] "Il principio di cooperazione non ha, in sé, alcun contenuto precettivo di chiara identificabilità". CASUSCELLI, Giuseppe, *Libertà religiosa e fonti bilaterali*, "ADEE", III, 1987, p. 91.

In respect of its practical use for defining a model for Ecclesiastical Law, things are not clear either. As we will see later on, the fundamental element of the model is common, without the concordat conferring privileged treatment in respect of that which is offered by a general legislator[39], but it may be argued that this is not the issue, that the purpose of the concordat is to encompass the special nature of the Catholic Church in relation to these groupings in such a way that the concordatory countries would be more sensitive to the needs of the Catholic Church than the non-concordatory countries. I do not believe that the Republic of Ireland is any less sensitive to the needs of the Church than the Kingdom of Spain. Nor can it be said that the concordat, at a technical level, enables structures to be created *ad hoc* to the advantage of the Catholic Church; you need only think of, if I am not mistaken, the French "associations diocésaines" that are the only exclusive categories for the Catholic Church designed by a legal system of the European Union which are obviously not supported by any concordat, but precisely by a separatist regime.

After analysing the different models of European Ecclesiastical Law, I had the opportunity, some time ago, to draw some conclusions in the area of comparison[40]. If I had to summarise this in relation to the question that we are addressing, I would say that there exists no such classification whereby we can group models together, and that, in reality, there exist only national models. The words that were historically employed to classify these models today lack a precise meaning, or, at

---

[39] "Gli accordi non possono disciplinare contenuti, facoltà, limiti delle libertà di religione che non abbiano un previo riscontro nel diritto comune posto dallo stato quale comune garanzia dell'espezienza di fede...Lo stato democratico non può accordare «nuove» libertà ai seguaci di una confessione stipulando accordi con essa: le libertà di tutti hanno radice e fondamento nella costituzione di tutti. L'affermazione conciliare che la chiesa non ripone le sue speranze nei privilegi offertile dall'autorità civile enuncia, in fondo, il medesimo principio: la libertà di una sola chiesa, o di alcune tra quelle che vivono nel territotio di uno stato, è la radicale negazione della libertà religiosa". Ibidem, p. 95.

[40] These were the conclusions that, in essence, I still maintain: "1ª, La diversidad de modelos es enorme; 2ª, No existen modelos puros. Tal vez no existen modelos; 3ª, La libertad religiosa no es plena en nigún caso; 4ª, Hay evidentes problemas de desigualdad; 5ª, Algunos problemas tienen su origen en la historia; 6ª, Otros lo tienen en situaciones absolutamente novedosas; 7ª, Las técnicas empleadas para solucionar las insuficiencias del modelo generan una creciente complejidad del mismo; 8ª, Tales técnicas pasan generalmente por una mayor intervención estatal; 9ª, Los campos de tensión han variado sustancialmente: el matrimonio no es ya un problema, y sí lo es la enseñanza, y 10ª, Las dificultades de generar un modelo uniforme aparecen casi como insalvables". IBÁN, Iván C., *Propuesta de conclusión*, in FERRARI, Silvio, IBÁN, Iván C., *Derecho y Religión en Europa Occidental*, McGraw-Hill, Madrid, 1998, p. 139.

least, they are not so clear as in former times[41]. In the same way, it seems that there does not exist any precise correlation between the legal position that the denominations occupy and how religious they are[42], nor do I believe that there exists any relation between the legal *status* that the Catholic Church has in a legal system and the treatment that it receives from the same.

But the absence of a unitary model in which all the existing denominations in each country can fit, and which corresponds to the traditional categories (separatist, denominational, etc.), does not mean that there are no common traits. In the first place, it is clear that religious confrontations, that were the basis for national models, have disappeared for sociological reasons[43]. In the second place, the extensive plurality of national models, is, in reality, more formal than real, since the differences, in real terms, are minimal[44]. What are these common traits that enable us to speak, if not about a European model of Church and State relations, at least about some basic common principles?

From my point of view, the first common trait is that we live in a secular European society, whereby such a term is understood in the sense that political power and religious power move on different planes and that the individual may withdraw from the scope of the latter, without this playing any significant role in his activities within society[45]. Naturally,

---

[41] "Laicità e separazione, neutralità e pluralismo non sono più sinonimo di anticoncordatarismo, di diritto unilaterale comune, di non disponibilità dei pubblici poteri a negoziare con l'autorità religiosa. Si è difussa in Europa, con modalità diverse, una prassi...che cerca di conciliare indipendenza e negoziazione, separazione e cooperazione, laicità e concertazione". VENTURA, Marco, *La laicità dell'Unione Europea. Diritti, mercato, religione*, G. Giappichelli, Torino, 2001, p. 111.

[42] "Il existe trés peu de relations entre le statut des confessions et le niveau de la religiosité dans les différents pays [de l'Union]". LAMBERT, Yves, *Les régimes confessionnels et l'état du sentiment religieux*, in BAUBEROT (ed.), *Religions et laïcité...*, cit., p. 257.

[43] "La diversificazione religiosa dell'Europa dei Quindici (e, a più forte ragione, di quella «allargata» verso est), la non indifferente presenza di non-credenti, il basso numero di praticanti tra gli europei più giovani, hanno imposto, nei fatti, il superamento delle antiche, profonde divisioni della cristianità". MARGIOTTA BROGLIO, Francesco, *Il fattore religioso nell'Unione europea. Continuità e nuovi problemi*, in AA.VV., *Studi in Onore di Francesco Finocchiaro*, II, Cedam, Padova, 2000, p. 1268.

[44] "The models prevailing in the member States of the European Union range from benevolent separation to cooperation, i.e. within quite narrow limits". FERRARI, Silvio, *Church and State in Europe. Common pattern and challenges*, "EJCSR", 2, 1995, p. 152.

[45] "Una «laicità europea» è configurabile solo -oltre le specificità nazionali- nell'ambito della storia della secolarizzazione in Europa e nel radicarsi in tale processo di attributi fondamentali del comune ethos costituzionale europeo quali la separazione del potere politico da quello religioso, l'affermazione dell'indipendenza dell'individuo e dello stato dall'autorità religiosa, la separazione fra norme giuridiche e norme morali (fra reato

that does not mean that numerous values of religious origin, and more specifically Christian origin, are not shared by a good part of society, but rather they have lost their religious connotation, or, if you like, they have lost their religious origins and are now secular values. Of course, there are also values in society that have strictly lay origins, but whose origin is not apparent when the said values are shared. There is a nucleus of values that are essential to the different societies of the Member States of the European Union, independent of their origins.

In the second place, in one way or another (and it is not the case to give examples), all the legal systems of the European Union contain a series of provisions that take religion into account, structured through organisations, or more definitely, through the churches[46]. Religion, expressed in this way, is protected by the State.

The third trait that identifies this "European model of Ecclesiastical Law" would be the general recognition of religious freedom as a fundamental right. Not only in the sense that a religious choice may be made and consequently acted upon, but also in the sense of the absence of discrimination with regard to the personal religious (or non-religious) choice.

It is true that these three common values (secularisation, a positive evaluation of religion and full religious freedom) are tendentious values; the limits of perfection can never be attained, but the process, even with many exceptions, is at an advanced stage in all European countries. They are values rooted in society. They are European values.

*

*   *

Up to now we have been talking about state legal systems and of common values at a sociological level; however, we have still not made any reference to the possible existence of European Ecclesiastical Law. The question that should be answered at this stage is whether the

___

e peccato), l'imputazione alla volontà popolare (e non più alla volontà divina mediata dall'organizzazione ecclesiastica) della sovranità, la strutturazione dei poteri pubblici e delle pubbliche istituzioni in senso inclusivo e non discriminante, quali casa di tutti, equidistanti (seppure coinvolti) dagli interessi e dalle credenze degli individui e dei gruppi. In questo nucleo si riconoscono oggi, pur con forti specificità, gli stati membri dell'Unione". VENTURA, *La laicità...*, cit., pp. 106-107.

[46] "Si dovrebbe essere fanaticamente anticlericali per definire l'opposizione Chiesa-Stato come uno dei più importanti motivi del conflitto de nostro tempo. Le Chiese godono oggi di una posizione ottima, grazie al fortunato concorrere di vari fattori". TORFS, *Stati e Chiese...*, cit., p. 19.

Community organs are issuing regulatory provisions that enable a system or regulation of the religious phenomenon to be built at a Community level. In a subsequent section, I shall endeavour to carry out the task of prognosis. For the time being, I shall make succinct reference to the current reality.

Any technical attempt to describe the current reality in this field comes across the typical difficulties at national level[47], in this case exacerbated by the lack of rules upon which to build a model. It is undoubtedly more important what may still happen in the field of the inevitable Community Ecclesiastical Law than what we can find at present.

It would be hard to describe any stance by the Community authorities on the subject, quite probably because, in principle, it cannot have one[48]. Despite this, some rules exist.

The starting point would inevitably be the "Declaration of the Status of the Churches and the non-denominational associations", the Declaration adopted by the Conference and that appears as an appendix to the Treaty of Amsterdam of 1997. The process of preparation[49] is illuminating in respect of what was debated at depth, but from reading the text[50], one automatic conclusion can be drawn: the European Union declared itself incompetent in respect of the subject of Ecclesiastical Law.

Such a reading seemed to me extraordinarily hasty. I do not believe that for any subject, including religious matters, there is a clear distinction

[47] "Tra le varie difficoltà incontrate si possono qui sinteticamente ricordare il problema della multidisciplinarietà degli studi giuridici sul nesso tra religione e diritto, il problema del raccordo tra sapere giuridico e altri saperi egualmente interessati al fenomeno religioso ed infine il problema della indipendenza o della confessionalità della ricerca in materia". VENTURA, *La laicità...*, cit., p. 95.

[48] "Le autorità comunitarie non possono dare per presupposto il «valore positivo» dell'apporto religioso...rispetto all'obbiettivo fondamentale dell'integrazione europea nella coesione sociale...In secondo luogo, l'apporto religioso deve essere relativizzato...va considerato come un contributo tra gli altri...Il riferimento al patrimonio spirituale e alla forza sociale coesiva delle confessioni non deve implicare una insufficienza costituzionale comunitaria...da colmare col riferimento ad un'autorità esterna...portatrice di una verità d'origine divina". Ibidem, pp. 227-228.

[49] For a description of this process of preparation: See JANSEN, Thomas, *Dialogue entre la Comission européenne, les Eglises et les communautés religieuses*, in CASTRO JOVER, Adoración (ed.), *Iglesias, confesiones y comunidades religiosas en la Unión Europea. San Sebastián, 25 y 26 de septiembre de 1998*, Universidad del País Vasco, Bilbao, 1999, pp. 77-85 and PIERUCCI, Andrea, *La posizione degli Stati dell'Unione europea nel dibattito sulle «chiese» nella revisione del Trattato di Maastricht*, in Ibidem, pp. 87-95.

[50] "The European Union respects and does not prejudge recognised status, by virtue of National Law, of the Churches and associations and religious communities in the Member States. Likewise, the European Union respects the status of philosophical and non-denominational organisations".

between the powers of the European Union and of the Member States. Phenomena that are susceptible to regulation have a certain inherent complexity, such that any claims to exact limitations of powers seem impossible to me, because they do not correspond to reality[51]. It is not only a question of whether Community provisions exist that fully enter into subjects of Ecclesiastical Law, such as not interrupting religious programmes of less than half-an-hour's duration with advertising[52], or of recognising decisions by canonical tribunals in matrimonial matters[53]. Nor is it a question of the existence of numerous references in the Treaties, in the case law of Luxembourg, or in parliamentary debates relating to religion[54]. It is simply a question of the existence of religious issues in everyday life, and that Community Law, like any regulatory system, attempts to regulate this social reality. It is not a question of positively or negatively evaluating this phenomenon called religion, but rather a question of regulating the social reality in which this phenomenon is present.

If, as far as the rest is concerned, you think as I do, that all regulatory systems have an expansive force that leads them to endeavour to continually regulate a greater number of subjects, perhaps you will agree with me that it will be inevitable in the medium term to be able to talk about European Ecclesiastical Law upon some real basis. But I shall return to this issue later.

After these references to the first cornerstone of the European Union-concordat relation that we intend to analyse, it is now time to look at the second: the concordat.

---

[51] "Diventa più che mai anacronistico porsi astrattamente la questione di chi, tra l'Unione europea e il singolo stato detenga La Competenza (con la maiuscola) in materia di religione. Anzitutto perché quella competenza è sia di fatto che di diritto tanto «condivisa» quanto è «condivisa» la sovranità dell'Unione nella cui prospettiva anche la nostra questione va ormai inquadrata. In secondo luogo perché l'individuazione di una vera e propria «materia religiosa» separata dalle altre su cui affermare la competenza dello stato ed escludere la competenza dell'Unione sembra impossibile tanto in astratto quanto in concreto". VENTURA, *La laicità...*, cit., pp. 181-182.

[52] See Art. 11, Dir 85 / 552 / EEC.

[53] See RODRIGUEZ CHACÓN, Rafael, *Unión europea y eficacia civil de resoluciones matrimoniales canónicas. El artículo 40 del Reglamento (CE) N° 1347/2000 del Consejo de la Unión Europea, de 29 de mayo de 2000*, "Laicidad y libertades. Escritos Jurídicos", 1, 2001, pp. 137-187.

[54] See a catalogue to that date in PAULY, Alexis, *Modestes réflexions à propos d'une recherche empirique*, EUROPEAN CONSORTIUM FOR CHURCH-STATE RESEARCH / CONSORTIUM EUROPEEN POUR L'ETUDE DES RELATIONS EGLISES-ETAT, *Religions in European Law / Les religions dans le droit communautarie, Proceedings of the colloquium. Luxembourg / Trier, November 21-22, 1996 / Actes du colloque. Luxembourg/Trèves, 21-22 novembre 1996*, Bruylant-Giuffrè-Nomos, Milan, 1998, pp. 163-192.

III. THE SECOND CORNERSTONE: THE CONCORDAT:
A VENERABLE INSTITUTION WITH AN IMPRECISE PAST
AND A CONFUSING FUTURE

In contrast to the opinion of some writers[55], I doubt that the expression
concordat has an absolutely precise meaning. Or, at least, that it would
be useless for our discourse to endeavour to find an exact definition.
I think that there are two elements that cause the imprecise nature of this
concept. The first is that certain regulatory acts of very different scope
and characteristics have been included under this name during the course
of time. The traditional definitions highlight some of the difficulties in the
use of the term[56], and that even such definitions derive from certain
assumptions that probably do not conform to reality. The second element
that complicates the use of precise technical categories of a general nature
in the legal world is the extreme peculiarities of one of the contractual
parties. The Holy See is the contractual party of the Catholic Church.
I do not believe that anyone would argue that we have here a subject that,
at least in the legal world, is quite singular. Both questions will be
addressed below.

It does not seem to make any sense to begin to discuss which of the
three main positions of the legal nature of the concordats[57] is currently
the most accurate. It is not simply a question of that in reality the so-
called theory of privilege has not transformed from being a theoretical

---

[55] "En droit canonique le mot concordat a le sens précis d'entente entre l'autorité
ecclésiastique et le pouvoir civil ayant pour but d'organiser les rapports entre l'Église et
l'État relativement à certains objects qui les intéressent tous deux". NAZ, *Concordat*, cit.,
c. 1353.

[56] "La convention concordataire est essentiellement le moyen dont se servent l'Église
et l'État pour établir, chacune des parties y apportant du sien, un ensemble de dispositions
normatives qui constituent une réglementation unique ayant pleine valeur à la fois dans
l'ordre interne ecclésiastique et civil. Du fait qu'elles adoptent pareille réglementation dans
un traité solennel, les parties contractent, en vertu de l'application de la norme supérieure
pacta sunt servanda, une obligation de droit public externe (de droit international, dirait-
on entre États), qui les astreint à rendre cette réglementation exécutoire par l'acte de sa
publication, et à lui maintenir dans la suite sa pleine efficacité. De là, dans le langage
courant, le mot «concordat» est un terme amphibologique, qui désigne tantôt le traité lui
même, tantôt la législation interne à laquelle il donne naissance". WAGNON, *Concordats
et Droit...*, cit., p. 225.

[57] "Les opinions professées par les auteurs au sujet de la nature juridique du concordat, peuvent, malgré des divergences parfois profondes, être ramenées à trois théories
principales: la théorie dite légale, la théorie des privilèges et enfin la théorie contractuelle.
Les deux premières refusent au concordat ce que lui reconnaît la troisième: la valeur d'un
traité bilateral". Ibidem, p. 2.

instrument which does not correspond to the reality[58], and that could even serve as the basis for justifying the opposite[59], but rather a question of that it would seem that there is a general consensus that the concordat is an agreement. Whilst not wishing to be the one to question such general unanimity, perhaps it is appropriate to spend a short while addressing the issue. Probably both the theory and the legal basis of privilege have never been manifested in a pure state. I believe that they manifest trends towards the relation of power between the Church and the State. At those times in which the Church exercised a clear position of superiority over the State, the theory by virtue of which the concordat was a privilege granted by the former to the latter would reflect the reality to a great extent. On the other hand, the theory by virtue of which the concordat was a state law to fix the position of the Church would accurately describe those historical moments in which the latter was in a position of inferiority, in terms of power, to the State. The contractual theory would reflect a situation of balance between the respective powers. I think that in the modern states of law, a series of legal elements can be found that perhaps enable us to imagine a tendency towards the legal theory. That is to say, that the states would be in a situation of superiority in respect of the Church. I am thinking about questions such as the consideration of the constitution as a higher level of law than the concordat, an appeal to an ordinary or constitutional court to the effect that such superiority can be effective, the intervention of parliaments in the passing of a concordat, etc. I outline the idea without developing it, since, for the time being, what interests us is the concept of the concordat.

---

[58] "La doctrine qui faisait du concordat une concession du Saint-Siège se heurtait à la leçon des faits. Les concordats ont toujours été l'objet des négociations, dans lesquelles la position du Saint-Siége fut, selon les circonstances, plus ou moins forte". GAUDEMET, Jean, *Conclusions de l'historien des institutions*, in BASDEVANT-GAUDEMET, Brigitte, MESSNER, Francis (eds.), *Les origines historiques du statut des confessions religieuses dans les pays de l'Union Européene*, P.U.F., Paris, 1999, p. 235.

[59] "Paradoxalement, c'est sur la base de[s]...discours, qui faisaient du concordat un simple privilège octroyé par le Saint-Siége, que s'est finalement construite la doctrine dite légale. Affirmée solennellement pour la première fois en 1770 par un ministre de l'électeur de Bavière, elle fut surtout développée, au cours du XIXᵉ siècle, par les juristes allemands au service d'États protestants. Pour la bâtir, ceux-ci reprirent les arguments des canonistes qui niaient le caractère contractuel des concordats, n'y voyant qu'une simple loi ecclésiastique susceptible d'être modifiée unilatéralement par le pape. Retenent cette qualification légale ces juristes rejetèrent par ailleurs toute ingérence pontificale à l'intérieur des États. Dans cette optique, les concordats allaient devenir des pures lois nationales prises par les États au bénéfice de l'Église considérée désormais comme une simple corporation". ROUMY, Franck, *Le concept de concordat dans la doctrine canonique des XVIᵉ-XVIIIᵉ siècles*, in Ibidem, p. 49.

Numerous definitions of the concordat have been compiled, but it is sufficient to refer to a manual of the *Ius Publicum Ecclesiasticum* to find one. It is sufficient to refer to a few of them[60] to see that some elements are always present. Such would be the case for the idea of agreement: "entente" (REBUFFE), "conventio" (CAPPELLO), "convention" (WAGNON), "conventiones" (OTTAVIANI and CONTE A CORONATA), "accordo" (CASORIA), "contrato" (HERRANZ) or "convenzione" (D'AVACK). We find less unanimity in the examples proposed when defining between whom such agreements are established: on some occasions it is a case of the Church and the State (CASORIA and HERRANZ), or other terms that we could consider to be equivalent, such as "Ecclesia et societatis civilis" (CAPPELLO) or "societatis civilis et ecclesiastica" (CONTE A CORONATA). A greater vocation towards technical precision is found when the expressions "S. Sede" and "Stato" (D'AVACK) are used,

---

[60] Without any claim to be exhaustive and by mere way of example, I shall hereby transcribe a few of them: "Le premier auteur à avoir tenté une réflexion d'ensemble sur les concordats est précisément un de ces docteurs *in utroque* à cheval entre la scolastique et l'humanisme juridique: Pierre Rebuffe (1487-1557). Dans un ouvrage, qui paraît en 1536, consacré au Concordat de Bologne de 1516 conclu entre Léon X et François Ier, Rebuffe livre la première tentative de définition juridique. Le concordat, écrit-il, est une «loi portée par la commune entente des princes, à savoir le pape et le roi». Ibidem, pp. 39-40; "Concordatum definiri potest: *conventio inter Ecclesiam et societatem civilem* ad mutuas relationes ordinandas, circa materias, quae *utriusque societatis interest, publico et solemni pacto inita*". CAPELLO, Felice M., *Summa Iuris...,* cit., p. 401; "Le concordat est une convention conclue entre le pouvoir ecclésiastique et le pouvoir civil en vue de régler leur rapports mutuels dans les multiples matières où ils sont appelés à se rencontrer". WAGNON, *Concordats et Droit...,* cit., p.23; "Conventiones inter S.Sedem et civitatum moderatores supremos initiae, quibus Republicae officia et privilegia Ecclesiaeque iura circa determinatas res, in bonum utriusque societatis definiuntur et pactorum sollemnitatibus firmatur". OTTAVIANI, Alaphridus, *Institutiones Iuris Publici Ecclesiastici. II. Ius Publicum Externum*[2], Typis Polyglottis Vaticanis, 1936, pp. 270-271; "Concordato è un accordo tra Chiesa e Stato per definire e rafforzare alcune relazioni giuridiche su affari di propria competenza". CASORIA, *Concordati e ordinamento...,* cit., p. 29; "El concordato es la conclusión pacífica de un contrato, o de una serie de contratos, establecidos entre la Iglesia y el Estado acerca del gobierno de los intereses espirituales y temporales de aquella, dentro del ámbito territorial de éste". HERRANZ, *La teoría concordataria,* cit., p. 24; "Conventiones inter societates civilem et ecclesiasticam ad earum relationes iuridicas melius determinandas et ad praxim facilius deducendas". CONTE A CORONATA, Matthaeus, *Institutiones Iuris Canonici*[4], Marietti, Romae, 1960, p. 140 and "Si designa col nome tecnico di «concordato» (*conventio, pactum, conventum, concordatum*) una convenzione bilaterale stipulata fra la S.Sede e uno Stato per regolare materie ecclesiastiche di comune interesse, in virtù della quale i due contraenti, facendosi reciproche concessioni, si obbligano, ciascuno per sua parte, ad assumere un dato atteggiamento e comportamento reciproco e a emanare in specie determinate norme per la disciplina giuridica di quella partizione della Chiesa cattolica che vive e opera nell'ordinamento dello Stato contraente". D'AVACK, *Trattato...,* cit., p. 185.

or "S. Sedem" and "moderatores supremes initiae" (OTTAVIANI). But the idea is probably most clearly expressed when the expressions "pouvoir ecclésiastique et pouvoir civil" (WAGNON) are used; which would be a more current way of referring to "le pape et le roi" (REBUFFE). I feel that a division is produced between the two groups of definitions employed in respect of the object. For the first group (WAGNON, CASORIA and CONTE A CORONATA) the concordat is the mechanism for defining and limiting the relations, to put it that way, without going into any type of valuation. This is expressed very clearly in the most mature definition used, when REBUFFE limits himself to describing it as a law derived from an agreement, but without any reference to its content. However, the other group of writers (CAPELLO, OTTAVIANI and D'AVACK) make reference to the idea of reciprocal interest[61]. Naturally, and it is sufficient to read the definitions proposed, the differences are far greater on other points; some (CAPPELLO and OTTAVIANI) demand a certain solemnity, some (D'AVACK) consider that the concordat undertakes to produce state legislation to develop itself, some (WAGNON) seem to view the concordat as an instrument to regulate all relations, whilst others (CASORIA) do not confer this global characteristic at all.

This brief example proposed is probably enough to reach the conclusion that there is only one common element in the definitions of a concordat: the idea of a bilateral agreement. Everything else remains open to interpretation.

Even the subject of who the contractual parties are remains open. On some occasions the expression State is used (CASORIA, HERRANZ and D'AVACK), but in others, more generic forms are adopted. It is quite clear that when Latin is used, this is due to the difficulties of finding an appropriate word to describe the State, but we can find such generic uses even in other languages, like "pouvoir civil", employed by WAGNON. It is probable that these authors are always thinking of the State, but on some occasions we can find explicit references to the possibility that the contractual part is a political entity of a broader nature.

This can be deduced from reading the current *Codex Iuris Canonici*[62], or it can be understood that the foreseeable way to overcome the

---

[61] A limited case would be that of HERRANZ, which exclusively realtes to the interests of the Church.

[62] "Il nuovo Codice canonico ha inserito, accanto alle «nationes», quali soggetti con i quali la Santa Sede può stipulare convenzioni, anche le «altre società politiche», intendendo come tali sia le molte organizzazioni internazionali governative con le quali il Vaticano intrattiene rapporti ufficiali, sia gli Stati membri di una federazione...(can.3)".

concordatory system would be via this path[63], or going into this complex world from a technical point of view, and unreal from a current perspective, of claiming the universal application of the so-called divine right It has been suggested that a form of universal concordat would be the way to achieve that[64].

In short, if it is difficult to state that in the past one of the contractual parties has always been the State, for the simple reason that the institution of the concordat is older than the existence of the State, nothing enables us to consider axiomatic the fact that the latter cannot be substituted in such a relation by other legal figures.

The term concordat has been used to describe many varied regulatory realities during the course of history, such that giving an omnicomprehensive definition seems an impossible task. The idea of an agreement seems to be the only historical constant, but an agreement between whom, between the Church and the State? I do not believe that the latter contractual party is fixed, we shall now proceed to see what happens with the former.

*

*   *

Relations between the State (or whatever institution may substitute it) and the Church occur at the level of International Law. In current terms, the Church acts at this level through the Holy See, so that formally

---

MARGIOTTA BROGLIO, Francesco, *Il fenomeno religioso nel sistema giuridico dell'Unione Europea*, in MARGIOTTA BROGLIO, Francesco, MIRABELLI, Cesare, ONIDA, Francesco, *Religioni e sistemi giuridici*, Il Mulino, Bologna, 1997, p. 179.

[63] "Ya que no de una superación por extinción o eliminación voluntaria del sistema y régimen concordatarios, ¿podría hablarse de *su superación por integrarse en figuras más amplias* que... rompieran la exclusividad de altas partes contratantes que de hecho la Iglesia disfruta... y el Estado y dieran lugar a un régimen general de convenios normativos como forma ordinaria de legislar en materia religiosa y eclesiástica atinente a la vida social de la comunidad política? La cuestión podría tratarse atendiendo a los sujetos en relación concordataria y a la materia de ésta. Nosotros *nos fijaremos en los sujetos*, por darse, respecto a ellos, el fenómeno de la expansión hacia otros nuevos... Respecto al Estado debe cuestionarse si otros órganos superiores... pueden a su vez concertar concordatos". CORRAL SALVADOR, Carlos, *La regulación bilateral...*, cit., pp. 196-197.

[64] "Un nuevo problema: el de las relaciones entre el Derecho canónico y el Derecho internacional, ambos universales, y una nueva posibilidad: la de que lleguen a existir convenios entre la Iglesia y la comunidad jurídica de los Estados, que también estarían insertos en los principios superiores de Derecho divino, que determinan las relaciones entre el orden político y el orden eclesiástico espiritual". MALDONADO, José, *Curso de Derecho canónico para juristas civiles*[2], Madrid, 1975, p. 73.

speaking, one of the contractual parties is the Holy See. We should not think that by giving this response all of the issues are resolved. And it is not only a question of whether the acts of the Holy See at an international level cannot all be extended to the same technical category, or that the Holy See always acts at the same level[65], fundamentally it is a question of the concept of the Holy See itself and that its position within the scope of International Law is very far from clear.

It is not a bad way of starting any attempt at working with the concept of the Holy See by remembering the words of WAGNON: "Le terme «Saint-Siége» ne désigne pas... un groupemente social, mais un gouvernement"[66]. But the singularities begin from that point on. In the first place it is a governmental organ of two distinct entities, on the one hand of the State of the Vatican City and on the other hand of the Catholic Church. The situation is thus in itself a strange phenomenon within the scope of International Law; this is further complicated by the fact that it is not clear whether it is either the Vatican or the Catholic Church itself.

The singularities of the Vatican State are so numerous (a nationality that is strictly functional and not achieved through birth, the manner of its creation, the probable necessity for its survival on the consent of the Italian Republic, etc.) that it makes no sense to refer to them. It is sufficient to think of its status as a non-member of the United Nations Organisation, and nowadays it is extremely exceptional that a State is not a member, that some consider it to be an undefined situation: the State of the Vatican City cannot form a part of that organisation[67].

---

[65] The following has been said by CARDIA: "discrasia tra la piena partecipazione vaticana all'OSCE e i diversi legami che collegano la Santa Sede alle istituzioni europee, al Consiglio d'Europa anzitutto (e alla Convenzione europea sui diritti dell'uomo e sulle libertá fondamentali) e all'Unione Europea". CARDIA, Carlo, *La soggettivitá internazionalle della Santa Sede e i processi di integrazione europea*, "I.E.", 11, 1999, [Also in *Studi... Finocchiaro*, cit., I, [379-428], p. 326

[66] WAGNON, *Concordat et Droit...*, cit., p. 34.

[67] "Las relaciones entre el Vaticano y las Naciones Unidas han seguido sustancialmente la línea trazada en los días de la Sociedad de Naciones. Una participación de la Ciudad del Vaticano como miembro parece prácticamente imposible para ambas partes. Por parte de la Santa Sede por su propósito de abstenerse de participar en toda controversia entre Estados; por parte de las Naciones Unidas, porque un número determinado de miembros se opondrían decididamente a toda representación Vaticana". PUENTE EGIDO, José, *Personalidad Internacional de la Ciudad del Vaticano*, Instituto Francisco de Vitoria. Consejo Superior de Investigaciones Científicas, Madrid, 1965, p. 88; "The real question is whether membership being granted under conditions consonant with its nature, the Holy See would desire to become a member of the United Nations as it is of many other international Organisations. The answer to that question, it would appear, is in the negative. Membership would involve the Holy See too directly in the political, economic and

It has even been maintained that, in contrast to what is rational, that is to say, the "Holy See" exists by virtue of the "State of the Vatican City", the situation, in reality, is quite the opposite: that the State exists because of the governmental organ[68]. Various writers, for whom its existence is justified all the time it fulfils its moral function, record the idea of the Holy See as a functional structure, which is not comparable with analogous classifications at state level[69].

But now our interest in the Holy See lies in its organisational leadership of the Catholic Church and not of the State of the Vatican City. We will also look at the purely instrumental nature of its international personality[70] and the possible need to overcome such categories[71]. The idea of functionality, of a merely instrumental nature, etc., should not, in principle, show anything. It seems clear to me that in the world of Public Law, and in particular of International Law, all of the categories are instrumental: the State, international personality, Parliament or the Head of State are all doctrinal and legislative creations to achieve an objective, to describe reality. What makes the case of the Church singular in its use of this category is something quite distinct.

commercial conflicts which arise between the States". CARDINALE, Hyginus Eugene, *The Holy See and the International Order*, Colin Smythe, Gerrards Cross, 1976, p. 259.

[68] "Solo accidentalmente la Santa Sede è riguardata quale soggetto di uno Stato che si trova con essa in un rapporto di immedesimazione organica funzionale, di uno Stato cioè che, in quanto tale, è in funzione dell'organo di governo, ed è oggetto dell'esercizio della sua potestà". BETTETINI, Andrea, S*ul titolo giuridico di partecipazione della Santa Sede alle organizzazioni e alle conferenze internazionali*, "DE", CVII-I, 1996, p. 718

[69] "La potenza della S. Sede, il suo ruolo, dipendano dal collegamento fra la sua azione e i valori morali che essa propugna e sui quali può mobilitare l'opinione pubblica internazionale. Questo spiega perché io sia favorevole, insieme a tanti altri autori, alla concezione, per la S. Sede, di una *personalità funzionale limitata*, cioè di una personalità che in tanto ha ragione di esistere in quanto sia collegata ai valori che costituiscono i fattori della "potenza" della Santa Sede, quelli con cui gli Stati sono obbligati a confrontarsi quando accettano la S. Sede come interlocutore nelle relazioni internazionali". BADIALI, Giorgio, *In tema di personalità internazionale della S. Sede*, in BARBERINI (ed.), *La politica internazionale...*, cit., p. 121.

[70] "La personalità internazionale non appartiene né definisce l'*essere* della Chiesa cattolica, è però una veste giuridica congruente con esso, attualmente operativa, strumentale per l'adempimento della sua missione, né più né meno". MARTIN DE AGAR, *Passato e presente...*, cit. p. 625.

[71] "¿No cabe pensar que la propia Santa Sede, y aún el Vaticano, encuentren más adelante otra fórmula de expresión de su naturaleza distinta de la calificación de personas internacionales? La búsqueda de estos caminos será una necesidad del futuro". DE LA HERA, Alberto, *El pluralismo y el futuro del sistema concordatario*, in AA.VV., *La Chiesa dopo il Concilio. Atti del Convegno internazionale di Diritto Canonico. Roma 14-19 gennaio 1970*, I, Giuffrè, Milan, 1972, p. 430.

Nobody doubts that the United States of America is a world power, but they, or Luxembourg or Spain feel at home in their use of the structures. However, the Catholic Church does not feel comfortable in their use, it has had to adapt to certain categories neither created by it or for it. The Church considers itself to be on another level (superior) to that of the rest of those who are subject to International Law[72]. The Church uses the categories of the State (the Vatican) and international personality (the Holy See), but in reality it does not believe that these are the ones that correspond to it. Pure grounds of historical convenience cause it to use them, and it was there that it placed all its efforts when it was necessary[73] to achieve that. In this sense, it seems to me that the Holy See is functional: it appeals to a category that it does not believe in, but to which it is obliged by reality. And this vocation to use the categories to the extent to which they are useful has been adopted in the way it has approximated itself to the European Union, i.e. it is present but it does not form a part of it[74].

Therefore, we can agree for our purposes to consider thinking of the Holy See as a subject of International Law, but with so many particular features in the way it acts, in the origin of such subjectivity, in its functions, and why not mention it, in the Church's lack of trust in such an instrument, that it is extraordinarily singular and unique in the field of

---

[72] "La Sede Pontificia... ha sempre rivendicato una posizione singolare, che non è (non accetta di essere: *non può essere*) *internazionale*: vale a dire *paritetica* a cospett o di questi altri Potentati. Ma è (postula di essere) dichiaratamente e francamente *sovranazionale* non *paritaria* ma *preminente*, rispetto a tutti quanti i membri (i comuni membri) della società internazionale. Sicché -anche se asserisce ogni momento di esser *soggetto* (*persona*) di diritto internazionale- in verità la Sede Pontificia non intende affatto di *restar subordinata* al diritto internazionale: *non può* intenderlo. E quindi -in sede negoziale- non esprime una concludente volontà d'impegnarsi internazionalmente: *non può* esprimerla. Semmai la Santa Sede può intender di *servirsi del diritto internazionale*: di *giovarsene ai suoi scopi*. Non per *vincolare giuridicamente se stessa*, ma per *vincolare a sé lo Stato* nei modi e nelle forme della vincolatività di diritto internazionale". BELLINI, *Natura ed eficacia...*, cit., pp. 95-96

[73] I am thinking about the rejection of the law of guarantees by the Kingdom of Italy, that provided the Holy See with a situation not entirely different from the present one, and which it rejected because it did not constitute a State. It considers itself to be something else (more), but it wants, at least, a state structure.

[74] "Nei riguardi delle istituzione comunitarie, la scelta è stata prima di un *pieno riconoscimento diplomatico*, con l'accreditamento di un ambasciatore con rango di nunzio apostolico, e poi di un qualche adeguamento strutturale (a livello di conferenze episcopali e di organismi di studio) alla realtà comunitaria. Non si è mai posto, invece, il problema di un rapporto in qualche modo diretto o organico con le istituzioni dell'Unione europea, dimodoché lo S.C.V. debe a tuttoggi considerarsi una realtà territoriale di tipo *extracomunitario*". CARDIA, *La soggettività internazionale...*, cit., p. 342.

International Law. Therefore, it is not surprising that the agreements that it signs are also singular. We shall now examine this.

To define a concordat as an international treaty between the Holy See and a State is a simple way to describe the reality, but is quite probably incorrect. There are those who adamantly deny such a classification[75], while there are others who make it, but point out that in order to extend it to the field of international treaties, it would be necessary to excessively extend the scope of International Law[76]. It insists on the special use of Concordatory Law in relation to International Law, stressing the fact that although the Holy See enjoys international subjectivity, it is not an inevitable condition that the agreements that it signs are international treaties[77]. And even in those cases in which it accepts its nature as an international treaty, it does so to confirm that this is not its real nature[78].

Nor is it the case here to get involved in doctrinal arguments. There are arguments both in favour of the internationalist position and against it. What is indisputable in my opinion is that if the Holy See is subject to International Law in a different way to other states, it would seem logical that the agreements that it signs cannot be easily extended to the technical categories envisaged as instruments of relations between the states. Whether Concordatory Law is external Law that falls under the scope of International Law, or, on the other hand, is situated outside it, appears to

---

[75] "El concordato no es un tratado internacional. Ni está concertado entre dos Estados nacionales, ni su existencia y vigor están colocados dentro de la órbita del Derecho internacional, ni entre las normas que rigen las relaciones entre sociedades políticas dentro de la comunidad jurídica de los Estados temporales". MALDONADO, *Curso...*, cit., p. 71.

[76] "Le critiche avanzate contro la soluzione internazionalista appaino invero assai convicenti e per superarle bisognerebbe avere del diritto internazionale una nozione ancora più ampia di quella generalmente adottata dall'odierna dottrina: bisognerebbe cioè ritenere che tale diritto abbia limiti così vasti da ricomprendere qualsiasi fenomeno giuridico che non sia ricollegabile a un ordinamento giuridico statale o all'ordinamento canonico". CATALANO, Caetano, *La natura giuridica dei concordati nella moderna dottrina*, in AA.VV., *La institución concordataria...*, cit., p. 34.

[77] "La specialità della materia concordataria è un dato indiscutibile, che rende vana la pretesa di esaurire o ridurre la problematica concordataria alla semplice preliminare adozione di una specifica nozione di ordinamento internazionale e alla conseguente determinazione della possibilità di riconoscere in seno a tale ordinamento la soggettività della S.Sede.... Non mi sembra, infatti, che esista una necessaria interdependenza tra i due problemi, in quanto la sussistenza di una personalità internazionale della S.Sede è sì condizione necessaria, ma non sufficiente per l'inquadrabilità dei concordati in seno all'ordinamento internazionale". CATALANO, Gaetano, *Problematica giuridica dei concordati*, Giuffrè, Milan, 1963, p. 131.

[78] "Che [i concordati]... abbiano la qualifica giuridica di accordi internazionali è un fatto che non intende esprimere tutta la loro specifica natura". MARTIN DE AGAR, *Passato e presente...*, cit. p. 626.

be a debate that lacks any practical basis. For that reason, it is perhaps more interesting to make a brief description of the current concordatory reality, focusing on the Member States of the European Union. That is what I shall move onto now.

*

*   *

It is clear that at the moment Community Law does not affect the validity of the concordats signed by various Member States of the European Union, and it is highly probable that such a situation is maintained in the medium term[79]. However, and as I mentioned before, I do not believe that such a situation can be considered indefinite, if, as I think, the legal unification process in the scope of the Community is unstoppable and in the end national legal systems will practically disappear, and so it seems to me that the existence of national concordatory systems such as those that we know now will be impossible to sustain. But even in the case that my prediction is correct, it is still a long way away, and hence it is appropriate to look at the present situation.

Four Community members have concordats that fully correspond to the standard concept of that institution in our time. That means, agreements of a general nature that regulate relations with the Catholic Church and its position within the state legal system[80]. They are those countries in which the argument maintained by some that the era of that type of concordat had concluded, and that they should be substituted by agreements to solve specific problems, has not triumphed[81]. It is quite clear that

---

[79] "Da parte degli Stati contraenti il Trattato di Amsterdam... si stabilisce con la *Dichiarazione* 11 che l'Unione Europea -con le sue finalità, la sua politiche e le sue attività normative e interpretativa- non si autolimita, ma piuttosto non può, né vuole, entrare in un ambito di competenza propria degli Stati membri. Questa interpretazione permette anche di cogliere la portata di attribuire all'espressione «rispetta e non pregiudica [quanto previsto] nelle legislazioni nazionali» e che negli ordinamenti interni gli accordi concordatari mantengono la loro natura di *lex specialis*, anche di fronte ad altra norma internazionale con carattere di «specialità» quale è el Trattato di Amsterdam". BUONOMO, Vincenzo, *L'Unione Europea e i regimi concordatori degli stati membri*, "IE", 11, 1999, pp. 362-363

[80] "Lo Stickler [Cfr. Stickler, *Der Konkordatsgedanke in rechtsgeschichtlicher Schau*, in *Oesterreichischen Archiv für Kirchenrecht*, 1957, pp. 25 ss], ha di recente sottolineato come il progressivo evolversi della funzione pratica del concordato si sia compiuto attuando un profondo mutamento della natura stessa dell'istituto, che da espediente per la risoluzione di specifici problemi è assurto a strumento per la generale disciplina dei rapporti fra la Chiesa ed i singoli Stati". CONDORELLI, *Concordati...*, cit., p. 227.

[81] "L'âge des Concordats semble terminé... la Saint-Siège s'est plutôt orienté dans la voie d'«Accords», qui n'entendent pas tout régler et qui, souvent, laissent la fixation des

many detailed issues cannot be resolved by concordats and that therein are contained mechanisms of evolution that imply the drafting of new regulatory texts, but I do not believe that this represents a lack of global foresight on the part of such concordats, but rather a reflection of the enormous complexity of modern legal systems that impedes the regulation of all aspects of a legal relation in one individual text that intends to be permanent, which thus obliges us to turn to general rules that are further developed in other more concrete ones. But this is not a characteristic of concordats, but rather of modern legal rules.

Be that as it may, the four concordatory countries that subscribe to such a model are Austria, Italy, Portugal and Spain. Four countries with a concordatory history and with a clear sociological majority of Catholics.

The case of the Federal Republic of Germany could also be quoted as a similar case. But I do not believe so. In Germany agreements at a federal or a state level with the Holy See or with the various dioceses fall within the general framework of agreements with the religious denominations. It is quite clear that Portugal, Italy and Spain have agreements made with other religious denominations apart from the Catholic Church; that is a very recent phenomenon. The concordat is much older.

I believe that in the four countries mentioned above, the concordat is the reflection of a concordatory tradition, while in the case of Germany a higher value is placed not on respect of the concordatory tradition, but rather on a general concept that questions of Ecclesiastical Law should be resolved through bilateral agreements signed by the religious denominations, which in the case of the Catholic Church happens to be a concordat, but this is purely by chance.

As is well known, together with the separatist French Republic, there is also a concordatory France. Due to a series of historical changes that are not necessary to describe here, the Napoleonic concordat remains in force in three "departments" in the east of the country.

Probably this Concordat of 1801 also regulates the relations between the Church and the State in Luxembourg, although its real effect is minimal[82] and it is unlikely that it will remain in force in Belgium.

---

points les plus délicats à des commissions qui devront négocier les détails de la convention". GAUDEMET, Jean, *Le concordat dans la republique laique*, "ADEE", VIII, 1992, p. 172.

[82] "It is not easy to analyse the current application of the concordat. Many of the provisions are too abstract and general to be applied directly or indirectly". PAULY, Alexis, *State and Church in Luxembourg*, in ROBBERS, Gerhard (ed.), *State and Church in the European Union*, Nomos, Baden-Baden, 1996, p. 195

This is the concordatory panorama in the European Union. I do not believe that it is necessary to proceed to discuss their contents, but I do believe that after the relatively recent processes of revision and substitution that have taken place in Italy, Portugal and Spain, it cannot be considered that they are situated within the former models[83] which would make their survival impossible due to their inability to adapt to the changing circumstances[84]. But I do not wish to stress all of that at this point. However, I do consider it important to make some comments about the concordatory situation within the European Union.

In the first place, it seems very clear to me that the concordatory regimes are only found in those countries where a majority of the population is Catholic. The countries with Catholic majorities in Europe are Belgium, Spain, France, the Republic of Ireland, Italy, Luxembourg, Austria and Portugal. In the majority of those countries there is a concordat currently in force. The exceptions are Belgium and the Republic of Ireland. As far as the first of these is concerned, we have already looked at how the Napoleonic Concordat could be argued to technically be in force, although quite probably this would be rejected. As far as Ireland is concerned, this clearly Catholic country in terms of its population and yet equally as clearly non-concordatory, the absence of a concordat can perhaps be explained, among other reasons, by the very recent independence, in historical terms, of the Republic from the United Kingdom.

There is only one country with a concordatory regime that cannot sociologically be considered Catholic: Germany. In the first place it should be pointed out that whilst German Catholicism in not in the majority, it is far from being a minority religion, since it has practically the same number of members as the Lutheran Church and between them we can find a clear majority of the German population[85]. This is a situation of two

---

[83] In reference to the now repealed Spanish concordat of 1953, which was graphically described as "una *Summula Iuris Publici Ecclesiastici*, matizada por el privilegio de presentación". LOMBARDÍA, Pedro, *Concordato, si, concordato, no*, in LOMBARDÍA, Pedro, *Escritos de Derecho Canónico*, III, Eunsa, Pamplona, 1974, p. 446.

[84] "Se si vuole mantenere la struttura concordatoria, si deve cercare di darle una dignità ed un valore storici che abbiano una portata valida per il futuro, cercare cioè di non fare un documento che fra pochi anni si richiederà di modificare nuovamente perchè non più rispondente alla ulteriore evoluzione dei tempi". MARGIOTTA BROGLIO, Francesco, *Sistema di intese e rapporti con la Chiesa cattolica*, in MIRABELLI, Cesare, (ed.), *Le intese tra Stato e confessioni religiose. Problemi e prospettive*, Giuffrè, Milan, 1978, pp. 145-146.

[85] See ROBBERS, Gerhard, *State and Church in Germany*, in ROBBERS (ed.), *State and Church...*, cit., p. 57.

majority churches. But moreover, as I have already pointed out, the German Concordat should be considered as one more piece in the German system of Ecclesiastical Law whose principle tenet is that the corresponding legal system should have a bilateral basis. The Concordat is simply another of the agreements with denominations.

My first conclusion is clear: the concordatory system, in general terms, exists in those countries that have Catholic majorities.

But there is a second element that I wanted to highlight, which is the sensation of confusion one has when looking at the European concordatory situation. Once again, without going into detail, I shall endeavour to describe the elements that cause this confusion. The bilateral Church-State texts in Spain that comprise a concordat, avoid the use of the term concordat. The substitution of the Italian Concordat of 1929 for a totally different one was not designed as such but as a simple reform. The fact that one part of France is concordatory as a result of this territory not belonging to French sovereignty at the time when the Napoleonic Concordat ceased to be in force is quite an unusual situation. As is the fact that it is arguable whether that Concordat is still in force in Belgium or in the Grand Duchy of Luxembourg. I am aware that behind all of these situations there are a series of concrete circumstances, but that does not detract from generating a sense of confusion. And why not mention that the institution is not strong enough to face the issues openly: by calling the Spanish agreements concordats, by speaking about a new concordat in Italy, by attempting to resolve bilaterally the situation in Belgium or Luxembourg, etc? A certain sensation remains that the institution is not a strong one and that it employs shameful mechanisms to survive.

IV. THE FUTURE: THE FORESEEABLE: THERE WILL BE EUROPEAN ECCLESIASTICAL LAW. THE UNFORESEEABLE: WHAT ITS CONTENT WILL BE AND WHETHER THE CONCORDAT WILL BE ONE OF THE INSTRUMENTS TO ESTABLISH IT

Inevitably all of these observations have a certain circular element: you always arrive back at the same place to start the circle once again, which leads us to the same goal. That is inevitable since they are observations about something that does not exist, or only exists in a minimal way. I shall now endeavour to draw a new circle, but trying to fix the elements in place in order to propose a conclusion. The last question, asked in a direct way would be: is it possible to imagine a European concordat? This requires us to answer a previous question: how do we see the future European Ecclesiastical Law?

I do not think that it is the role of a jurist to determine what the function of religion should be in the process of European integration. In spite of that, I do not think that it can be said whether it constitutes a favourable factor or not in the said process[86]. Of course it will not be, if the intention, as is made by some lines of thought[87], is to use the process of unification as a means of "rechristianising" society. Religion is an element in the structure of European society, which also has a strong lay tradition. Neither the Community institutions nor Community Law may take sides in these options. The Law must respect social values and should reflect them. A Community Law that tried to instil certain values not shared by society would inevitably lead to disaster. There is no place for Community Law that resembles a totalitarian state in which the dominant structures impose their will upon society. European society is not willing to go through what some national societies have already had to got through. The problem is much graver than one of "technical competence"[88] and goes much further than whether the European Union may or may not intervene in the regime of Church and State relations[89]. It is quite simply

---

[86] "On peut à la fois soutenir que la religion est un facteur favorable ou, au contraire, qu'elle est un facteur défavorable à l'intégration européenne. En effet, s'il est incontestable que les efforts entrepris du côté politique pour renforcer l'unité européenne et la concrétiser dans les institutions comme la Commission de Bruxelles et le Parlement de Strasbourg incitent les religions à se rapprocher pour apporter leur pierre à cette vaste enterprise, il est non moins incontestable que la construction même de l'Europe réactive un certain nombre de tensions interreligieuses et interconfessionnelles. La construction de l'Europe est oecuménogène au sens où elle vient renforcer un certain nombre des collaborations interconfessionnelles entre les différentes Eglises chrétiennes. Mais elle est aussi, à certains égards, oecuménicide, au sens où elle vient aussi renforcer des processus de reconfessionnalisations". WILLAIME, Jean Paul, *Unification européenne et religions*, in CASTRO JOVER (ed.), *Iglesias, confesiones..*, cit., pp. 37-38.

[87] "Dans le discours catholique sur l'Europe, on perçoit souvent comme une nostalgie: celle d'un passé glorieux où les peuples européens, après avoir élaboré le modèle de civilisation occidentale dans la matrice de la chrétienté médiévale, répandaient cette civilisation à travers le monde". VANDERMEERSH, WEYDERT, *Le catholicisme*, cit., p. 144.

[88] "Quello che si nota avvicinandosi al complesso fenomeno dell'Unione Europea, è la mancanza di una esplicita competenza europea, o a dir meglio comunitaria, in materia religiosa: si ravvisa come esistente un *deficit religioso*, per un verso ampiamente giustificato dalle finalità proprie e dall'esperienza delle Comunità". BUONOMO, *L'Unione Europea...*, cit., p. 350.

[89] "Bisognerebbe... che l'assenza nella maggior parte degli Stati membri di un regime «concordatario» impedisse la realizzazione degli obiettivi comunitari (mercato comune, unione economica e monetaria, politiche e azioni comuni da cui agli artt. 3 e 3A), per legittimare un intervento della Comunità nel settore delle relazioni formali tra Stati e

a question of the substantial inability of a democratic legal system, as only the European one can be, to impose values upon society, whatever these may be.

But as a result of the fact that the future (or the present) European Union cannot have an ideological orientation based on religion that leads it to favour one concrete opinion on the matter, does not lead us to deduce that it cannot assume some of the regulatory powers which, in matters of Ecclesiastical Law, the Member States exercise at the moment. I do not believe that it can assume all of them, not because some remain under the scope of the current members, but because that type of rule will disappear. What I mean to say is that in the long term, it seems improbable to me that certain internal rules of one particular church will be approved by a European Parliament, as happens in the United Kingdom now, or that the church, as is the case of Denmark, is considered part of the Public Administration, or that the judgments of a canonical court have civil effects, as is the case of Italy and Spain, since these seems to be to be an untenable situation in the long term, whether at a Community level or at a national level. In any case, this is an idea relating to the long term and it would be better to start with the present reality.

I shall repeat, in an attempt to order things, the reasons why I believe it is possible to imagine a future European Ecclesiastical Law that will progressively take the place occupied by national Eccelsiastical Laws.

In the first place, there is one reason that is not exclusive to our field, but present in any subject. That is what I would call the expansive vocation of the Law. The purpose of any legal system is to regulate all those issues capable of legal regulation. Or at least to consider that it has national competency to regulate it, even though it may "delegate" its concrete regulation to another regulatory jurisdiction. Using the term coined by ROMANO[90], the European Union has the vocation to set itself up as an "ordinamento giuridico primario". Of course the truth of my assertion will only be tested when the process has concluded and that is still a long way off.

A second factor that enables me to imagine that such European Ecclesiastical Law is possible in general is quoted as evidence to the contrary. I am talking about the afore-mentioned Declaration number 11 appendix to the Treaty of Amsterdam. The standard interpretation of this

---

confessioni religiose (art. 3 B). Il che, francamente, non sembra, allo stato, possibile". MARGIOTTA BROGLIO, *Il fenomeno religioso...*, cit., p. 192

[90] See ROMANO, Santi, *L'ordinamento giuridico*[3], Sansoni, Florence, 1977, passim.

Declaration is that the Union states that issues of Ecclesiastical Law should be regulated at state level and not at Community level. Apart from the fact that such an interpretation is excessive, since in reality what it is referring to is the status of religious denominations and other analogous organisations, which does not in any way exhaust the scope of Ecclesiastical Law, there is a much deeper issue at stake. Of legal philosophy, if you prefer. When the Union states that it respects the status of the denominations that is recognised by national law, it is not saying that it is incompetent to regulate this status, but rather it is saying just the opposite: whilst I am competent to regulate it, I renounce doing so. It does not make any sense to proclaim that it is incompetent to do something if it is essentially incompetent. My interpretation of Declaration number 11 can be summarised by saying that the Union is concerned about the status of the denominations, but is saying, for the time being, that it is not interested.

In fact, and as we have already seen, the European Union has been dealing with certain issues that are typical of Ecclesiastical Law. The Directive relating to matters of television, or Article 40 of the Regulation of May 29, 2000[91], which supposes the recognition of the effects of Canon Law at a Community level, by concordatory means, are examples of that, even though it would be excessive to speak about Community Ecclesiastical Law, there do in fact exist at least some Community rules extending to that area of legal science.

Neither is the religious element indirectly irrelevant at a Community level. From the strange situation of Mount Athos that the Greek treaty of accession respected, to exceptions in matters of application of the hygiene rules in the sacrifice of animals if there are religious rites implicated[92]. It is also becoming involved, although in a parliamentary and police area, in a fundamental issue of Ecclesiastical Law: the concept of religious denomination, since on the various occasions that the European Parliament has alluded to the question of the "new religious movements", it indirectly concludes by giving a definition of denomination.

But we are still at the fledgling stage of this potential European Ecclesiastical Law, and perhaps now is the right time to briefly outline the way in which it will be created. It seems to me that in general, Community Law is being built upon two cornerstones: on the one hand we have the

---

[91] Regulation (EC) n° 1347/2000 of the Council of the European Union.

[92] See, among others, the Council Directive of November 18, 1974 (77/577/EEC) or that of December 22, 1993 (D. 93/119/EC).

idea of "common constitutional traditions" and on the other the "principle of subsidiarity". It seems to me that both ideas reflect the extraordinary realism with which they are attempting to develop Community Law.
You cannot impose a new system of law that is in conflict with the
national legal systems, so it is necessary to search for common factors
between the different legal systems of the Member States. It could be
said that what is currently national law is being transformed into Community law. This would be a simplified interpretation of what the expression "common constitutional traditions" encapsulates. But if it is not
possible to go directly against the national legal systems, nor may Community Law be something prejudicial for the individual citizen, the European Union should make the development of the lives of its citizens
easier, and only act in those areas in which advantages may be derived
from for the individual. That is the idea around which the "principle of
subsidiarity" revolves; that is to say, problems should be resolved at the
hierarchical level most beneficial to achieve that.

Now, it is not enough to simply announce these pillars in order to
achieve the existence of effective Community Law, they have to be implemented in practice: by creating this law. There are two essential meth-
ods being used to achieve this, that are no different to those used at
national levels. On the one hand there is the activity that we could call
legislative, that is the drafting of general legal rules. This method is the
most effective, but should be used with extreme caution, since national
law, like all law, naturally resists change. But together with that, there is
another much slower and more deliberate method of creating Community
Law. I am referring to Community Case Law. The European Court in
Luxembourg may only act by basing its arguments on legal texts of a
legislative nature, but, and the examples are numerous, it draws certain
conclusions from them that are not always evident at first sight. I believe
that the Case Law of that Court is, and will continue to be, an essential
pillar for creating such law.

And what is clear at a general level is also clear at the level of Community Ecclesiastical Law. Independently of what may be advisable,
(we could call it "Community preferences" for a certain model of relationship with the religious phenomenon)[93], it seems clear to me that since

_____

[93] "Les relations Eglises/Institutions européennes... au niveau de la pratique des ces
relations...on peut dire que c'est plus un modèle allemand de relations Eglises-Etat qui pré-
vaut qu'un modèle francais. Les Eglises y sont en effet beaucoup plus reconnues comme
interlocuteurs réguliers et légitimes du pouvoir politique que ce n'est le cas en France".
WILLAUME, Unification européenne..., cit., pp. 46-47.

a common model does not exist for all the Community countries, as we saw previously, it is hard to imagine a certain model constituting a "common constitutional tradition". Numerous features of national models cannot be considered to belong to this common tradition[94]. In reality, I believe that the only feature common to the constitutions of the Member States in religious matters is the idea of religious freedom. But a certain concept of religious freedom which results from multisecular evolution. Religious freedom that implies the establishing of relations to facilitate co-operation and not confrontations with the religious denominations, but that, simultaneously is situated within the cultural sphere that we could call pluralistic laicism[95]. National legal systems tend not to favour or discriminate on religious grounds, and tend to value the religious phenomenon, without that resulting in any undervaluing of those who do not form a part of a religious group. This is the norm and this is what the basis for Community Ecclesiastical Law will be, not as now, a tendency, but rather as the culmination of a multisecular process.

If the idea of "common constitutional traditions" is translated to the field of Ecclesiastical Law, it does not seem particularly problematic to me and in all probability will culminate in being based around the idea of religious freedom as I have defined it above, without that presenting any particularly serious problems. However, I think that the practical formulation of the "principle of subsidiarity" will be considerably more complex.

It would seem that Declaration number 11 of the Treaty of Amsterdam had resolved this issue to the extent that we can deduce that we are faced with a power exercised at a national level. I do not believe that things are so simple.

---

[94] "L'unica tradizione costituzionale comune ai paesi membri è il riconoscimento dell'indipendenza sostanziale dei culti. Non possono, infatti, essere considerati principi generali del diritto comunitario né il sistema di bilateralità delle fonti che regolano in alcuni Stati il trattamento di Chiese, confessioni, associazioni ecc. religiose, né il carattere di enti di diritto pubblico che altri Stati riconoscono ad alcune confessioni religiose, né la previsione di finanziamenti statali, diretti o indiretti, per i culti, né il diritto degli Stati di controllare la vita interna delle chiese né quello delle chiese di vedersi protette penalmente dal vilipendio della religione". MARGIOTTA BROGLIO, Francesco, *L'evoluzione dei rapporti tra Chiesa e Stati durante il pontificato di Giovanni Paolo II. Tavola rotonda*, "QDPE", 1999-1, p. 19.

[95] "La sistesi che sembra possibile operare tra i diversi elementi sottolineati articola in due momenti fondamentali le «tradizioni costituzionali comuni» in materia di libertà religiosa: il primo momento riguarda la collocazione del diritto di libertà religiosa nell'orizzonte della laicità europea (intesa come espressione del principio di pluralismo democratico); il secondo riguarda la cooperazione tra stato e confessioni che tende ad imporsi come atteggiamento trasversale ai diversi sistemi nazionali di relazione tra confessioni e poteri pubblici". VENTURA, *La laicità...*, cit., p. 105.

As I have already pointed out, a good deal of Community Ecclesiastical Law will be created by indirect means, in the sense that it is not a case
of provisions that try to regulate the religious phenomenon directly and
comprehensively, but rather of rules with a different objective, but which
still influence the religious phenomenon. A first example of this could be
at the level of taxation. This is a field in which national powers clearly
prevail over Community powers, but in which the process of unification
is absolutely unstoppable. In a system with complete freedom of movement, residence, etc., both of legal entities and individuals, it is impossible to maintain distinct tax systems, since that would cause migratory
flows of companies and individuals towards the most beneficial tax areas,
which would end up distorting the trade systems. It is clear that taxation
enters into the realms of religious denominations, so this hypothetical
Community Tax Law will end up influencing Ecclesiastical Law.

A typical area of co-operation with the churches is that of the conser-
vation of historical and artistic heritage. It is not impossible to imagine a
European system of co-operation in this field, which would require,
among other things, the naming of a spokesman, if it does not want to fall
into a type of neojurisdictionalism[96], and it would probably have to operate through spokesmen at supranational levels.

One final example to examine in which it is impossible to imagine the
application of the principle of subsidiarity in the sense that all Ecclesiastical Law will come under national authorities is the phenomenon of the
new religious movements.

I am convinced that there is co-operation between the police forces of
the different Member States for the purpose of exchanging information
relating to what we could call the "destructive sects". This is an issue,
as I have already mentioned, that goes right to the core of Ecclesiastical
Law: the definition of the concept of religious denomination. When there
is a European police force, when certain mechanisms exist to determine
what is a religious denomination, all of this will be carried out at a Community level.

If European Law is being built based on legislation and case law, the
same processes will be used to build Ecclesiastical Law. For the time being
very little exists at a regulatory level, but denominations are starting to be

---

[96] "La selettività della cooperazione implica il rischio di un giurisdizionalismo
pluriconfessionista, di trattamenti differenziati palesemente discriminatori, di indebite
penalizzazioni delle minoranze e implica soprattutto la necessità dell'identificazione... del
soggetto confessionale". Ibidem, p. 114.

involved, albeit very tentatively, in the Community process[97], and this will end by them achieving a "religious" presence at the regulatory level. However, in the short and medium term, I believe that the case law method will be the most effective one to create this Community Ecclesiastical Law. Some steps have been taken, but this is not the time to analyse them.

To summarise, I am aware of not having proven anything, but I believe it is a case of something more than a mere personal intuition; European Ecclesiastical Law will come into existence and its central feature will be the idea of a religious freedom that is derived from common traditions, and which, upon their separation from national structures, will result in greater respect for religious equality, since national traditions tend to benefit certain churches more than others.

Will the concordatory institution play a part in this new Law? We will now deal with this question.

*

*   *

The starting point to try to give a rhetorical answer to such a question is perhaps to remind ourselves of two important facts. In the first place, the Catholic Church has always had a marked presence in the world of international relations, but perhaps at the present it is finding it more difficult than in the past to combine this presence with the fact that its objective is strictly religious[98]. And secondly, relations between the Holy See and the European Union have not followed a homogeneous and consistent process over the years[99].

Probably both facts are connected with the question now before us. The European Communities were created with clearly economic

---

[97] "Malgré l'absence d'une base juridique, la Commission européenne, à l'initiative des Presidents Delors et Santer, a commencé depuis quelques années à développer et à entretenir des relations avec les Églises chrétiennes et d'autres communautés religieuses. Ces relations informelles, mais néanmoins régulières, se sont nouées pour l'essentiel à la demande des Églises et des communautés religieuses". JANSEN, *Dialogue entre la Commission...*, cit., p. 81.

[98] "Se la Chiesa è stata, sostanzialmente, sempre presente nella realtà internazionale, bisogna verificare come, nell'attuale assetto giuridico della comunità internazionale, le sia consentita di operare senza confondersi con la società a fini politici". PETRONCELLI HUBLER, *Chiesa cattolica...*, cit., p. 112.

[99] "La singolarità del rapporto tra Santa Sede e processi di integrazione europea sta nel fatto che essa si è sviluppato in modo nettamente disomogeneo, in relazione alle diverse fasi storiche e alle specifiche istituzioni comunitarie". CARDIA, *La soggettività internazionale...*, cit., pp. 316-317.

objectives; perhaps the Holy See did not manage to grasp that behind this objective there was a vocation for a certain political union, and thus it did not take an interest in a phenomenon that was so distant from its own religious objectives as economic issues are. It was only once the process had advanced considerably that it started to show an interest. Of course, nowadays we have every right to speak about relations between the Holy See and the European Union, but that is not what we wish to analyse, rather whether it is possible to imagine that such relations can be channelled through a concordat.

Before starting to evaluate the grounds on which such a potential concordat would be made possible or not, it is necessary to look at one fact: the concordat is not an institution that can be considered to be widespread within the Union, and therefore, extendible to the imprecise world of "common constitutional traditions", since the majority of the Member States do not have such an institution; nor is it a case of something unknown, since at least one-third of Community countries have signed such an agreement.

I will attempt to outline first of all, the reasons that will make the idea of a European Concordat difficult or even impossible. I will classify them in three groups: firstly, a potential lack of interest of the Holy See, secondly, what we might call political hurdles and lastly, technical reasons.

We have already seen how the attitude of the pontiffs towards the process of integration have not been uniform and have not been enthusiastic towards it[100]. As regards the present pontiff, he would seem to prefer a larger Europe which respects the present nations[101]. In principle, the pontiffs' lack of enthusiasm towards the process of European unification seems totally logical, since it is highly likely that the relations would not be based at a European Union – Holy See level, but rather a European Union – European Church level[102], which would thus mean that the Holy

---

[100] "La petite Europe supranationale vers laquelle semblent se porter les faveurs de l'ultime Pie XII ne sera pas celle de son successeur, Jean XXIII, qui marquera une certaine distance à l'égard des nouvelles institutions et appellera, dans l'unique message du pontificat consacré à l'Europe, à construire «une communauté vraie», «non pas close sur un cercle élargi d'intérêts égoïstes, mais ouvert aux intérêts universels et supérieurs de l'humanité» (message aux Semaines sociales de France de Strasbourg, juillet 1962)". CHENAUX, Le Saint-Siège…, cit., p. 59.

[101] "Il Papa [GIOVANNI PAOLO II] non si è mai espresso sulle varie formule possibili di integrazione europea, lasciandone l'elaborazione alle parti interessate. Ha invece chiesto che il processo rispetti le identità nazionali e, in particorare, il patrimonio culturale e religioso nel quale esse affondano le proprie radici". MIGLIORE, Celestino, Relazioni tra la Santa Sede e gli stati europei, "IE", 11, 1999, p. 391.

[102] "Quali siano le sollecitazioni che giungono alle autorità confessionalli…[l']esigenza…. che gli interlocutori religiosi… abbiano una dimensione strettamente europea e

See would lose some of its importance in the process, thereby supporting the reappearance of the phenomenon of the XVIII century, not of national Churches but of a European Church.

We cannot properly speak about the lack of interest of the present pontiff in relation to Europe. What has probably happened is that during previous pontificates, the creation of a united Europe seemed far enough away for it not to be considered dangerous, and there were even some statements made in favour of a federal Europe[103]; the thoughts of Pope John Paul II perhaps show a fear of this strong European Community, in which Catholicism would be on the same level as other religions. And this, without underestimating the fact that the previous pontiffs who had made declarations about the process were Italian, and so belonged to a country that has been a member since the beginning of the European Communities, while the present pontiff was born in a country that continues to be extracommunitarian. A Europe that goes beyond the limits of the Community fits better with the ideas of the present pontiff, who wishes to overcome the Europe that was created in Yalta[104]. This Europe that rose from the ashes of the Second World War was not prejudicial for the citizens of what is today the European Union, but it was prejudicial for those citizens in Eastern Europe, which include Poland. This interest in a more extensive but not a federal nor a supranational Europe is thus understandable by this pontiff in particular[105], who suffered the effects of Yalta. Dedicated towards the construction of this other Europe, he would have left the Community process in the hands of others[106].

---

soprattuto che dialoghino con l'Unione in quanto organizzazioni europee". VENTURA, *La laicità...*, cit., p. 202.

[103] "Pie XII... n'avait pas manqué à plusieurs reprises de marquer son attachement aux thèses fédéralistes et souhaité ouvertement le dépassement des souverainetés nationales au nom du bien commun". CHENAUX, *Le Saint-Siège...*, cit., p. 61.

[104] "Giovanni Paolo II ha costantemente posto il problema di un recupero europeo della sovranità confiscata dopo il 1945 e di un superamento della logica di Yalta con la costruzione della «casa» e della «famiglia dei popoli europei»". CARDIA, *La soggettività internazionale...*, cit., pp. 317-318.

[105] "Un interesse che progressivamente non ha più privilegiato l'Europa comunitaria -la CEE- ma si è allargato sempre più all'Europa dall'Atlantico agli Urali, con la partecipazione alla CSCE e, soprattutto, con la linea politica manifestatasi prepotentemente con il pontificato di Giovanni Paolo II". BARBERINI, Giovanni, *La presenza della Santa Sede nella politica internazionale. Introduzione ai lavori del Seminario*, en BARBERINI (ed.), *La politica internazionale...*, cit., p. 11.

[106] "Tout se passe comme si le Vatican de Jean Paul II préférait laisser aux évêques et aux laïcs le soin de gérer l'acquis communautaire a fin de mieux se concentrer sur ce que paraît être l'objectif fondamental du pontificat: la réconciliation de l'Europe tout entière avec elle-même et avec sa propre histoire". CHENAUX, *Le Saint-Siège...*, cit., p. 66.

But although the Holy See is probably not very enthusiastic towards the Community process, and that particularly in the event that, as I believe, it will end up by becoming a unitary political entity, this does not mean that it ignores the process and rejects being present to the extent of its possibilities. We must not forget that the Holy See, at least since the pontificate of JOHN XXIII, has opted to be present on as many international stages as possible[107] and, obviously the European Community is one of the main ones.

The most evident formal presence of the Holy See is the existence for more than three decades (December 10, 1970) of an Apostolic Nuncio as a representative of the Holy See in the European Community, which is the only case of an Apostolic Nuncio accredited by an institution that is not a state.

If the figure of the Nuncio in the Community is unusual, so is that of the Commissio Episcopatuum Communitatis Europaeae (COMECE). This is not a representative organ of the Holy See, that much is obvious, but neither is it an Episcopal conference, nor even a co-operative entity between Episcopal conferences, but rather episcopacies[108]. Unlike other co-operative entities between episcopacies and Episcopal conferences, its specific objective is to form relations with an interstate entity for those matters deriving from the existence of the Community itself, and not to go beyond those bounds[109]. That is to say that here we have an entity whose only reason to exist is derived from the existence of the European Community[110].

---

[107] "[Da Giovanni XXIII] sia prevalsa la scelta a favore di una presenza generalizzata della Santa Sede in tutti gli organismi e i congressi internazionali quasi prescindendo dalle materie che vi si trattano, e dallo «specifico» che essa può apportare in quanto órgano di governo della Chiesa universale". CARDIA, La soggettività internazionale…, cit., p. 314.

[108] "Si tratta di un organismo di collegamento organico e di cooperazione pastorale non, propriamente, tra le «Conferenze Episcopali» ma tra gli «episcopati» dei Paesi dell'Unione Europea". NICORA, Attilio, La Commissione degli episcopati della Comunità Europea, "IE", 11, 1999, p.414.

[109] "[Gli] organismi di collegamento tra conferenze non si concepiscono come partners o interlocutori di correspondenti organizzazioni di carattere intergovernativo, con l'unica, interessante eccezione costituita dalla Commissione degli episcopati della Comunità europea (COM.E.C.E.). Tale Commissione, infatti, non si propone, come il Consiglio delle conferenze episcopali europee, di realizzare una collaborazione di carattere globale che investa tutte le esigenze pastorali comuni ai paesi che non fanno parte, ma si interessa esclusivamente dei problemi derivanti dall'esistenza e dall'attività della Comunità europea". FELICIANI, Giorgio, Il ruolo delle Conferenze episcopali nella politica internazionale della Santa Sede, in BARBERINI (ed.), La politica internazionale…, cit., p. 125.

[110] "Nella struttura e nelle competenze… la COM.E.C.E. si distingue dagli altri organismi di cooperazione episcopale, nettamente caratterizzati dall'esigenza di una

Apart from these two institutional presences of the Catholic Church in the European Community, there are others at a different level[111]. Therefore, the presence of the Catholic Church is established at two levels: an institutional level and that of Catholic organisations[112].

I do not believe that the presence of the Holy See (or of the Catholic Church) in the Union can be exclusively justified by its vocational support for the process. It does not depend on that. It depends on its wish to be present in order to achieve better treatment for itself. Without doubt it would like a "Catholic" Europe[113] to be established, but it probably appreciates that that is not possible. I would say that more than participating in the process, what it intends is to be present when the process is concluded.

In summary, although the institutional Catholic Church is probably not particularly enthusiastic about the unification process of the Union, with the characteristic realism of centuries of historical hindsight, it has set up the basis, apart from its own influence during the process, for being present when decisions are taken. This is not to be involved in the process of decision taking, but rather to be a spokesman for those who have taken them.

Perhaps a European concordat is unrealistic, but at least the elements for it to happen exist: a political authority (the EU) and bodies that represent the Catholic Church (the Nuncio and the COMECE) recognised by that political authority.

But if the initial lack of interest towards the European Community is not an obstacle for the possible attainment of a Community concordat, since the Church has institutionally placed itself in such a way that it is recognised as a spokesman for it, then perhaps the political objections of the Union, on the other hand, will carry more weight.

coesione degli episcopati di fronte a problemi socio-culturali territorialmente definiti. Qui, la ragione del lavoro comune è integrata dai problemi pastorali, che può proporre una realtà politica ed economica di tipo sovranazionale, e dall'esigenza di studiare quali proposte di dialogo si diano con essa, per gli episcopati e per la S.Sede". PETRONCELLI HÜBLER, *Chiesa cattolica...*, cit., pp. 217-218.

[111] See a relation of those organisations, not only the Catholic ones, in JANSEN, *Dialogue entre la Commission...*, cit., p. 82.

[112] "I molteplici volti della rappresentanza cattolica presso l'Unione sembrano oggi comporre un sistema a doppio binario: relazioni diplomatiche, da un lato, e dialogo tra Unione e varie organizzazioni cattoliche, in quanto espressioni della società civile". VENTURA, *La laicità...*, cit., p. 213.

[113] "The presence of the Holy See at the various European Organisations is a sign of its commitment to support the eventual unification of Europe on the basis of those spiritual and moral principles which constitute the common heritage of European countries and the backbone of European culture and civilisation". CARDINALE, *The Holy See...*, cit., p. 263.

The fact that this would be discriminatory to believers of other religions is one argument against the possibility of such a type of concordat, as this would go against the spirit of the European Convention and the common constitutional traditions[114]. I do not think that the first objection is insurmountable, since I do not believe that religious equality is respected to any less degree in some concordatory countries (Italy, Germany, Spain, etc.), than it is in some non-concordatory countries (Greece, Denmark, etc.). The second objection carries much more weight.

Any attempt to homogenise Church-State relations at a Community level would be extremely problematic[115], and it would be difficult to manage the incorporation of Ecclesiastical Law institutions from one country to the whole of the Union. Should any such homogenisation occur, it would more than likely be the result of the inverse process, whereby national institutions would be eliminated. The elimination of a certain system of financing (Germany), the elimination of the idea of a national Church (Denmark, Finland), the elimination of constitutional references to religious dogmas (Greece, Republic of Ireland), and the elimination of the concordatory system itself.

There would not only be political opposition of a general nature, but also that deriving from the other religious denominations. If the mere fact of European integration perhaps means some risk of the denominations losing their identity, especially in the cases in which they are closely tied to a certain State[116], the idea of creating a specific instrument of relations for one of them, as would be the case of the concordat, then I think the only thing that would happen would be the rejection of the rest.

---

[114] "La... prospettiva di un «maxiconcordato» dell'Unione con la sola Chiesa cattolica, si rivela ancora una volta impraticabile in quanto violerebbe anche il principio generale del diritto comunitario sul rispetto dei diritti fondamentali (così l'uguaglianza dei culti e dei loro fedeli senza distinzione di religione) garantiti della Convenzione europea e risultanti dalle tradizioni costituzionali comuni degli Stati membri". MARGIOTTA BROGLIO, *Il fenomeno religioso...*, cit., pp. 191-192.

[115] "La construction européenne... ne comporte aucun programme visant une quelconque homogénéisation des relations Eglises/Etat dans les différents pays. Ces relations sont tellement liées aux spécifités historiques, culturelles et religieuses de chaque nation que vouloir une homogénéisation dans ce domaine risquerait d'être interprété comme une tentative d'uniformisation portant directement atteinte à l'identité de chaque société nationale". WILLAUME, *Unification européenne...*, cit., p. 44.

[116] "Les orthodoxes grecs...voient dans l'intégration européenne un risque de dissolution de l'identité orthodoxe, l'Europe étant ici identifiée à «la civilisation matérialiste anglo-saxonne»...Des pasteurs protestants des pays du Nord ont aussi tendance à voir dans l'Europe de Bruxelles la main de Rome, réactivant la peur protestante d'une «Europe vaticane»". Ibidem, pp. 39-40.

I would even dare state that this foreseeable political opposition to a concordatory formula would perhaps make a European concordat impossible. It seems extremely unlikely to me that countries in which a certain church receives more favourable treatment than the Catholic Church, would be prepared to accept at a Community level that the Catholic Church has its own special instrument of relations, which, at the least, would be a formal show of favourable treatment for Catholicism. Even less likely would be that these countries would accept a concordat, if you take into account that it is not out of the question that the Community process means that such countries would have to alter their systems of Ecclesiastical Law precisely so that no specific denomination received favourable treatment. Naturally, not only those countries with a clearly privileged denomination (Denmark, Greece, etc.), or with, at the least, one formally privileged one (the United Kingdom), would be opposed to a European concordat, but in all probability France would as well (in spite of the situation in the Eastern "Départments") We might also imagine that those religious denominations other than the Catholic Church would be especially fervent in their opposition to those potential agreements.

And it is not only on political grounds that would make the existence of a concordatory regime at a European level difficult to attain, but also it is worth looking now at the possible technical reasons that would be in opposition to it.

The list of technical difficulties to achieve a concordatory process at a European level is extensive[117]. However, I feel that these difficulties can be divided into two clear groups. In the first place, one of background: the incompetence of the European Community in the matter; and secondly what we could call practical difficulties of a technical origin.

It is clear that neither the usual content of a concordat is found among the objectives of the texts that regulate the European Union in the current

---

[117] "La strada di un «approccio concordatario» europeo per garantire la libertà religiosa soprattutto nei suoi aspetti collettivi (essenzialmente ecclesiastici) non mi pare percorribile, sia perché riserverebbe a solo alcuni, pochissimi soggetti abilitati a stipulare convenzioni internazionali la possibilità di «collegarsi» con l'Unione Europea, sia perché le tradizionali materie «concordatarie» non trovano posto tra gli obiettivi e le competenze della Comunità, sia perché tale approccio dovrebbe essere oggetto di una esplicita proposta di un paese membro o della Commisione inteso a modificare i trattati con le procedure previste dal diritto comunitario. Quello che puó rivelarsi necessario per raggiungere gli scopi della Comunità é la difesa della libertà di coscienza, di religione o credenza non la sistemazione di rapporti con le confessioni religiose in quanto tali potendo essi soli legittimare una sorte di «maxiconcordato» europeo. MARGIOTTA BROGLIO, Francesco, *La tutela della libertà religiosa nell'Unione Europea*, in CASTRO JOVER (ed.), *Iglesia, confesiones...*, cit., pp. 75-76.

state, nor is there room for the concordatory techniques[118]. However, I do not believe that we should view those texts as fixed. It is clear that any regulatory text may be modified, despite having to manoeuvre around many political and technical difficulties, and this is the same whether it is Community Law or national laws. Naturally, in order for such a reform to occur it is necessary to have a political perception that such a reform is necessary. It is highly likely that this political will does not exist, yet that is not a technical question, but rather a political one, and we have already looked at that previously.

In respect of the practical difficulties of a technical origin, one of them is that the European Community as such, has not signed international treaties that have a similar level of importance to the concordats, such that it does not seem very likely that concordats would begin to take that route.

The second difficulty derives from the fact that the Holy See should sign a concordat, and the singular nature of that party under International Law would only cause obstacles in the execution of such agreements. On the one hand, the Church tends to place itself on a supranational level rather than an international one; to this effect the following words by PAUL VI on October 4, 1965 to the United Nations General Assembly are very significant: "Nous serions tentés de dire que votre caracteristique reflète en quelque sorte dans l'ordre temporel ce que Notre Eglise Catholique veut être dans l'ordre spirituel, unique et universelle. On ne peut rien concevoir de plus élevé sur le plan naturel, dans la construction idéologique de l'humanité"[119]. The Church works at a universal level, as

---

[118] "Del tutto non percorribile... risulta la strada... di un «approccio concordatario» a livello di Unione Europea che, a parte la esclusiva limitazione alla Chiesa cattolica unica abilitata a stipulare convenzioni internazionali, non trova posto alcuno tra gli obiettivi delle Comunità. Difficile anche sostenere che il sistema concordatario di relazioni con le Chiese possa rientrare tra gli obiettivi di cui agli artt. 2 e 3 del Trattato istitutivo o nelle previsioni dei successivi articoli o nell'ambito delle politiche comuni in materia di relazioni esterne (art.11 del Trattato sull'Unione) o immaginare che l'azione comunitaria in materia di rapporti con le religioni possa rivelarsi necessaria per raggiungere gli scopi della Comunità e, quindi, legittimare una sorta di maxiconcordato con la Chiesa di Roma avente come riferimento territoriale quello dell'Unione (art. 34, o e art. 308, Trattato istitutivo)". MARGIOTTA BROGLIO, L'evoluzione dei rapporti..., cit., p. 19; "Non si potrebbe certo far rientrare quella concordataria tra le competenze esplicite della Comunità, che possono essere ampliate, «Quando un'azione... risulti necessaria per raggiungere, nel funzionamento del mercato comune, uno degli scopi della Comunità, senza che il presente Trattato abbia previsto i poteri d'azione a tal uopo richiesti», con deliberazione unanime del Consiglio, su proposta della Commissione e udito il Parlamento europeo (art. 235 Trattato della Comunità)". IDEM, Il fenomeno religioso..., cit., p. 188.

[119] AAS, 1965, p. 888.

if it were a kind of United Nations at a spiritual level. It does not seem that that is the most desirable position in order to negotiate with the European Union, which works at a regional level. This formal superiority does not help negotiations of that class.

This difficulty could perhaps be insurmountable, if, as it has stated, the Union will only undertake negotiations on matters relating to concordats in the field of associations at a European level, and no higher[120].

And all the above without forgetting the difficulties of placing the Holy See at the level of International Law, since it cannot simply be considered as a representative body of a State[121], and should this be the case, it would further complicate the process, since it would not be understood why an extracommunity state should come in and regulate the religious freedom of European citizens.

In summary, I appreciate that although the technical grounds may be overcome, the possibility that a concordat in the classical sense might be signed, is highly remote. Now, are there any grounds for believing that things could work out differently?

The process of European unification revolving around the European Union represents a kind of historical revolution in the legal-political structures of our continent. The concordatory history shows that many concordats are the result of profound legal-political changes, that require Church and State relations to adapt to the new situation[122]. It would not be surprising if, in an advanced phase of the process of European unification, the Catholic Church should try to reach some kind of agreement in order to position itself in this new reality.

It should also not be forgotten that the system of agreements with the religious denominations is very far from being anomalous to the traditions of several Community countries, so it is not unforeseeable that they should draw on this kind of technique at a Community level[123].

---

[120] "Tale collegamento... sarebbe formalizzabile solo con associazioni e fondazioni nazionali (e non con le... «case madri»)". MARGIOTTA BROGLIO, *Il fattore religioso...*, cit., p. 1274.

[121] "Nè l'esistenza dell'antico Stato pontificio prima del 1870, nè la creazione dello Stato della Città del Vaticano possono fornire una spiegazione sufficiente di questo stato di fatto che nessuno può negare; l'intervento della Chiesa nella vita internazionale, tra l'altro anche con i concordati". CASORIA, *Concordati e ordinamento...*, cit., p. 75.

[122] "Tutte le risoluzioni concordatarie, di ogni epoca, all'investigazione storico-critica dichiarano sempre la medesima motivazione: la Chiesa ricercava i concordati per adeguarsi a situazioni post-rivoluzionarie e di riassetto politico-costituzionale degli Stati". CILIENTO, Lorenzo, *Concordato e diritto comune*, in COPPOLA, R. (ed.), *Gli strumenti contituzionali per l'eserzicio della libertà religiosa*, Giuffrè, Milan, 1982, p. 100.

I have already mentioned that it does not seem that unlikely to me that at an advanced phase, the European Union could end up establishing European Ecclesiastical Law. A fundamental element of this Law would be the positions that the religious denominations occupied within this legal system. In the recent history of democratic countries, the idea that the rules on a particular subject cannot be imposed by Parliament, but that the participation of the individuals affected by them is necessary, has become more widespread. The religious denominations are not alien to this process[124]. Within European political systems, mechanisms of co-operation between the political and the religious authorities are becoming more widespread, not necessarily at the highest level of the respective organisations, but at all levels[125]. There is nothing stopping the Catholic Church from acting in collaboration with other religious denominations in these negotiation and agreement processes between political and religious authorities[126].

Having looked at the panorama, I do not think it impossible that after a preliminary process of nominating spokesmen, the European Community could evaluate the possibility of establishing relations with a series of religious denominations with bases in Europe, provided that they strive to unify their positions; a relationship that would possibly lead to a framework of activity being established. Of course, it would not be an agreement under the scope of International Law, and not because other mechanisms cannot be found to "internationalise" the process[127], but

---

[123] "Non dovrebbe essere esclusa a priori la possibilità di accordi con le confessioni a livello comunitario, proprio perchè il punto di partenza per non pochi Stati membri è il sistema di concertazione". MARTIN DE AGAR, *Passato e presente...*, cit., p. 659.

[124] "Gli odierni rapporti pattizi che gli Stati tendono ad instaurare con le Confessioni religiose, vengono da taluno ascritti al filone della «partecipazione politica» tipica delle moderne democrazie; in virtù della quale si cerca di spezzare il tradizionale circuito della «sovranità/rappresentanza», in favore del coinvolgimento dei vari gruppi di interessi organizzati nei procesi di formazione delle scelte e della stessa legislazione". TOZZI, Valerio, *Pactos y diversidad de fines del Estado y de las confesiones religiosas*, "ADEE", IV, 1988, p. 63.

[125] "Il modello separatista va... riletto alla luce della disponibilità degli stati alla rinnovata politica concordataria della Santa Sede, dell'estensione del sistema bilaterale a nuove confessioni..., ma soprattutto della accentuata e diffusa tendenza alla cooperazione tra autorità pubbliche (ai vari livelli) e autorità religiose". VENTURA, *La laicità...*, cit., pp. 110-111.

[126] "La Iglesia puede concurrir al mundo de la tutela jurídica del fenómeno religioso en unión de otras confesiones religiosas". DE LA HERA, *El futuro del sistema...*, cit., p. 19.

[127] "Per le.....confessioni religiose [diverse dalla Chiesa cattolica]... si dà, di certo, soltanto la possibilità di operare quali organizzazioni internazionali non governative". PETRONCELLI HÜBLER, *Chiesa cattolica...*, cit., p. 100.

quite simply because it is not necessary and probably because it is not possible, since the Union would not accept the issue to be couched in terms of negotiations between sovereign entities.

The concordatory reality has changed during the course of history, from agreement between absolute monarchies to becoming international texts ratified by parliamentary democracies. If my intuition is correct, then we are faced with a new phase in this evolutionary process.

Any changes would be radical, but not essential. The Church would not act as a sovereign entity, it should co-ordinate its activities with other denominations, it would not operate at the level of International Law, etc. But all of these are mere instruments used during the course of history. I imagine that what is essential from a concordat is to try to establish the position of the Church at the core of the legal system, relying for that on both the State and the Church. If this is what is needed, this agreement between the European Union and the religious denominations, with a format that I am unable to imagine, would respect the essence of the concordatory institution.

It is not clear in what way the Holy See would act in this process, perhaps it would be necessary to add an additional function to the two traditional ones in the field of agreements, and as well as being the representative of the State of Vatican City and of the Universal Church[128], it may also have to act as co-ordinator of the episcopacies of the Community countries through the COMECE, or as spokesperson with other denominations in "representation" of the said episcopacies.

It may well be that this agreement between a series of denominations and the European Union, justified on the basis of the vocation of the latter to attend to the needs of its citizens[129], requires in turn, for its practical application, some subsequent agreements to further develop the initial agreements. In the area of the concordats with Member States, this format

---

[128] "L'État de la Cité du Vatican a aussi adhéré officiellement aux nombreuses conventions internationales... Dans tous ces actes, le Saint-Siège n'est intervenu qu'en tant qu'organe de l'État du Vatican... Il n'est pas besoin de faire remarquer que des accords de ce genre sont totalement différents des concordats dans lesquels le Pontifice figure à titre de Chef de l'Église universelle". WAGNON, *Concordat et Droit...*, cit., n. 2, p. 62.

[129] "La funzione degli accordi tra lo stato e le chiese debba appunto essere quella di supplire la naturale incapacità del primo di strutturare ed articolare in modo operativo l'appagamento degli interessi religiosi, ed in via congiunta di ridurre la difficoltà od impossibilità delle seconde (se non altro per la atipicità delle strutture ordinamentali costitutive) di organizzare in modo adeguato le proprie attività, di esplicitare tutte le originarie competenze, di predisporre tutti i servizi mirati a tal fine". CASUSCELLI, *Libertà religiosa...*, cit., p. 95.

is becoming ever more frequent. These types of agreement can be justified nowadays on the basis of their increased flexibility compared with the concordatory instrument, which is necessarily slow in its negotiations and approval[130]. It is not infrequent in this type of agreement that different administrative bodies participate, both on behalf of the Church and of the State. One example in relation to my own country is enough to appreciate how such a mechanism of "cascade agreements" can operate. Catholic aid in hospitals is recognised as a right in an agreement made between the Spanish State and the Holy See[131], that is laid down in an agreement signed between the Secretaries of State for Justice, for Health and for Consumer Affairs and the Chairman of the Episcopal Conference "duly authorised by the Holy See"[132], which, in turn, is laid down by means of a new agreement between the Director General of the National Health Service and the Chairman of the Episcopal Pastoral Commission "on behalf of the Spanish Episcopal Conference"[133], but since a large part of the health powers are currently exercised by the regional political authorities that are called "comunidades autónomas", the real exercise of such rights of religious aid has required new agreements to be made between the self-governing regions and the bishops of those regions. I could provide further example, but it seems unnecessary for these purposes.

The hypothesis that I am proposing could be formulated in the following way. Perhaps the European Union will end up making an agreement with a group of religious denominations, either of a comprehensive nature or in order to resolve a specific problem. The second option seems more likely to me. I do think it absurd to foresee that, should the creation of a European Armed Force occur, the way in which chaplains are

---

[130] "Accordi più agibili, semplificati che di materia in materia, di momento in momento consentano di rilevare gli effettivi interessi religiosi della comunità nel loro mutevole divenire per approntare quegli strumenti in grado di comporre in modo democratico tensioni e conflitti di lealtà di cui l'individuo si fa portatore, per realizzare una maturazione ed una liberazione consapevole del singolo attraverso lo specifico, puntuale rilievo della sua personale responsabilità di scelta nei confronti delle contrastanti regole di condotta di cui è destinatario". CASUSCELLI, *Concordato...*, cit., pp. 129-130.

[131] Art.IV, Acuerdo de 3 de enero de 1979, entre el Estado Español y la Santa Sede, sobre Asuntos Jurídicos.

[132] Orden de 20 de diciembre de 1985 por la que se dispone la publicación del Acuerdo sobre asistencia religiosa en los Centros hospitalanos públicos ("Boletín Oficial del Estado", 21 de diciembre)

[133] Convenio de 23 de abril de 1986 sobre asistencia religiosa católica en los Centros hospitalarios del Instituto Nacional de la Salud ("Boletín de la Conferencia Episcopal Española", 10, abril – junio 1986)

attached to that body would be negotiated with a joint body of religious denominations. But the practical reality of the situation perhaps would require individual agreements with each of the denominations. In the case of the Catholic Church, it would perhaps be essential to negotiate with the COMECE, which "would represent" the national episcopacies and who would be the ones to provide the resources for these chaplians. In the recent past, it has often been pointed out that in concordatory matters, it is necessary to count on the national episcopacies, but without defining the way in which they should participate[134], and all with extreme caution. In the hypothesis that has enabled me to set out the problem, it is exactly the opposite. What would the function of the Holy See be?

It would probably participate in the negotiation process of this, what we could call "the framework agreement" and which would establish the general guidelines, in the example given, of the attachment of chaplains to the Armed Forces. But, would it be prepared to act on an equal footing with the representatives of the rest of the denominations? Would the European Union accept negotiating with a group of denominations, but where one of them is represented by an entity endowed with international subjectivity? Would the Union accept negotiating, for the effects of creating legal rules of application within its territory, with an entity with powers that exceed this territorial scope? Could an agreement in which one of the negotiating parties, the religious denominations, endowed with international subjectivity, work under the scope of International Law?

But there are probably more uncertainties in the case of what we might call the "development process" of the "framework agreement". Let us turn to the example given above: A European Armed Force and an agreement with the religious denominations whereby chaplains are attached to the former. It is easy to imagine that the Holy See would not participate directly in this agreement. In all probability, the practical application of this type of agreement would require negotiating the way in which these chaplains would be provided for each denomination. This would be the development agreement. In the specific case of Catholic chaplains, a common method of structuring it is by means of the Military ordinariates, of

---

[134] "Un épiscopat national ne pourra guère faire figure d'interlocuteur valable dans de négociations concordataires par manque de véritable indépendance vis à vis du pouvoir civil; de toute façon l'accord qu'il signerait ne pourrait bénéficier de la garantie d'ordre international attachée aux seuls accords diplomatiques. Ceci dit, il résulte nèanmoins des principes inaugurés par Vatican II que l'épiscopat d'un pays ne pourra plus désormais être tenu à l'ecart des négociations concordataries, mais qu'il devra y être activement associé". WAGNON, L'institution..., cit., p. 16.

which there are several dozen established among which are included nine of the Member States of the European Union: Austria, Belgium, France, Germany, the United Kingdom, Italy, the Netherlands, Portugal and Spain. It would come as no great surprise to find that this model would be chosen to provide Catholic chaplains to this potential European Armed Force. Although the creation of this "personal diocese" formally corresponds to the Holy See and, therefore, would be a question of a unilateral decision; in the reality of the example quoted, it would be an evolutionary process, probably agreed under this "framework agreement". We would find ourselves faced with a very strange concept in comparison with tradition: an agreement not at an international level, the negotiation of which would not necessarily include the Holy See and whose evolution would require the participation of the Holy See and very possibly negotiations between the latter and the European Union, who may well adopt a concordatory formula.

Of course, the Holy See has already negotiated and concluded other agreements with the European Union, at the time of the introduction of the Euro as the single European currency[135], but in such cases represented by the State of the Vatican City and should not be taken as a precedent for a potential European concordat. We are working on a different level that does not allow over simplistic answers[136], since the reality of the European Union is complex and prone to change, and to which traditional formats cannot and should not be applied. We can only use hypotheses.

V. BY WAY OF CONCLUSION: OR LIKE THE WRITER, BETRAYING HIS STARTING HYPOTHESIS, WILL CARRY OUT THE TASK OF PROGNOSIS

If by concordat we understand, as has been the case during the course of the last two centuries, an agreement signed by two sovereign entities at the level of International Law to establish the position of the Catholic Church within a State, then it seems highly unlikely to me, if not

---

[135] See, among others, the Monetary Agreement between the Italian Republic, in the name of the European Community, and the State of Vatican City and, in its own name, the Holy See, of December 29, 2000 (2000/ C 299/01).

[136] "Possibilità che l'Unione possa stipulare direttamente accordi in materia religiosa, anche nella forma di concordati, magari accanto a quelli conclusi dai singoli Stati membri quanto al rispettivo ambito di sovranità". BUONOMO, *L'Unione Europea…*, cit., p. 362.

impossible, that we will see something of that nature within the European Union.

However, it seems quite likely to me that in some specific way, the authorities of the Catholic Church, in co-ordination with authorities of other religious denominations, negotiate an agreement with the authorities of the European Union, to regulate some aspects that affect the religious interests of its citizens. We should not even discard the possibility that such a type of agreement requires subsequent development through further agreements in which the parties would be a body of the Union and another of the Church. The function of the Holy See, of the national episcopacies and of the COMECE in this process is still uncertain and I am unable to imagine what it would be like. Would this be a concordat? We should probably call it this if we intend that the term continues to have some meaning in Europe.

PERSONALIA

THOMAS J. GREEN was born in Bridgeport, Connecticut (USA) in 1938. He was ordained a priest for the diocese of Bridgeport in 1963. He obtained his STL in 1964 and his JCD in 1968 at the Pontifical Gregorian University. After serving in the chancery and the tribunal of his diocese, he began teaching canon law at the Catholic University in Washington in 1974, where he chaired the department from 1984-1987. He also fullfilled several functions in the Canon Law Society of America and was for several years a consultor to the NCCB Canonical Affairs Committee. In 1992, he was chosen to occupy the Stephan Kuttner Distinguished Professor of Canon Law chair. He is also a member of the Polish National Catholic-Roman Catholic Dialogue. Since September 2000, he has been editor of *The Jurist*. He is the author of several publications in the field of canon law.

IVÁN C. IBÁN was born in Madrid (Spain) in 1952. He has a degree in Economics (1974), a degree in Law (1976) and a doctorate in Law (1978) at the Universidad Complutense of Madrid. He held the Chair of Canon Law at the Universidad de Cádiz (1983-1989), and since 1989 he holds a Chair of Church and State Law at the Universidad Complutense. He is a member of the Executive Committee of the *European Consortium for State-Church Research* since 1989 and member of the Editorial Board of *Il diritto ecclesiastico* (Milano), *Anuario de Derecho Eclesiástico del Estado* (Madrid) and *Nomokanonika* (Athens).

RIK TORFS was born in Turnhout (Belgium) in 1956. He studied law (lic. iur., 1979; lic. not., 1980) and canon law (J.C.D., 1987) at the Katholieke Universiteit Leuven. After one year of teaching at Utrecht University (The Netherlands), he became professor at the Faculty of Canon Law (K.U. Leuven) in 1988. He is dean of the Faculty of Canon Law since 1993 and visiting professor at the University of Stellenbosch (South Africa) since 2000. He is currently president of the *European Consortium for State-Church Research*. R. Torfs published seven books and more than 200 articles on canon law, law, church and state relationships. He is editor of the *European Journal for Church and State Research*.

PUBLICATIES / PUBLICATIONS
MSGR. W. ONCLIN CHAIR

Editor Rik TORFS
Editoral assistant KURT MARTENS

Canon Law and Marriage. Monsignor W. Onclin Chair 1995, Leuven, Peeters, 1995, 36 p.

R. TORFS, *The Faculty of Canon Law of K.U. Leuven in 1995*, 5-9.
C. BURKE, *Renewal, Personalism and Law*, 11-21.
R.G.W. HUYSMANS, *Enforcement and Deregulation in Canon Law*, 23-36.

A Swing of the Pendulum. Canon Law in Modern Society. Monsignor W. Onclin Chair 1996, Leuven, Peeters, 1996, 64 p.

R. TORFS, *Une messe est possible. Over de nabijheid van Kerk en geloof*, 7-11.
R. TORFS, *'Une messe est possible'. A Challenge for Canon Law*, 13-17.
J.M. SERRANO RUIZ, *Acerca del carácter personal del matrimonio: digresiones y retornos*, 19-31.
J.M. SERRANO RUIZ, *The Personal Character of Marriage. A Swing of the Pendulum*, 33-45.
F.G. MORRISEY, *Catholic Identity of Healthcare Institutions in a Time of Change*, 47-64.

In Diversitate Unitas. Monsignor W. Onclin Chair 1997, Leuven, Peeters, 1997, 72 p.

R. TORFS, *Pro Pontifice et Rege*, 7-13.
R. TORFS, *Pro Pontifice et Rege*, 15-22.
H. PREE, *The Divine and the Human of the Ius Divinum*, 23-41.
J.H. PROVOST, *Temporary Replacements or New Forms of Ministry: Lay Persons with Pastoral Care of Parishes*, 43-70.

Bridging Past and Future. Monsignor W. Onclin Revisited. Monsignor W. Onclin Chair 1998, Leuven, Peeters, 1998, 87 p.

P. CARD. LAGHI, *Message*, 7-9.
R. TORFS, *Kerkelijk recht in de branding. Terug naar monseigneur W. Onclin*, 11-20.
R. TORFS, *Canon Law in the Balance. Monsignor W. Onclin Revisited*, 21-31.

L. ÖRSY, *In the Service of the Holy Spirit: the Ecclesial Vocation of the Canon Lawyers*, 33-53.
P. COERTZEN, *Protection of Rights in the Church. A Reformed Perspective*, 55-87.

Church and State. Changing Paradigms. Monsignor W. Onclin Chair 1999, Leuven, Peeters, 1999, 72 p.

R. TORFS, *Crisis in het kerkelijk recht*, 7-17.
R. TORFS, *Crisis in Canon Law*, 19-29.
C. MIGLIORE, *Ways and Means of the International Activity of the Holy See*, 31-42.
J.E. WOOD, JR., *The Role of Religion in the Advancement of Religious Human Rights*, 43-69.

Canon Law and Realism. Monsignor W. Onclin Chair 2000, Leuven, Peeters, 2000, 92 p.

R. TORFS, *De advocaat in de kerk, of de avonturen van een vreemdeling in het paradijs*, 7-28.
R. TORFS, *The Advocate in the Church. Source of Conflict or Conflict Solver*, 29-49.
J.P. BEAL, *At the Crossroads of Two Laws. Some Reflections on the Influence of Secular Law on the Church's Response to Clergy Sexual Abuse in the United States*, 51-74.
CH.K. PAPASTATHIS, *Unity Among the Orthodox Churches. From the Theological Approach to the Historical Realities*, 75-88.

Canon Law Between Interpretation and Imagination. Monsignor W. Onclin Chair 2001, Leuven, Peeters, 2001, 88 p.

J. CORIDEN, *Necessary Canonical Reform: Urgent Issues for the Future*, 7-25.
R. PAGÉ, *Full Time Lay Pastoral Ministers and Diocesan Governance*, 27-40.
R. TORFS, *Kerkelijke rechtbanken* secundum *en* praeter legem, 41-61.
R. TORFS, *Church Tribunals* secundum *and* praeter legem, 63-84.

Many Cultures, Many Faces. Monsignor W. Onclin Chair 2002, Leuven, Peeters, 2002, 112 p.

R. TORFS, *Dwarsverbindingen*, 7-17.
R. TORFS, *Cross-connections*, 19-29.

J.R. TRETERA, *Systems of Relations Between the State and Churches in General (Systems of State Ecclesiastical Law) and Their Occurence in the Czech Lands in Particular*, 31-56.
A. MENDONÇA, Bonum Coniugum *from a Socio-Cultural Perspective*, 57-108.